MIREI SHIGEMORI—REBEL IN THE GARDEN

Layout and cover design:
Vera Pechel, Basel

Photographs:
Christian Lichtenberg, Basel

Project Management:
Henriette Mueller-Stahl, Berlin

Copy-Editing:
Lucinda Byatt, Edinburgh

Production:
Heike Strempel, Berlin

Lithography:
DillierundDillier, Basel
Christian Lichtenberg, Basel

Paper:
150 g/m² LuxoArt Samt New

Printing:
Optimal media, Röbel/Müritz

Library of Congress Control Number: 2020937892

Bibliographic information published by the Deutsche Nationalbibliothek
The Deutsche Nationalbibliothek lists this publication in the Deutsche Nationalbibliografie; detailed bibliographic data is available in the Internet at <http://dnb.ddb.de>.

P.O. Box 44, 4009 Basel, Switzerland
Part of Walter de Gruyter GmbH, Berlin/Boston

ISBN 978-3-0356-2175-4

e-ISBN (PDF) 978-3-0356-2176-1

9 8 7 6 5 4 3 2

www.birkhauser.com

CHRISTIAN TSCHUMI

MIREI SHIGEMORI—REBEL IN THE GARDEN
MODERN JAPANESE LANDSCAPE ARCHITECTURE

WITH PHOTOGRAPHS BY CHRISTIAN LICHTENBERG

SECOND AND REVISED EDITION

BIRKHÄUSER
BASEL

CONTENTS

ACKNOWLEDGEMENTS

This volume owes its existence to a great number of helpful people, some fans and followers of Mirei Shigemori, others my own friends and colleagues, as well as persons attracted by the topic of the Japanese garden. Some gave information, advice or access, others provided a link or a photo. For all these contributions, regardless of their size and importance, I am very grateful. I want to take this opportunity to thank all those who made them.

The following people and organizations deserve special mention for their particular support in one of the two important phases of this project.

The book's creation
The Japanese Ministry of Education (Monbusho), who generously supported my research on site in Japan; my advisors, Prof. Vittorio Magnano Lampugnani, Prof. Christophe Girot and Prof. Yukihiro Morimoto, who guided me through the adventure and made sure it was up to academic standards; Prof. Michel Conan and Prof. Kendall Brown who were instrumental in refining the arguments; Prof. Günter Nitschke who, in many conversations, gave me valuable insights into the Japanese Garden; Peter Goodman who published my very first book and generously allowed me to reuse part of the garden descriptions here; Christian Lichtenberg, who is responsible for most of the wonderful photographs in this book; Vera Pechel, who gave this material a magnificent face; and Henriette Mueller-Stahl, who was the responsible editor and project manager.

The book's sponsors
The following sponsors supported the publication of this book with generous financial contributions: JT International AG, Diethelm Keller Holding / DKSH Management, Sika AG, Credit Suisse Jubiläumsstiftung, ETH Zurich / Network City and Landscape / Institute of Landscape Architecture, Maria and Henry Wegmann-Müller, Bund Schweizer Landschaftsarchitekten, Metron Holding, Metron Kultur Stiftung, Rotzler Krebs Partner, Raderschall Landschaftsarchitekten AG, Verband Schweizer Gärtnermeister, Trüb AG, Enea GmbH, Villiger Gartenbau, Lüscher Gartenbau, Tanner Gartenbau, Nussbaumer Gartenbau, Berger Gartenbau, Alfred Forster AG, Syngenta International and the Swiss-Japan Chamber of Commerce.

Of course, none of this would have been possible without the support of the Shigemori family, especially Geite Shigemori, Mitsuaki Shigemori and Chisao Shigemori.

Last but not least, I want to thank my family, friends and colleagues in the office for being patient with me over the course of the last months while I was working on this book, and finally my wife, Nao, for her enormous support and silent encouragement.

白砂

THE SPIRIT OF THE ROCKS by Christophe Girot

To many of us Japan remains an extraordinary culture where the archaic meets the modern in the most diverse and surprising ways. The Japanese landscape and garden tradition seems to have escaped this rule and remained, at least to Western eyes, a place of immutable secular tradition where man and nature remain in contemplative harmony. It is as if the spirit of the Shinto rocks from the remote Muromachi era were still distilling its sacred substance to this day. The fact is that we have ignored most developments in Japanese garden design over the past century. Outside a few generalist books, there is scant literature written in English, and it is hard to think of a garden design or a landscape architect from this recent period, which is well known outside Japan. With all the dramatic changes that the country underwent over the last 100 years, it is, however, quite difficult to imagine that this could not have had an effect on the secular Japanese garden tradition.

This first English monograph on Mirei Shigemori is a breakthrough with respect to the question of recent evolutions in the Japanese garden tradition. The book enables us to enter the realm of the modern *karesansui* garden, and to understand a significant shift towards nature that has happened in Japanese society over the past century. This is of invaluable importance because it enables us to break away from the archetype of the Japanese garden as an immutable sphere, impermeable to change and innovation. With Mirei Shigemori we see how the spirit of the rocks is transmogrified into undulating waves of colored concrete, how rectangular checkers of stepping-stones dissolve into a background of moss and shrubs. The work that is comprised in this book incorporates not only his gardens, but also his writings and his teachings. It is impressive and consistently shows the birth and evolution of what one could call the modern Japanese garden.

The works of Mirei Shigemori coincide with important periods of change in recent Japanese history. It is interesting to note how spiritual and respectful of a certain order these gardens remain, but it is also interesting to note how they reflected the radical changes in Japanese society. Mirei Shigemori never left his native island. He only knew of the Western world through books and pictures. He probably embodies the last authentic period in the evolution of the Japanese garden, one where the influence from Europe and America was still relatively minimal. The way his projects are oriented spatially, and the way in which the elements are arranged, coincides with some of the canons of the *karesansui*. But there is also an important degree of individual creativity and fantasy in all the projects; Mirei Shigemori had the courage to transcend the established garden tradition that he learned, altering also its spiritual significance.

There is something both unique and delectable in this book; the extraordinary compilation of original plans, combined with excellent photographs and text, casts light on the most intricate details of Mirei Shigemori's digressions from the established canons of his times. There is something personal in his design approach that is quite strong and dedicated. What appears different on the surface and in the style in fact reflects a deep commitment and consistency toward a certain understanding of nature. One could say that Shigemori is probably one of the last Japanese landscape designers not to have been affected by American culture. The work is therefore of prime importance to both professionals and scholars of Japanese garden design. The microcosm that is represented here reveals an extremely diversified and rapidly changing oeuvre. One could say that everything in Shigemori's garden has an underlying meaning. A meaning that is much deeper than what appears to the naked eye, a meaning that is drawn from the substantive spirit of the rocks.

Tradition would like old stones to symbolize islands, but Mirei Shigemori has succeeded in making liquid stone, that is to say concrete, symbolize the cosmic waves of a *karesansui* garden from the Muromachi period. These waves of concrete, which flow and then solidify, incorporate the essence of matter in their very shaping. It is a clear break from tradition, and may even be a comment on the end of a way of seeing and believing the world. The carefully flowing and ever-changing sand grooves of a temple garden become suddenly petrified and set in their patterns of concrete. What does this shimmer of an instant cast in concrete really mean? I have learned from this book to leave all my preconceptions about the modern Japanese Garden behind. Mirei Shigemori offers a refreshing voyage through the evolving 20th century tradition of Japanese gardens. It conveys a deeper and better understanding of an epoch, which, although quite recent, has remained a black hole to Westerners until this day. It is thanks to the courage and determination of Mirei Shigemori that his oeuvre now stands as an uncontested achievement. It is also thanks to the relentless determination and astuteness of Christian Tschumi that Shigemori's work will finally receive all the international attention that it deserves. Let us hope that, beyond the milestone period described in this book, the spirit of the rocks will continue to permeate the Japanese gardens of tomorrow.

CONCEPT GARDENS by Günter Nitschke

Mirei Shigemori was the best known and most extensively published Japanese garden artist of the 20th century. One of his gardens (Yûrin no Niwa) has even been preserved by being disassembled and moved over hundreds of miles to a different location. And since 1938, when Mirei Shigemori finished working on the original publication of the (still untranslated) 26 volumes of his *Nihon Teienshi Zukan*, or "Illustrated Book on the History of the Japanese Garden", anyone exploring the history and principles of the Japanese garden—including myself—has been deeply indebted to him as an erudite and endless source of information on traditional garden design.

Even after the publication of Christian Tschumi's comprehensive study of Mirei Shigemori's work as a scholar and a designer, it might be still too early to identify him unequivocally as the first great reformer of Japanese garden art or the last traditionalist hanging on to a beloved past. Moreover, by now, that is 30 years after Mirei Shigemori's death, the *really* modern garden in Japan often boasts rivers and cascades carved in plastic, rocks cast in glass and trees sculpted from sheet metal; in addition, their creators justify their modern garden designs with the claim that they are creating a "second nature." To my way of thinking, the garden has arisen as an urban phenomenon and has always existed as a delicate overlap of nature and architecture. It is neither purely one thing nor the other. In the best examples, it discloses both in the form of art. Therefore, our minds and our hearts are needed to make or appreciate a garden. Searching here for a possible message and legacy in Mirei Shigemori's life and work, I wish to draw the reader's attention to three major aspects of it.

First, the main leitmotif running through his work is an enduring ambition, or rather an obsession to "modernize" the garden art of Japan. This question of modernizing the garden probably arose because Mirei Shigemori approached garden design similarly to architectural design. From the 20th century on, architecture was driven by novelty and it fed off constant manifestos and sales drives for ever new forms. There have been massive changes in architecture over the last hundred years. But modernizing the garden is a different story, since nature obviously is beyond concepts of traditional and modern. What can one possibly modernize in nature? We can never ask trees, rocks or mountains to adopt more modern forms just because we have become bored with their traditional or old-fashioned looks. Mirei Shigemori might not have quite understood what it truly was he wanted to renew and what he possibly could and should have renewed: nature, architecture, or perhaps himself.

Second, *bummei kaika*, officially translated as "civilization and enlightenment of the West," was the cultural order of the day during Mirei Shigemori's lifetime. His enthusiastic absorption of European art, religion and philosophy must have unconsciously infected him—like it infected most other Japanese intellectuals and avant-garde artists shortly after the Meiji Restoration—with the same split so characteristic of all three, namely the split between god and man, the human being and the earth, body and soul, culture and nature. Even when Mirei Shigemori refers to Shinto deities, he speaks of them as one speaks of God in the West. If you look carefully at any of his designs in this book, your attention is drawn to the mental concepts, such as Yin and Yang, the five sacred mountains, the isles of the blessed, the gods of the four cardinal directions, rock groups as the abodes of ancient Shinto deities, bundle patterns on kimono designs, or even large pictographic interpretations of particular Chinese characters. His gardens are primarily mindscapes rather than landscapes, their themes are concepts. His designs should be understood as garden versions of conceptual art.

Admittedly, Mirei Shigemori continued to use mainly natural materials, rather than plastic or metal, but he definitely already used cement. Nowhere in his gardens are we drawn to sensual delights, such as seasonal flowers or the murmur of a river. His gardens point to a modern, self-conscious individual and to a self-proclaimed innovator, disinherited from his past, just quoting from it, and estranged from nature, equally just quoting from it. Here I sense the basic weakness of Mirei Shigemori's gardens. His designs emanate the energy of one separate ego, not of someone working in unison with nature as a whole. Their novelty will make them the first gardens the coming generations will want to replace, unlike any garden from the Muromachi or Edo era we seem to be able to enjoy for ever.

Third, we have come to realize, mostly in hindsight, that the work of artists often expresses a vision or premonition of things to come, as well as a hidden warning. Of the approximately 250 gardens Mirei Shigemori designed, more than three-quarters are dry landscape gardens, some of them comprising vast areas, such as in the "Garden for Appreciating Clouds" at Kôzen-ji Temple in Kiso Fukushima (see page 107). The dry landscape garden type per se is not at all a modern invention. It existed in Japan from the early Middle Ages on. The mesmerizing effect the empty garden has had on the modern Western psyche as either being inducive to or resulting from meditation is due to a fairly recent misunderstanding. Or does it foreshadow—unconsciously and even despite Shigemori's recorded intentions—a fate our planet might face in the future, namely to become a barren moonscape with sparse patches of green or rocks , and no water or place for animals? Even the smallest and most innocent weed or daisy that pops up through the sand in his white gardens is usually eliminated immediately so that it does not disturb the seeming purity of the design-concept. Sometimes I wonder why we have come to accept such raked white surfaces as gardens in the first place?

I had the chance of meeting Mirei Shigemori several times and I found him to be a serious but humorous person, outgoing, helpful and generous, not a charlatan. He was probably not aware of the message his designs would convey once they became divorced from their original Shinto context or Zen temple setting and spread globally. The value of this exhaustive monograph by Christian Tschumi lies in the fact that now, for the first time, Westerners can also judge for themselves whether Mirei Shigemori's life work succeeded in his aim to renew the spirit of the traditional Japanese garden. Do Mirei Shigemori's gardens nourish the contemporary Japanese and Western mind and heart equally or more than traditional gardens still do?

Already during Mirei Shigemori's lifetime, there was a growing realization that there could no longer be any meaningful landscape design without recognition of the need to heal our earth from its progressive devastation and desertification. Only such an awareness, accompanied by a real, not just romantic, re-discovered sense of unity with nature—transcending our dominant Judeo-Christian-Islamic dualistic vision of man versus nature—could give a new content and form to a modern garden. Today the search for a separate modern Japanese garden, as such, appears to be futile.

MIREI SHIGEMORI AND MODERN JAPANESE ARTISTIC CREATION by Kendall H. Brown

A confession: as an art historian specializing on Japan, I teach three lecture courses on modern Japan—painting and prints, sculpture and ceramics and architecture. Although I have taught seminars on premodern gardens, visited many recent gardens and published on Japanese-style gardens in North America, modern gardens are absent in my formal classes. In similar fashion they are given short shrift in most books on modern garden history and on recent Japanese culture. Clearly most academics consider modern Japanese gardens peripheral to the dominant concerns of Japanese visual culture and to international garden history.[1] Yet, that supposition becomes untenable after reading Christian Tschumi's study of Mirei Shigemori. In the contours of his biography as in the content of his design and writing, Mirei Shigemori was a paradigmatic Japanese modernist. Indeed to understand Japanese modernism more fully we must examine Mirei Shigemori.

As a dynamic creator in several media as well as a prolific historian and engaged theorist, Mirei Shigemori embodied the interdisciplinary nature of much 20th century Japanese art and its overtly historical and theoretical underpinnings. By seeking a Japanese avant-garde within an avowedly Japanese context, he confronted the central artistic quest of his era—a new direction in Japanese creativity founded on the desire to overcome a fundamental tension between the perceived polarities of dynamic Western culture and the relative stasis attributed to Asian tradition. Although East–West cultural interface had occupied Japanese artists since the dramatic westernization of the late 19th century, it acquired a new urgency in the mid 20th century when Japanese artists accommodated the overt nativism of the war era, then, in the wake of defeat and occupation, were further compelled to demonstrate both the persistence of an "essential" Japanese culture and its world relevance.

The profound paradox of the simultaneous search for Japanese uniqueness and universalism that animated Mirei Shigemori's design and theory is first encountered in his biography. Like many of his contemporary painters and sculptors at the prestigious Tokyo School of Fine Art, Mirei Shigemori's academic art training (around 1917–20) was in the native idiom known self-consciously as *nihonga* ("Japanese painting" as opposed to *yoga*, or "Western painting"). Nonetheless, his education unfolded within a largely European intellectual milieu dominated by ideas of the artist as heroic, anti-authoritarian creator and of art as a revolutionary practice. Mirei Shigemori's maturation coincided with the emergence of abstraction in painting, manifest in Japanese versions of Futurism, Cubism, Constructivism and Surrealism, all of which he surely imbibed despite the Romanticist tendencies exhibited in his taking a new name based on that of the painter François Millet.

Even as he was naming his children after European cultural heroes—Kant, Hugo, Goethe and Byron—Mirei Shigemori was building his first gardens in the *karesansui* genre and helping reform ikebana. Following (and surpassing) the fascination with historiography displayed by so many modern Japanese artists, in the 1930s he published a 9-volume history of ikebana then a 26-volume survey of Japanese gardens. Part of a desire by intellectuals to chart Japan's cultural trajectory, these efforts were nurtured by a nationalistic pride in Japanese historic achievement and by the realization that understanding history, and thus better defining "Japaneseness," was conducive to fresh creation. The study of traditional arts to spur radical art was central to Japanese modernism, and occurred most dramatically in ikebana when Sôfû Teshigahara (1900–1979) founded the progressive Sôgetsu school. Abetted by Mirei Shigemori, he revolutionized the moribund world of flower arrangement by connecting it with painting, photography, design, pottery and music. Teshigahara's addition of unconventional items to his arrangements and conception of flowers as Surrealist objects surely influenced Mirei Shigemori's gardens with their peculiar combinations of materials and compositional disjunctures.

Teshigahara's postwar embrace of the aesthetics of the "modern primitive" may also have stimulated Mirei Shigemori to explore these ideas which resonate in his theoretical essay *New Sakuteiki* and appear in his later gardens. As conceived by Surrealist poet turned ikebana theorist and art critic Shûzô Takiguchi (1903–1973), and further articulated visually and verbally by figures including painter Tarô Okamoto (1911–1996), architect Kenzô Tange (1913–2005) and potter-sculptor Shindô Tsuji (1910–1981), the "primitive modern" addressed the debate on tradition by uncovering a vital and transformative energy in Japan's prehistoric culture that allowed artists to radicalize existing practices within the Japanese cultural framework and thereby transcend the dichotomy of Japanese "tradition" and Western "modernity." The formative, "original" and "essential" components of Japanese culture and indeed of all creative endeavor were located in the material products of the Jômon (c.10,000–300 BC) and Yayoi (c.300 BC–AD 300) periods. Thus, since true Japanese tradition was marked not by the refined elegance or lyrical naturalism previously associated with the Japanese past but instead by primitive force and dynamic tension, it was not merely congruent with contemporary Western art but even universal.[2]

In his book *Modern Art* (1938), Takiguchi linked ikebana and *karesansui* stone gardens, interpreting both as precursors of the Surrealist object. A year later the Surrealist painter Noboru Kitawaki (1901–1951) depicted an emblematic *karesansui* garden in his painting, *Ryôan-ji Vector Construction*.[3] The discovery of *karesansui* by Surrealists was part of a broader modern discourse on stones and stone gardens in which they could stand for many things, including the non-duality of Zen. While Mirei Shigemori's interpretation revolving around Shinto *kami* was relatively rare in the 20th century, his idea of adapting *karesansui* forms was not. Most notably, Isamu Noguchi (1904–1988) designed modernist stone-oriented gardens at the Reader's Digest in Tokyo in 1951 and UNESCO in Paris in 1958, and in that same year Tange constructed Brutalist stone gardens at the Kagawa Prefectural Office in Takamatsu and at Teshigahara's Sôgetsu Kaikan in Tokyo.

Mirei Shigemori criticized these types of gardens as creatively sterile Western imitations. For him, a key lesson of modern art was that successful abstraction demanded strong content—"the artist's idea." A nativist, he held that Japanese gardens by definition should manifest Japanese ideas. To supply this meaning, Mirei Shigemori sought to connect his gardens with the particular cultural memory of their locations and, more broadly, with East Asian belief systems including Daoism, Confucianism, orthodox Buddhism, Zen and, most importantly, Shinto. The primordial power attributed to nature in (modern) Shinto ideology served Mirei Shigemori both as the locus of a universal creativity (consistent with the "modern primitive") and as the bedrock of a unique Japanese identity. When it came to producing form for that content, Mirei Shigemori applied elements of modern painting and ikebana, resulting in the chromatic brightness, rapid movement of line, and overt compositional dynamism of his typical postwar gardens.

Perhaps Mirei Shigemori's strongest link to modern art was neither thematic nor formal but born from the idea of artist as fountainhead, independent from all but the authority of ancient traditions and universal paradigms. His insistence that the power of gardens derives from the power of the garden maker and that the artist's will must be as strong as that of the gods parallels similar statements by avant-garde theoreticians. For example, in his famous book *Art of Today* (1954), Okamoto stressed the fundamental creativity of the artist, railed against ossified styles and moribund institutions, argued for a dynamic concept of tradition, and located the "raw power" of creation in the artist's intervention between object and practice.

Mirei Shigemori's intellectual connections with his peers do not diminish his creativity or accomplishment. To the contrary, they increase the intellectual depth and cultural relevance of his work. His gardens exist in a complex relationship of mutual inspiration with the art of his fellow painters, sculptors and garden makers. There is no doubt that Mirei Shigemori's garden at Tôfukuji Hôjô (1939) was one of the seminal works of mid-century Japanese culture, bridging the naturalistic geometry of early modernist gardens, like the Okada House garden (1934) by Sutemi Horiguchi (1895–1984), and modern primitivism that flowered after the war. Moreover, his impact likely transcended modernism. The accumulation of forms and symbols in some of his late gardens so overwhelm modernist ideas of elegant simplicity or elemental power that Mirei Shigemori might be seen as the inspiration for postmodern Japanese landscape design.

1 A notable exception is Marc Treib, "Converging Arcs on a Sphere: Renewing Japanese Landscape Design," in Marc Treib, ed., *The Architecture of Landscape, 1940–1960* (Philadelphia: The University of Pennsylvania Press, 2002), pp. 270–298.

2 For an overview of the "modern primitive," see Niimi Ryû, "The Modern Primitive: Discourses of the Visual Arts in Japan in the 1950s," in Louise Allison Cort and Bert Winther-Tamaki, eds., *Isamu Noguchi and Modern Japanese Ceramics, A Close Embrace of the Earth* (Washington D.C.: Arthur M. Sackler Gallery, Smithsonian Institution, 2003), pp. 87–101.

3 For the latter, see Marc Treib, *Noguchi in Paris: The UNESCO Garden* (San Francisco: William Stout, 2003). Noguchi's gardens, particularly his Ryôan-ji inspired works, are studied by Bert Winther, "Isamu Noguchi: The Modernization of Japanese Garden Design," *Nihon teien gakkaishi* 1:1 March 1993, pp. 30–44.

REBEL WITH A CAUSE by Christian Tschumi

Mirei Shigemori **[002]** had a real cause to be a rebel. There were two issues that profoundly concerned him about the Japanese garden in 20th century Japan. One was the continuous imitation of past styles and the other the loss of the ancient spiritual roots of the garden. Both were right at the center of his understanding of life and culture as a whole, and artistic creation as an important part of it. And both he constantly addressed when making gardens or when writing about them.

Artistic Creation in the Present

Mirei Shigemori regarded the making of a garden as an artistic creation. Art for him meant engaging with life and, in the case of the garden, with nature, which by definition is subject to continuous change and constant renewal. This view of garden art left little room for imitating past styles, a practice he viewed with great suspicion. Mirei Shigemori wrote: "One can make gardens according to the ancient meanings or according to the ancient shapes, but actually the person who is designing the garden and building it is from the present time and no other. The significance of the fact that we are people who live in the present is that we cannot make gardens that embody the meaning of the old times or have the shape of those times. So, in this case, we can only make a garden that is an imitation and this is meaningless."[1] This shows how much he saw art as rooted in the present, drawing from the current life-world. In his view gardens should connect to people's everyday experiences and should reflect modern times. In this way art is pregnant with meaning as it mirrors the situations that people deal with and creates a specific moment in time. As a person looking into the future, Shigemori felt it was wrong to imitate past forms at the cost of present artistic inventiveness. Although, in general this was an attitude not unlike that proposed by the Western modernists, it did not imply that Shigemori assumed that European garden styles should be adopted in Japan. Quite the contrary, in fact; he argued that Western garden culture was not relevant to the renewal of the Japanese garden, as it did not engage at all with the culture of the place or build on its long history **[003]**.

The historical survey of gardens all over Japan (see also pages 35–37) certainly opened up a new perspective on garden history for Shigemori. Analyzing what he had seen, he naturally wrote his own version of the history of the Japanese garden, and also came to some interesting conclusions and interpretations. Shigemori explains that from the Heian through Momoyama periods, court nobles, priests and warriors constantly introduced fresh ideas to the creation of gardens. He writes: "Sadly, among the gardeners of the Meiji period (1868-1912) and thereafter, as well as among the landowners of that time, there was hardly anybody who had an eye for true beauty."[2] But, over the course of the Edo period, parallel to the fading of the daimyos' power, merchants and other wealthy city folk increasingly started to make gardens. This growing body of amateurs was in search of design advice, a need well recognized by Kitamura Enkin, the author of *Tsukiyama Teizôden*, a book that quickly became a bestseller as a result. But despite the author's intention of teaching ordinary people how to make gardens, the book also established a standard

1 Mirei Shigemori, "Shin-Sakuteiki," in *Shigemori Mirei Sakuhinshû: Niwa Kamigami e no Apurôchi* (Tokyo: Seibundô Shinkô Sha, 1976), p. 292. This text was first published as a series of 11 essays in the *Kintaifu* pamphlets nos. 16 to 27 (with no essay in no. 19); after Mirei Shigemori's death his son, Geite Shigemori, compiled the above book and republished the essay for the first time in one piece.

2 In Kintaifu 5, „On Tea Ceremony and the Garden", p. 2.

[002] Mirei Shigemori, about 1970

[003] Yûrin no Niwa

[004] Plan of Kibitsuhiko Jinja

[005] Ryôan-ji *kami-ike*

way of making gardens. People did not just use *Teizôden* as a source of inspiration, but rather as a set of guidelines. This meant that Japanese gardens became stereotypical in layout, stone setting and even planting. Eventually, even professional gardeners started to abide by the *Teizôden* style, as this was what they were judged against. At this point, gardens had lost much of the creative character of earlier times, and garden-making largely became about imitating old forms. He states that, "If one takes a look at the buildings of the Meiji period and later, as well as the gardens, everywhere all but fragments are to be found. This is a tendency that continues until this very day." Shigemori concluded that after the middle of the Edo period, the Japanese garden had lost the vitality that was its most important feature and the desire to recreate its forms took precedence over the process of garden-making as a creative act.

Rediscovering the Spiritual Roots

In addition to his fierce opposition to simple imitation of the past or assimilation of European styles, Shigemori pointed to what he saw as an enormous deficit in contemporary Japanese gardens: a significant loss of spirituality, which was usually replaced by interchangeable and meaningless form. People in the modern world had lost this important connection to the world of the gods, a link the ancient Japanese gardens had been testament to. The old references had been dropped or simply forgotten and new ones contained no spiritual dimension. To Shigemori most new gardens were dull, often unimaginative reiterations of past forms. Hence, he saw this desecration as leading to much poorer gardens that clearly lacked the profound aesthetic experience of their predecessors.

When Shigemori imagined a garden, he saw the *kami*, the native Japanese gods, and the *iwakura*, the shrine rock. He saw the ancient roots of the Japanese garden in the memory of nature and the spirits that occupy it. In his writing Shigemori developed a myth of the Japanese origins and he asserted that when people lived in primitive huts or caves, as hunters and gatherers did, they enjoyed intimate contact with nature and the gods. But this changed when the ancient people built houses and started to spend more time inside, protected from direct contact with nature and its forces. So the process of civilization in this respect was a path toward alienation from the gods in nature, creating an increasing distance between people and nature. Then, according to Shigemori, there came a point when people, fearing the absence of the gods, started to bring nature back into their lives and close to their houses in the form of gardens. Hence the oldest gardens we know were created as places for the gods, called *kami-ike*, literally "god-ponds." They would contain an island with a stone or a small shrine where the gods would reside **[004 | 005]**.

The pond symbolized the ocean and the *shima*, which literally meant "the silent mountain floating on the waves," was the island where the gods lived. Therefore, in old Japanese *shima* came to signify garden, a meaning many people still remember. So the early "god-ponds" and their islands were a way of worshipping the gods, of reconnecting with the other world. Shigemori understood the creation of gardens as first and foremost an attempt to reengage with nature as it is inhabited by the gods. This was the aspect of the past that previous generations of garden makers had emulated, and this should be put into practice in the present. He wanted to reestablish this important connection that had been lost when people had become overpreoccupied with imitating old garden styles. For him the memory of garden-making was the capacity to create things like the ancients did when they were in direct contact with the gods in nature.

These two points, the continuous imitation of past styles and the loss of the ancient spiritual roots of the garden, were the main criticisms that Mirei Shigemori formulated. Later, in the chapter on selected gardens, we will look at the solutions he proposed in his own garden designs.

Making Gardens and Making History

The situation of garden designers in the second half of the 20th century in Japan was not much different than today. In the already cited *Kintaifu* 5 essay, Shigemori gives us an interesting glimpse into his everyday practice, as he states a common problem: "I myself have been asked to do many gardens and in most cases the building already had been finished. Even though often a lot of money has been used for the building, there are in fact a lot of structures that I find rather disappointing." Certainly this is an issue that many contemporary garden designers can well relate to. As a reason he sees that, "Usually the building is left in the hands of an ordinary carpenter, who usually does not have an eye for true beauty, hence the buildings show hardly any architectural distinction. I can't stand the situation, having been asked to do a garden next to such a building." Nevertheless Shigemori took on numerous design projects and was always ready to fight for a good solution. As a true rebel he felt that, "Ideally building and garden should be designed and directed by the same person, if not that, then from the beginning they are to be designed simultaneously. With the current situation, where this is not paid attention to, buildings and gardens are as a result not well harmonized, and ultimately outstanding things cannot happen." A position that today certainly is as valid as in Shigemori's time.

Few people in the field of the Japanese garden have made history to the extent that Mirei Shigemori has. With his built gardens he has left us a staggering body of work—living history really—that still impresses many today and inspires garden makers all around the globe. But from an academic point maybe even more important, he has researched and composed the history of the Japanese garden as it was accessible to him in the 20th century. Some parts he has copied from old sources and hence re-written, while others are his genuine thinking, surprising discoveries and his own true contributions. Not a shy person, Shigemori also made sure he had a place in his story and that we would look at his work the way he felt appropriate.

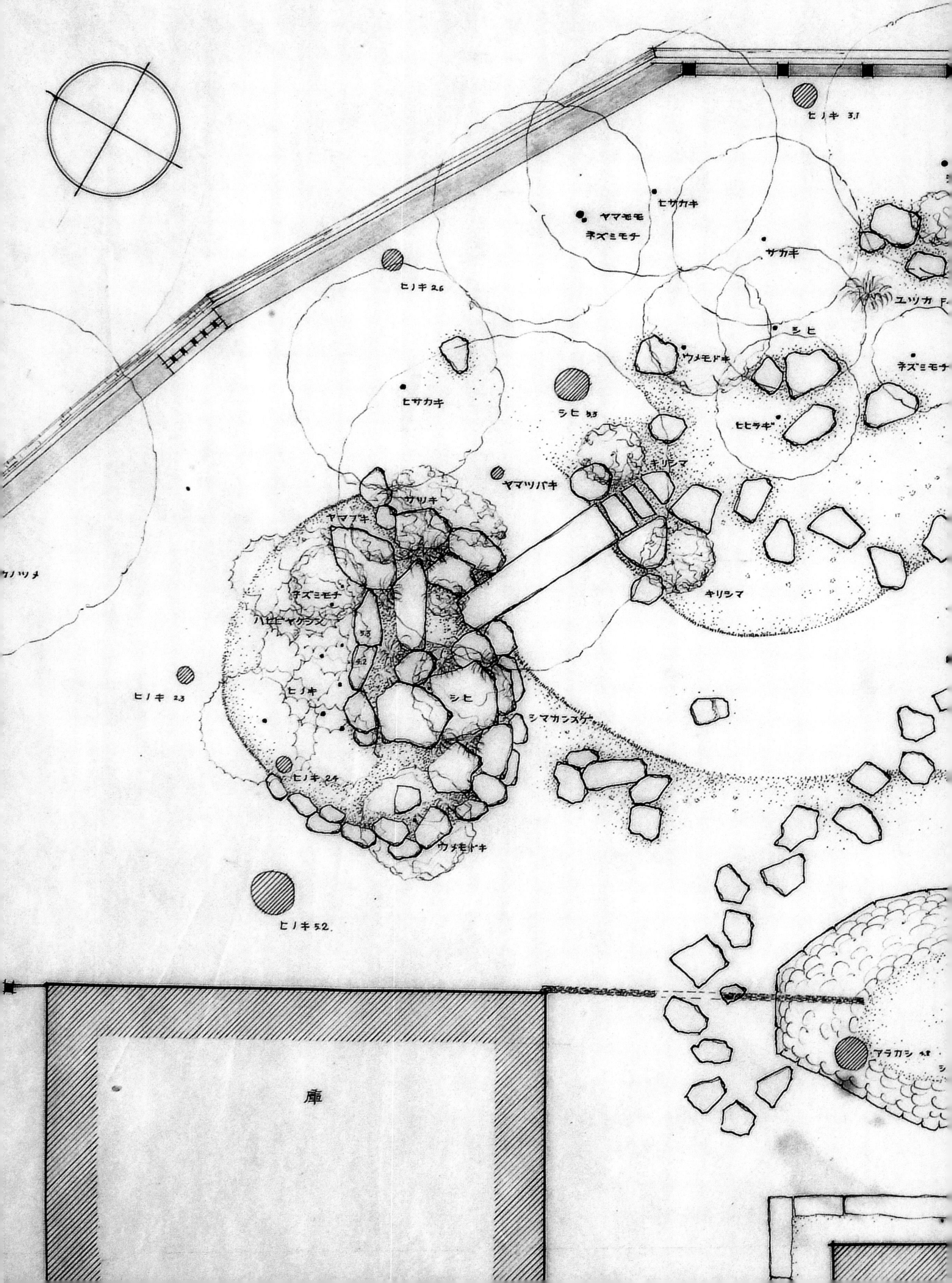
ヒノキ 3.1
ヒサカキ
ヤマモモ
ネズミモチ
サカキ
ユツカ
ヒノキ 2.6
シヒ
ウメモドキ
ネズミモチ
ヒサカキ
シヒ
ヒヒラギ
キリシマ
ヤマツバキ
サツキ
ヤマブキ
キリシマ
ネズミモチ
ヒノキ 2.3
ヒノキ
シヒ
シマカンスゲ
ヒノキ 2.4
ウメモドキ
ヒノキ 5.2
アラカシ
庫

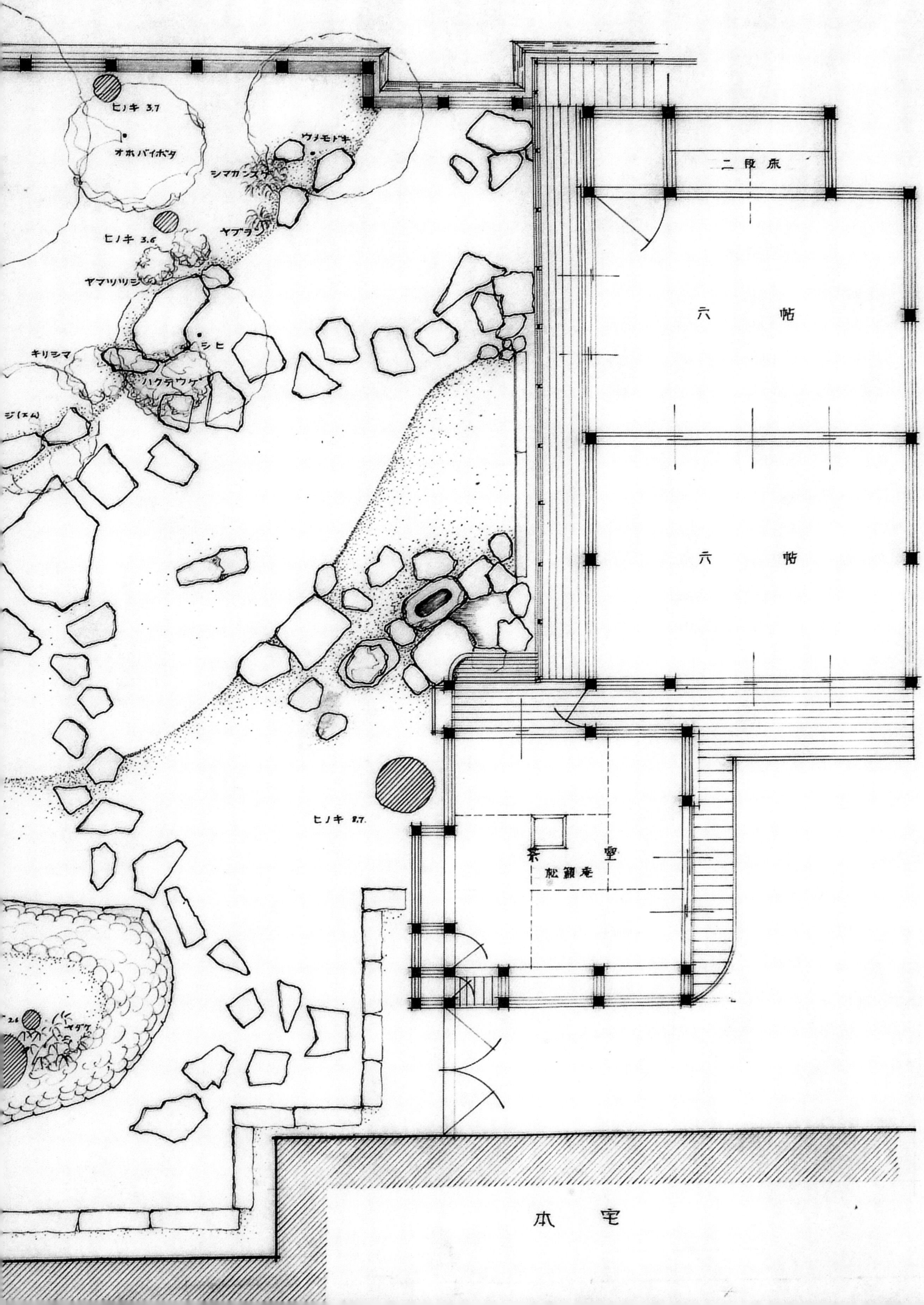
ヒノキ 3.7
オホバイボタ
ウメモドキ
シマカンスゲ
ヒノキ 3.6
ヤブラン
ヤマツツジ
シヒ
キリシマ
ハクチョウゲ
ジ(エム)
二段床
六帖
六帖
ヒノキ 8.7
茶室
松籟庵
本宅

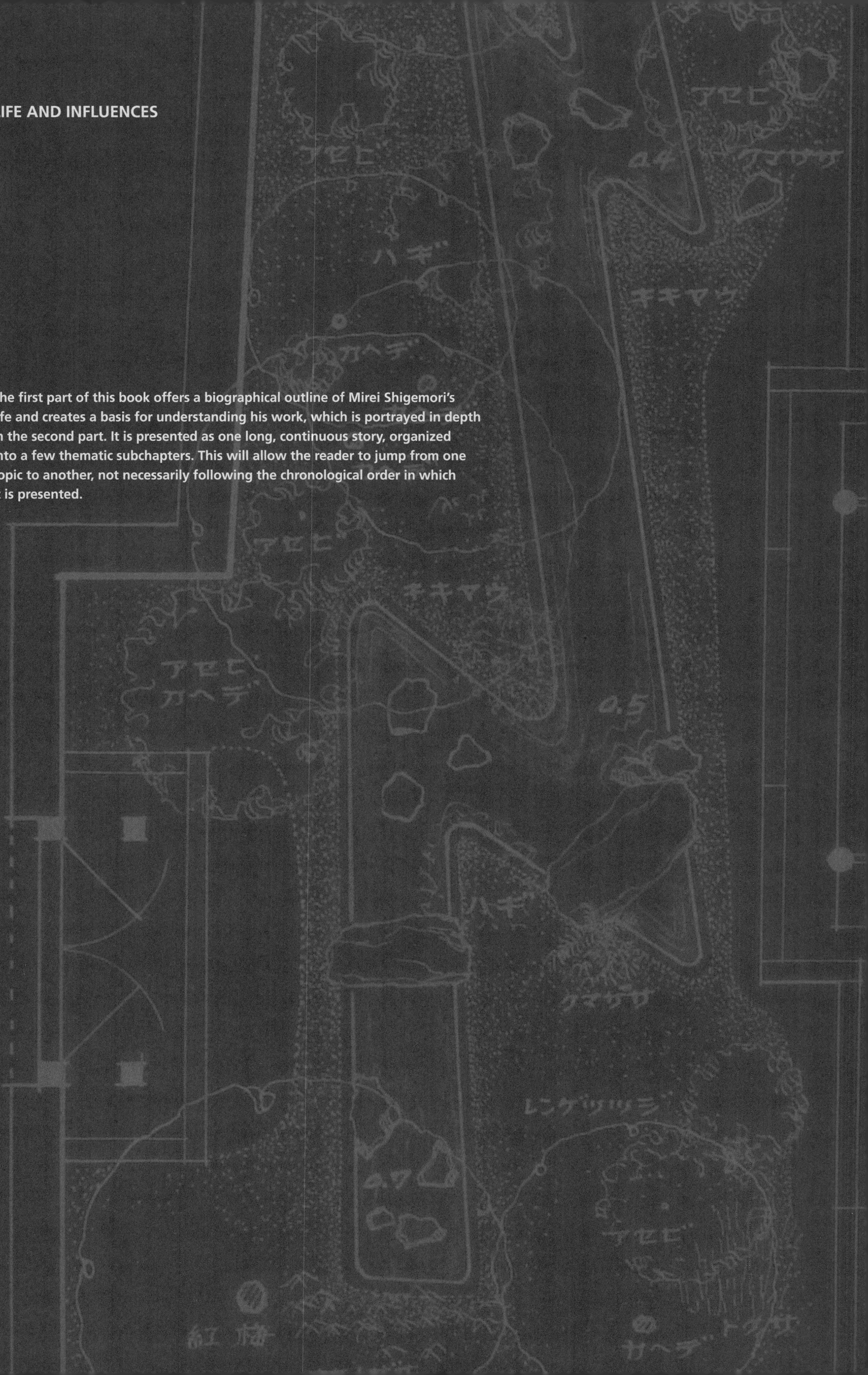

LIFE AND INFLUENCES

The first part of this book offers a biographical outline of Mirei Shigemori's life and creates a basis for understanding his work, which is portrayed in depth in the second part. It is presented as one long, continuous story, organized into a few thematic subchapters. This will allow the reader to jump from one topic to another, not necessarily following the chronological order in which it is presented.

THE EARLY YEARS

Growing up in the Countryside of Okayama

When Mirei Shigemori was born on August 20, 1896 in Kayô-chô, Okayama Prefecture, this was still very much Japanese countryside **[007]**. His father Ganjirô Shigemori was a real estate dealer and traded in "mountains and fields," as Mirei notes in an essay on his hometown.[1] His mother Tsuruno was busy entertaining the occasional visitors from the city and doing the farm work. The family was relatively wealthy and had a rather large house just outside the center of Yoshikawa, a small town up in the hills, about 40 kilometers northwest of Okayama city. Three generations of Shigemoris lived there together: Mirei with his parents and his four sisters, and his grandparents. The house had been planned by Mirei Shigemori's father and was built in 1894. The person closest to him was apparently his grandfather. And it was this relationship that kept Mirei Shigemori in his hometown; only when his grandfather died did he leave and go to school in faraway Tokyo.

Even though his father was the respected head of the family and the one who often disciplined him, Mirei Shigemori much valued his practical skills: "My father also liked working as an architect, did carpentry work and became good at carving and sculpting. As an amateur at around age 30, he made Buddhist altars and household Shinto altars."[2] Eventually they even built a tea house together when Mirei Shigemori was about 18 years old.

His First Garden

The garden at the family's house is actually the result of another collaboration between father and son. Ganjirô Shigemori had left an open area near the house in preparation for a garden to be built. After completing the house, he started to collect stones from the nearby mountains. As stones are usually seen as the most important part of a Japanese garden, this was a logical first step. At that time though Mirei Shigemori must have been too young to be of much help. And so the project for the garden was put on hold until 1907 when a stone and earthen wall was built. This, at least in Japan, often marks the real beginning of work on the garden. But still nobody seemed to be in a hurry. Mirei and his father did not actually work together on the waterfall stone setting **[008]** and the stepping-stones until 1913. He notes: "I was impressed how enthusiastically my father studied about the garden. He worked out the design [made a plan] and sometimes even asked me for my opinion." But even though he apparently had been asked for his opinion, he was not entirely happy with the outcome, as is shown by his comments on the waterfall stone setting: "I thought it could have been changed a little in order to look more like the Daisen-in one." In fact, a little more than a year after his father passed away, Mirei Shigemori decided to renovate it and change that part of the garden to look more like the famous Kyoto example. The work on the garden was officially completed in honor of Dr Tadashi Sekino's visit to Yoshikawa on January 2, 1925. Mirei Shigemori recalls: "While he was enjoying my garden, he said that it reminded him of Daisen-in in Kyoto."[3] The garden was named Shôrai-en **[006 | 008]**.

[007] Shigemori residence in Yoshikawa
[008] The first stone setting
[009] The famous model at Daisen-in

[006] Previous pages: A plan of Shôrai-en

1 In *Kintaifu 22*, "My Hometown," p. 1; translated by the author.
2 Ibid.
3 *Nihon Teienshi Zukan*, vol. 21, p. 43.

[010 | 011]

[012]

[013 | 014]

A BROAD EDUCATION

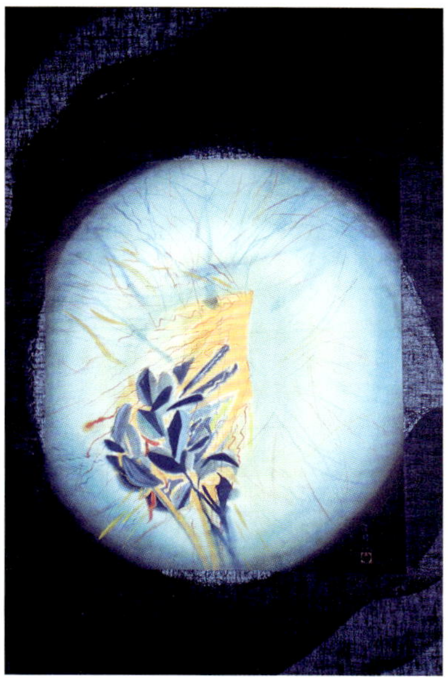

[015] A World Beyond Experience (Pupil)

The National Art Academy in Tokyo

As the oldest child and the only son, Mirei Shigemori was given the privilege of going to study in Tokyo. This was an expensive undertaking for his family at that time. Tokyo was still regarded as being very far away, in terms of both distance and in people's minds. But Mirei Shigemori was ready to leave his hometown. So in 1917, at the age of 21 he moved to Tokyo. Life in the city must have been quite a culture shock for a young man who had grown up in the remote countryside. He enrolled in Tokyo Fine Arts School to study *nihonga*, Japanese painting **[010–015]**. But even though he worked very hard to learn *nihonga*, he was not at all happy with the results. He had come to Tokyo full of self-confidence and convinced that his painting skills were actually quite good. But now that he was in a school surrounded by other similarly talented students, he began to get discouraged. Also many of the other students had been to a cram school prior to entering the university, so in his eyes they were more advanced. When he decided to approach his teacher with his worries, he was scolded but also received some good advice. His painting teacher, Professor Kii, told him: "Even though you say you are the worst painter, your paintings are the purest and so they are even better than those of the others. The other students' paintings look good because they all went to cram school. But their works are conventional and therefore not very interesting, they just look good in your eyes. It will take time for them to free themselves from these conventional stereotypes, but you came directly from being a farmer to study painting, so your work is pure and that is the best."[4]

This response might have comforted him in the short term, but it certainly didn't eliminate his worries. He realized that maybe his real talent lay elsewhere, and so he started to become more interested in history of art, aesthetics and philosophy. In 1919 he graduated from the undergraduate program at Tokyo Fine Arts School and continued into the graduate program at the same university. There he was able to pursue his specific interests and did his research more or less independently.

Studying Art History, Aesthetics and Philosophy

Mirei Shigemori's interests had definitely shifted away from *nihonga*, and as Tôyô University was offering classes in Indian philosophy, he decided to enroll in their program as well. So for a while he was attending the lectures there in the morning and studying at Tokyo Fine Arts School in the afternoon. But then he became increasingly dissatisfied with the classes and he went much more to the library. He writes: "While I was doing that, I realized that to understand what art history and Japanese aesthetics are all about, I had to study the tea ceremony, the Japanese garden and ikebana. This is how I ended up devoting myself to these topics. So I often went to libraries and visited many scholars to talk with them [about these topics]."[5]

In 1920 he graduated from the Research department of Tokyo Fine Arts School. This must have been a life-changing moment for Mirei Shigemori, when he realized that art history in general, and Japanese aesthetics specifically, were inextricably related to some of the things he had been doing all along. At this stage he had been practicing ikebana and the tea ceremony for close to ten years. In fact, since coming to Tokyo, he had even been teaching ikebana to other students. So many of the subjects he already knew started to make more sense because of his studies in art history. Without doubt, this time of studying and talking to other scholars was a very fruitful moment in Mirei Shigemori's life and laid the basis for much of his later thinking. He himself notes that: "This is how I started to study gardens and how it became the most important thing in my life. But when I studied the art of the garden, investigating its beauty, it was very useful that I had already learned about painting, aesthetics, art history and philosophy. That turned out to be very important for me. What I had been doing before was not at all a waste of time."[6]

[010] Untitled
[011] Three *bodhisattva*
[012] Struggle of Reason and Sense (Self-Portrait)
[013] Untitled
[014] Silence

4 Mirei Shigemori quotes Professor Kii, in *Kintaifu 3*, "Study Time," p. 1; translated by the author.
5 Ibid.
6 Ibid.

And in the end it was this broad spectrum, this wide understanding of Japanese culture that allowed him to approach the modernization of the Japanese garden from a totally new point of view.

Consequently, Mirei Shigemori later also argues for a different way of studying gardens. To understand the inherent beauty of each garden, he says, it is necessary for everybody to survey and research them thoroughly on site. It is important to understand why a garden is beautiful, where in the garden the beauty is to be found and what historic period it was created in. And according to Mirei Shigemori this cannot be taught, but only experienced. Of course, this comment stems from his later experience of the work on the big garden survey. Moreover, he recommends that one should go and see the same garden several times, saying that a garden is not something that can be understood in two or three visits. Of course he is right, because something as complex as a garden, changing over the course of a day as well as through the seasons, is never the same. His conclusion then is that, even after experiencing all this, the only way to really know gardens is to actually make them. Creating gardens is the best way of learning about them. Anybody who has ever made a garden knows how true this is.

The "University of Culture" Project

Mirei Shigemori's view of art within the broader sphere of culture was a very integrative one. His studies had shown him that there were many common interrelated roots within the arts. But in his own education his chosen subjects of study had all been segregated. So he felt that these subjects should be taught together in one single place. Building on this experience, he wanted to found his own school. The ideal image he had of this institution was not that of an ordinary university, but rather a place where all aspects of culture could be studied in an integrated way. The name of the university was supposed to be Bunka Daigakuin (University of Culture). However, as he didn't have enough money to embark on this project alone, he contacted the Yasuda *zaibatsu* to ask for support. Somebody must have introduced him, as it would be difficult to go to such a powerful family and just knock on the door. Also he was only 26 years old at the time. Apparently, Mr Yasuda was unwilling to approve his request immediately and wanted to see how the project would develop. Therefore, as a trial run Mirei Shigemori started a long-distance education program, which he called Bunka Daigakuin. He knew how to organize long-distance education as he himself had taken such classes. Also he edited a booklet called *Gendai Bunka Shichô* ("Trends in Modern Culture") as a textbook for the program. It was mailed to all the subscribing students on a monthly basis. This was how his long-distance education program actually got started. Interestingly, the word *gendai* (modern) appeared in the title of every topic, for example "Trends in Modern Society" and "Trends in Modern Economics," and so on. The topics were as diverse as education, literature, art, aesthetics, romance and drama. And the teachers were among the best, many of them from the prestigious Tokyo University. Mirei Shigemori himself was in charge of all the art courses. He did this for one year and then brought the twelve-lecture course book to Mr Yasuda, who recognized the effort and decided to support the project. An advertisement was then placed in the newspaper to announce the official establishment of Bunka Daigakuin. Finally, everything was ready to start and Mirei Shigemori was on the way to Mr Yasuda to show his gratitude, when the great Kantô earthquake hit. As he could neither go to Mr Yasuda's house nor return home, he decided to take a Chûô-line train and travel via Nagano to his hometown in Okayama Prefecture, still wearing the formal *hakama*. If the earthquake had not occurred, Mirei Shigemori would have probably established the Bunka Daigakuin and would have become its principal.

SOME MAJOR CHANGES

[016] **Yoshikawa Hachimangû shrine**

Return to His Hometown

Mirei Shigemori's time in Tokyo came to a sudden and unexpected end on September 1, 1923, the day the great Kantô earthquake struck. And given that his wife and his first son had already gone to his hometown earlier to escape Tokyo's summer heat, he naturally followed them there. At the time, he probably did not imagine that he would end up reestablishing himself in the small town of Yoshikawa for the next six years. According to Tanaka Hisao, Mirei Shigemori absorbed himself in his studies while enjoying farming in the countryside.[7] He continued to read philosophical books and even taught a local class on this topic. This is a time that neither Mirei Shigemori nor anybody close to him wrote much about. So there are few records for this period of his life. But there are some things we know.

It was during this period that Mirei Shigemori became interested in protecting the local shrine in Yoshikawa **[016]**. When he came back from Tokyo, his studies in art history must have made him realize what an extraordinary structure the local shrine was. He decided to ask the village mayor to apply for formal protection of the shrine as a national monument. But when the mayor returned empty handed from a meeting with the prefecture government, Mirei Shigemori realized he needed to use other methods in order to reach his goal. His efforts eventually led to the visit of Dr Tadashi Sekino. As mentioned above, for this important visit Mirei Shigemori finally finished his own garden, which he had started together with his father more than ten years before. His efforts paid off and the Yoshikawa Hachimangû shrine was eventually registered as a national treasure, much to Mirei Shigemori's credit. Soon after he had finished his own garden, he built another one at his friend Iga's house. And then Mr Nishitani, the village mayor, asked Mirei Shigemori to create a garden at his house as well. In hindsight we can see these months, late in 1924, as the start of Mirei Shigemori's career as a garden maker, a career that would occupy him for much of the next 50 years. But eventually Mirei Shigemori became tired of the easygoing life of a part-time farmer and he longed to return to Tokyo.

Changing His Name

Around the time when Mirei Shigemori was working on his first gardens, he must have decided that his old name did not suit a burgeoning artist. When he was born, his parents had actually named him Kazuo (計夫), a name that was commonplace in the rural towns of Japan at the time. But it seems to have been too common and ordinary for someone like him, so eventually, at the age of 29, he decided to change Kazuo to Mirei (三玲) **[017]**. The inspiration for his new name came from the French painter Jean-François Millet (1814–1875), whose work he must have learned about in school. To this day, the naturalism of Jean-François Millet's work is very popular in Japan. But Millet's work never really matched Mirei Shigemori's preference for abstract art, by artists such as Kandinsky or Monet. It is also an interesting detail that he took Millet's family name and turned it into his own new first name. Moreover, the correct pronunciation of the two characters is "mi–re," so the sound is close but not exactly the same as the original.

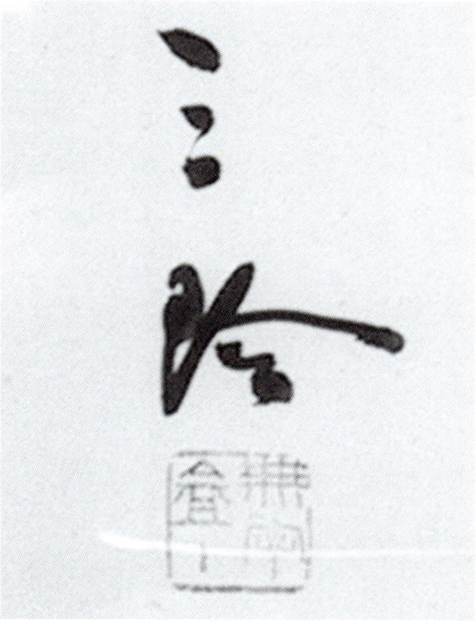

[017] **Mirei-signature**

Moving to Kyoto

In 1929 Mirei Shigemori decided that country life was definitely not for him. He wanted to move back to Tokyo, together with his wife and two sons aged three and seven. The story goes that they actually boarded a train in Okayama city that was bound for Tokyo. Apparently, while he was on the train, Mirei decided that he would like to spend a little more time in Kyoto first. So they got off the train there, not knowing that this was where they would spend the rest of their lives. The family eventually settled in a house at 45 Shimo Ôji-chô in the Sakyô ward, in the northeastern part of Kyoto city. At this time, Mirei Shigemori had no real job. He had embarked on his career as a scholar and was studying and writing a lot. So his wife, Reiko, was responsible for supporting the family.

7 In Hisao Tanaka, "The Basis of the Formative Artist Shigemori Mirei" in: *Shigemori Mirei's Collection of Works, Gardens—Approach to Gods* (Tokyo: Seibundô Shinkô Sha, 1976).

[018] **Working on a manuscript in his study**

[019] **Manuscripts**

THE SCHOLAR AND WRITER

Mirei Shigemori was as dedicated to writing about gardens as he was to actually building them. His body of written works is so extensive that compiling a complete list requires a substantial effort. The appendix of this book contains a detailed catalogue of his published works. Many of the original manuscripts were found in the family *kura*, the traditional earthen storage house next to the residence **[019]**. The following chart provides an analysis of the many books he wrote, organized by subject:

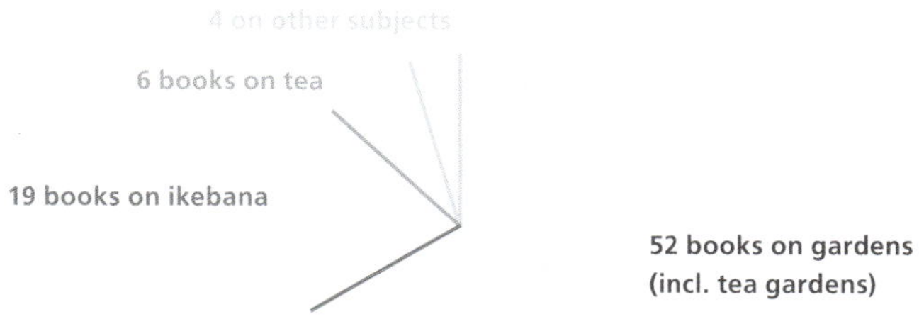

The 81 books written by Mirei Shigemori divided by subject.

[020–022] ***Complete Works of Japanese Flower Arrangement Art***

His first written work was not about gardens though, but rather about ikebana, the Japanese art of arranging flowers. In 1919 Mirei Shigemori had met Ryôsaku Hiramoto who at that time was the publisher of the ikebana magazine, *Kadô*. Hiramoto was eager to publish Shigemori's innovative ideas and asked him for a contribution. His first essay was published in the April issue of *Kadô* in 1919, after which Mirei Shigemori became a regular contributor to the magazine. He was only 22 years old at the time. His first contributions to a book were his essays for *Gendai Bunka Shichô* ("Trends in Modern Culture"), which served as a textbook for the trial run of the long-distance education program for Bunka Daigakuin (see above). His essays were entitled "Lecture on the Trend of Thought on Art," "Lecture on the Trend of Thought on Philosophy" and "Outline of the Aesthetics of Flower Arrangement," giving us a good indication of the range of his interests and areas of competence at the time.

The great Kantô earthquake and Mirei Shigemori's subsequent return to his hometown, Yoshikawa, caused a break of several years in his writing, which lasted until he moved to Kyoto. He resumed writing with a rather unusual piece. In 1930, one year after he had arrived in Kyoto, his *Japanese History of the Unification of Opposites* was published by the Tôshinkaku Shobô Company in Kyoto. There is absolutely no connection with gardens as this is basically a book about Mirei Shigemori's understanding of sex. At that time he was very interested in the origin of things and the origin of creation. The book was a commercial success and sold so well that a second edition was printed a year later.

His next major writing project was the *Complete Works of Japanese Flower Arrangement Art* **[020–022]**, a nine-volume book that he started in 1930 and which kept him busy for over two years. It was basically a book on the history of flower arrangement, written by using old ikebana books as empirical proof. He published it by himself under the name Kadô Bijutsu Kenseikai. It was produced in two cloth-lined boxes: a first set of six and a second set of three volumes. In volume six of the first set, work number 149 is by Mirei Shigemori himself **[022 | 037]** (see also page 39). It is titled "Exploration" and appears in the section labeled "contemporary," together with a rather critical essay. The artwork is credited to him and states that the creator is from the Bunka Daigakuin. So nine years after the earthquake that had ruined his plans to found the university, he was still using the name. It would fill this entire volume to discuss all 81 books in detail, so I will refrain, but his first book on gardens is certainly a key work and deserves some attention **[023–025]**. It is interesting that it was not his idea to write a book on this topic. It was in fact Mr Nakano[8] who asked him to write it. While working on this project Mirei Shigemori visited

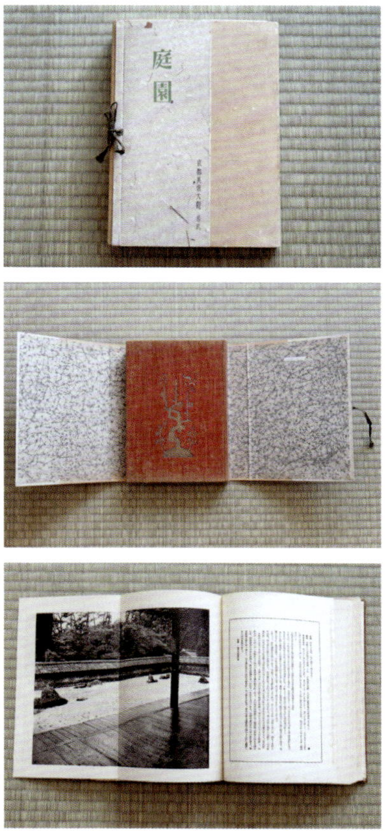

[023–025] ***Art in Kyoto*** **(Garden Edition)**

8 Mr Sokei Nakano was the owner of the Nakano Art Studio, a little west of the intersection of Marutamachi and Karasuma Street in Kyoto, and a pioneer in photography as well as the first president of Kyoto Rinsen Kyôkai.

[026] **Reading a book and having a coffee**

[027] **A sketch of the big survey**

[028] **Tessar F24 camera, bought second-hand in 1934 for ¥38**
[029] **Glass negatives and case**

over one hundred gardens in and around Kyoto. This was really the start of what later would become an even bigger project, the 26-volume *Nihon Teienshi Zukan* ("Illustrated Book on the History of the Japanese Garden").

As part of his research Mirei Shigemori also collected a lot of books and data, which completely filled his studio of 4.5 *tatami*, measuring about 9 square meters. The walls of the room were so densely packed with shelves full of reference books that no light could penetrate from the *shôji* screens behind. Mirei Shigemori suggests that one reason for this state of affairs was that he didn't employ a secretary or assistant to tidy up. But, in fact, he seemed to like being surrounded by clutter, which he regarded as a creative mess not chaos.

Writing was something that Mirei Shigemori loved, and when he was working on a manuscript he wanted to spend every minute of his time on it. Many people say that he was a fast writer, but for him, what was most enjoyable was "...not so much the [writing] speed I think, as working hard every moment."[9] He would spend entire days from sunrise to sunset in his studio, only leaving to have his meals in the kitchen. Mirei Shigemori took his writing very seriously indeed and made every effort to meet a deadline for a manuscript. However, he did plan a few escapes from his writing, probably in search of new thoughts and inspiration. Moreover, he made it a habit not to snack in between meals. Instead, to relieve the stress he took to cigarettes, although he was aware of the dangers: "However, instead I have the bad habit of smoking a lot of cigarettes. Occasionally I tried to stop smoking but couldn't do so. I can't drink sake or anything else that contains alcohol, and I usually don't eat sweets or the like, either. But tobacco is my only pleasure, and since I think that is okay, I continue to use it to this very day. Everybody tends to live with his good and bad sides. I don't think I could become a saint anyway."[10] Mirei Shigemori was a chain-smoker and eventually died from cancer. But who would have wanted him to give up his only pleasure?

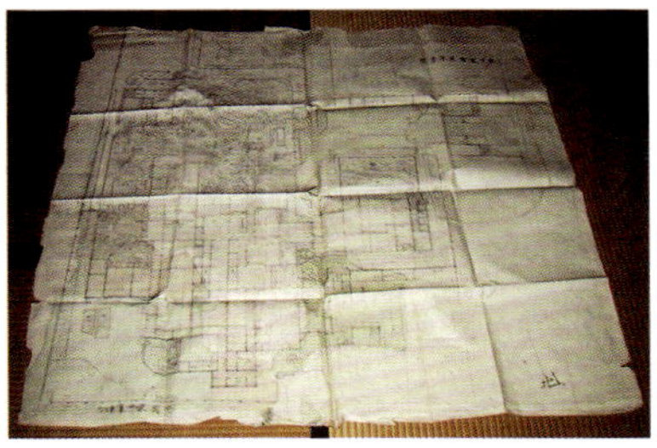

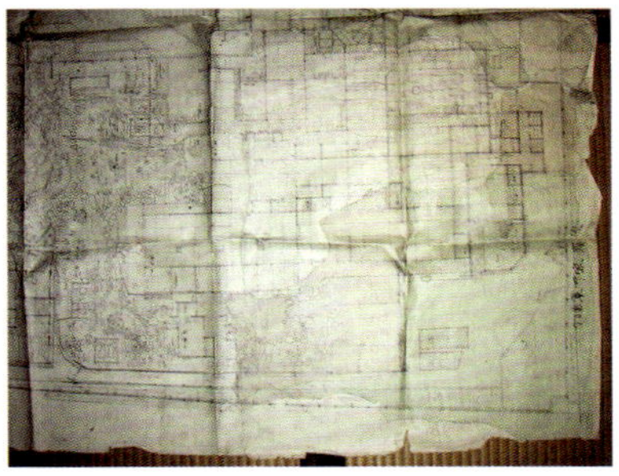

[030 | 031] Plans made during the survey

The Big Survey of All Gardens in Japan

Nihon Teienshi Zukan ("Illustrated Book on the History of the Japanese Garden") is certainly one of Mirei Shigemori's most important bequests **[032–036]**. It was the first time in the history of Japan that someone set out to survey gardens all over the country. The resulting work captures the state of the Japanese garden at a unique moment in time, hence it is a time capsule of sorts, and a great resource for the study of gardens, right up to the present-day.

It all started when, on September 21, 1934, the Muroto typhoon hit Kyoto and severely damaged many historic gardens. This event made a strong impression on Mirei Shigemori and he was concerned as to how these gardens could be restored when hardly any records of their original layout were available for consultation. Again he approached the government, this time the Ministry of Education, Science and Culture, and suggested that a survey of all historic gardens should be made. But again he was unsuccessful in getting the government to do something he deemed important. So, as nothing had happened by early 1935, he decided that if nobody else was going to do this survey, he would go ahead and do it himself. After all, another typhoon could hit Japan anytime. He visited almost 250 gardens all over Japan, surveyed them, took pictures, made sketches and checked their documentary records **[027]**. This must have also been the time when he became increasingly opposed to bureaucratic red tape and he showed a growing desire for independence from the governmental system.

The *kura* at the Shigemori residence actually contained the camera that was used on the survey project, still nicely wrapped in a velvet cloth **[028]**. It is a wooden travel camera from the F24 series made by Tessar in 1903. Unfortunately, the wide-angle lens that he bought with it was missing, but the wooden plate holder for the glass plates was there. It accommodated two 16.5 x 12.5 centimeter glass plates, one on each side. Along with the camera several hundred glass negatives were stored in the *kura*, all in boxes of ten, many of them made by Agfa or Fuji **[029]**. The fact that the negatives had to be carried around

9 From his last essay, in *Kintaifu* 32, "Mirei Shigemori's Last Writing," p. 2; translated by the author.
10 Ibid.

in wooden holders suggests that this was all rather heavy equipment to travel with. The developing was done later in a professional darkroom. The publisher requested *nakaban* (10.5 x 15 cm) or *yatsugiri* (15.2 x 20 cm) prints for the books.

Another remarkable thing stored in the *kura* was the actual survey plans **[030 | 031]**. The paper itself was glued together using many small and often irregularly shaped pieces of different paper. The reason for this is not certain, but in view of Shigemori's financial situation when he started the project, it was probably more economical to do it this way than to buy big sheets of paper in a store. The plan information is then drawn in pencil and looks quite sharp and precise. Most of the drawings have been folded at some point, it seems. Back in Kyoto the drawings were always redrawn, using a technique to copy them onto tracing paper. Black ink was used for this purpose. So in the end every single plan required dozens, if not hundreds of hours of work.

[032 | 033 | 034 | 035] ***Illustrated Book on the History of the Japanese Garden***

According to his grandson, Mirei Shigemori could read original Chinese texts and copied much information from the temple records using shorthand notes. He then filed these notes in his study and used them for quotes in his books. Obviously the photocopy machine had not made its way into every temple office yet. All in all, the survey became a substantial project. In his last essay, Mirei Shigemori wrote, on the subject of *Nihon Teienshi Zukan*: "I prepared a manuscript of more than 8,000 pages for the chronological table and the text on the gardens. Also I collected a lot of books and other data, and even to this day I have not been able to look through all of it, and so there is still a lot I have to read through."[11] No wonder it took him nearly four years to publish all 26 volumes with Yûkô-sha, a publisher based in Tokyo. The following table shows all the books in the order they appeared:

Order of publication	Period covered by the volume	No. of Gardens	Date of publication	Vol.
1	Momoyama period (2)	13	**6/22/1936**	6
2	Early Edo period (1)	12	**8/18/1936**	8
3	Meiji, Taishô and Shôwa period (3)	11	**10/3/1936**	21
4	Mid Edo period (1)	12	**11/18/1936**	13
5	Early Edo period (4)	13	**12/25/1936**	11
6	Momoyama period (3)	9	**1/25/1937**	7
7	Late Edo period (1)	12	**2/23/1937**	17
8	Meiji, Taishô and Shôwa period (1)	9	**4/10/1937**	19
9	Early Edo period (3)	9	**5/23/1937**	10
10	Mid Edo period (2)	11	**6/23/1937**	14
11	Muromachi period (1)	6	**7/23/1937**	3-1
12	Muromachi period (2)	6	**8/23/1937**	3-2
13	Early Edo period (2)	10	**9/20/1937**	9
14	Meiji, Taishô and Shôwa period (2)	10	**10/20/1937**	20
15	Mid Edo period (3)	10	**11/22/1937**	15
16	Early Edo period (5)	9	**12/25/1937**	12
17	Momoyama period (1)	13	**1/30/1938**	5
18	Late Edo period (2)	11	**3/20/1938**	18
19	Mid Edo period (4)	11	**4/25/1938**	16
20	Kamakura, Yoshino period (2)	6	**5/25/1938**	2–2
21	Kamakura, Yoshino period (1)	4	**7/20/1938**	2–1
22	Early Edo period (supplement 1)	9	**8/20/1938**	24
23	Meiji, Taishô and Shôwa period (4)	13	**9/23/1938**	22
24	Ancient, Asuka, Nara and Heian period	7	**11/5/1938**	1
25	Muromachi period (2)	6	**12/23/1938**	4
26	Chronological table of Japanese gardens	–	**3/13/1939**	23

The 26 volumes of *Nihon Teienshi Zukan* listed in the order of publication.

11 From his last essay, in *Kintaifu 32*, p. 1.

The survey was the most comprehensive ever performed at the time in Japan on this subject: a total of 26 books containing 242 gardens. Each book covers between four and 13 gardens, and every garden has its own chapter, containing information on history, style, technique and appreciation. Furthermore, sketches, plans and photographs are provided for illustration. It is organized systematically and chronologically and completed by an index volume. The books were published at an average pace of almost one per month, quite an impressive speed. When he began the survey in 1936, Mirei Shigemori managed to finish five volumes by the end of that year. Then, in 1937, he completed a total of eleven volumes; this was the most productive year of his work on *Nihon Teienshi Zukan*. But by the end of 1937 Mirei Shigemori had completely exhausted his funds and he realized he would have to stop work on the survey. It was then that Mr Usaburô Yomo from Kyoto decided to sponsor the project by donating ¥1,000 (about ¥ 570,000 in today's money, i.e. about € 3,890), and by doing so made it possible for the *Nihon Teienshi Zukan* to be finished.[12] So in 1938 nine more books were published, leaving only the index with the chronological table, which came out early the following year. When the books finally were all finished, Mirei Shigemori was understandably very proud and presented them together with a stone setting **[036]**.

[036] The first presentation of the 26 volumes

There is no comparable publication in the field of garden history in Japan, as other books usually cover a few dozen gardens at best. Moreover, the wealth of illustrations, especially the plans, makes the *Nihon Teienshi Zukan* immensely valuable. It has become the reference book on the Japanese garden and has made its way into all the universities and many private libraries. To date nobody has produced anything nearly as extensive and only Mirei Shigemori himself could outdo his own work. Thirty-three years later, just three years before his death, he decided to update and republish the historical survey. This time Mirei Shigemori, together with his son Kanto, produced 35 volumes and called them the *Nihon Teienshi Taikei*. Much like the earlier earthquake, the typhoon changed Mirei Shigemori's life again quite dramatically. However, this time, the effect of the natural disaster was not bad in the end, at least from an outsider's point of view. It influenced his future career dramatically in that it created a very unique basis for his further creative work. Nishizawa Fumitaka finds the right words to describe it when he says: "This experience comes to life in his technique of arranging rocks. The task of painstakingly surveying actual gardens is equivalent to being taught by his predecessors."[13] Looked at in this way, Mirei Shigemori was blessed to have so many good teachers. Needless to say, all this would hardly have been possible without the amazing support of his wife, Reiko. While he travelled all over the country surveying gardens, she ran a boarding house and a store to make ends meet. It was a time of serious financial hardship for the whole family.

In spite of his efforts, there are those who are critical of his work. Some experts rightfully point out that the survey plans are not always one hundred percent correct and others say that Mirei Shigemori misinterpreted some of the documentary records that he used as a base. Evidence can probably be found to support both points of view. However, the results are impressive and even critics acknowledge the sheer volume of data that Mirei Shigemori and his helpers collected. With this in mind, and considering the relatively brief time it took to complete this enormous project, a few shortcomings are inevitable.

12 Mr Usaburô Yomo was a client and Mirei Shigemori's had just worked on the garden at his second house in Nagaokakyô, Kyoto Prefecture, from 1934 to 1936.

13 From Nishizawa Fumitaka, "My View of Shigemori Mirei's Landscape Design" in: *Shigemori Mirei's Collection of Works, Gardens—Approach to Gods* (Tokyo: Seibundô Shinkô Sha, 1976).

IKEBANA—A LIFELONG PASSION

Ikebana is probably the creative activity that Mirei Shigemori cared most about, besides making gardens of course. Every morning he collected a few branches and flowers to decorate the various *tokonomas* in the house. It was an art that he had started quite early: "From the age of 15 or 16 years old I learned Fumai style tea and Ikenobô style flower arrangement."[14] Mirei Shigemori's father and his uncle did ikebana in the Yôshin style and his mother's older brother did ikebana in the Senkei style. This made a strong impression on him as a child and he wanted to try to learn it himself. By chance a widow, who had just moved back from Kure, started to teach flower arrangement and the art of the tea ceremony in a neighboring village. So with five or six friends from elementary school he went there to learn flower arrangement. She belonged to the well-established Ikenobô school.

After moving to Tokyo Mirei Shigemori started to teach ikebana right away. But while doing so, he continued to study under Mr Kawabata from the Ryûsei school. So he taught while being a student at the same time. Later, though, he was more involved with the Ikenobô school, which to this day is the most progressive, diverse and internationally minded. Not surprisingly, Mirei Shigemori had his own particular take on doing ikebana **[037]**. He hated the hobbyist approach, often symbolized by the "waterfall-coming-out-of-the-mountain-gorge" style, and disliked the idea of ikebana as a pastime for the masses. "First," he writes, "we have to dismantle the old methods in a positive way, and put the emphasis on taking a genuinely new position in *kadô* [ikebana]. Secondly," he insists, "that while respecting the individual style of every artist, we should dismantle all the *kadô* styles. The reform of Japanese *kadô* should then come from the artists themselves."[15] Mirei Shigemori was an intellectual and he advocated the establishment of the individual, within the context of both the rapidly changing art scene as well as all of society; moreover, he was opposed to traditional ikebana.

For Mirei Shigemori, the so-called *iemoto* system was at the center of the problem. He claimed that, "Once people learn a style, that is when they go to hell [that is what kills art]!"[16] Mirei Shigemori strongly resisted these traditional styles. He founded his own school and eventually became a master himself. He believed that it was necessary to break out of the *iemoto* system because it was the enemy of art. But what was Mirei Shigemori's own style? The start of the Shôwa period (from 1925) marked the introduction of two new and distinct ikebana styles, *nageirebana* and *moribana*, that epitomized the taste of the new times. But for Mirei Shigemori they were still too deeply rooted in naturalism. He called for a surrealist development in ikebana. "By destroying nature, and not just physically, we must establish art. The lines and colors of art must be guided by pure creativity."[17] Here his education as a painter, his profound interest in art history and even his extensive philosophical readings are clearly evident. This broad background gave him quite a different view of ikebana and allowed him to break out of the established styles. Mirei Shigemori sums up his basic approach to ikebana as follows: "It is true that in the art of flower arrangement the most important thing is to bring nature to life. But this doesn't necessarily mean bringing it alive in a realistic way. Bringing nature to life means translating it inside myself. And in order to make it a thing of myself, all or part of nature has to be transformed: transformed from the field of nature to the field of art, emphasizing the distinction between nature and art. In order to bring nature to life, the lines and colors of nature are made into the lines and colors of art."[18]

Eventually Mirei Shigemori completely turned away from the 19th century naturalism of the European art world to the modernism of the 20th century. And later he devoted himself deeply to surrealism. Hôjô Akinao points out another reason that might have fostered this development: "Usually Shigemori hated to be called *sensei*, as he had a deep-rooted, defiant attitude toward authority. So we can easily imagine that Dadaism, and Surrealism [...] were fascinating and fresh for him as they carried a certain

14 In *Kintaifu 22*, "My Hometown," p. 1.
15 In Hôjô Akinao, *History of Ikebana People* (Tôkyo: Shibundô, 1997), p. 152.
16 Ibid., p. 153.
17 From Shigemori Mirei, "Exploration—The Art of Flower Arrangement"; text together with work no. 149 in: *Complete Works of Japanese Flower Arrangement Art*, vol. 6 (Kyoto: Kadô Bijutsu Kenseikai, 1930–1932).
18 Ibid.

anarchistic character. Dadaism, introduced to Japan from Europe after WWI, denied existing authority and discipline, and had reached acceptance in the world of literature and art at the time."[19]

In whatever field Mirei Shigemori was involved, he always tried to be at the forefront of development, always looking for what was new and exciting, and ikebana was no different.

[037] Ikebana by Mirei Shigemori titled "Trial"

The *New Ikebana Declaration*

In view of Mirei Shigemori's position in the field of ikebana, it is no surprise that he was instrumental in the development and writing of the now famous *New Ikebana Declaration*. Already in 1930 Mirei Shigemori had established contact with Teshigahara Sôfû and Nakayama Bunpo, and the three of them eventually founded a group called the *New Ikebana Association*. Mirei Shigemori, the main promoter, argued that just as the Futurists and the Cubists had done in their respective fields, they should start a new movement in the field of Japanese ikebana. Teshigahara Sôfû, who later became a famous artist in his own right, was four years younger then Mirei Shigemori. Apparently during that time he often visited Kyoto to study some of the ikebana classics under Mirei Shigemori and together they discussed how this art could evolve. According to Mirei Shigemori's diary, the *New Ikebana Declaration* was then drafted in 1933. As it is a unique text that almost perfectly reflects Mirei Shigemori's attitude toward art, it is reproduced here in full:

> **Declaration**
> New *ikebana* rejects nostalgic feelings.
> We can't find a vivid world in anything nostalgic.
> There is nothing but calmly sleeping beauty in the nostalgic world.
> New *ikebana* rejects formal fixation. Creation always brings forth a fresh form. Fixed form is like a gravestone.
> New *ikebana* rejects the concept of moral principles. Ikebana is neither a religious lecture nor a created moral story. If anything, it is art.
> New *ikebana* rejects botanical limits. Ikebana is an art and certainly not about plant samples or botanical teaching materials. Plants are the only and most important materials.
> New *ikebana* uses the flower vase freely. We accept no limits regarding the flower vase and its use is unrestricted. Either we can make it painstakingly with our own hands, or we can cooperate with a good vase maker. The vase must also follow our new spirit; we must give a new life to old things and make them alive.
> New *ikebana* undergoes constant development; it doesn't have a standard form. It adapts to the lifestyle of our time, but it is always tied to an artistic conscience. It is neither a traditional old pastime nor a metaphysical existence departing from life. If we take the biased viewpoint and blind obedience of conventional ikebana, our work would indeed be different. The new spirit will be expressed by a completely new appearance.[20]

We will later find much of this thinking in Mirei Shigemori's approach to the garden. It is rooted in the Modernism of the Taishô period, advocating an art that was adjusting to a new way of life.

19 In Hôjô Akinao, *History of Ikebana People*, p. 156.
20 Translated from Japanese by the author, based on a reprint from Endô Nozomu, *Sofu Teshigahara—The Postwar Avant-Garde Era* (Tokyo: Setagaya Museum, 2001).

[038]

[039]

CHADÔ—THE WAY OF TEA

"*Chadô*, or the way of tea, is about making only one cup of tea and drinking it. But in fact, that single cup is equivalent to drinking a palace of beauty, drinking the universe."[21]

The word tea in this context refers to a green and very foamy drink that the Japanese call *maccha* **[048]**. It is made from the pulverized leaves of the tea plant (*Camellia sinensis*) and hot water. But more important than these rather simple ingredients is the entire procedure surrounding the making of this beverage. And this is probably the reason why in the West it is often referred to as the tea ceremony.

Tea culture was originally imported from China, but the Japanese profoundly altered it over time. Famous to this day are the tea masters Sen Rikyû (1522–1591), Furuta Oribe (1543–1615) and Kobori Enshû (1579–1647), all of whom Mirei Shigemori greatly admired. However, it was Kobori Enshû, who was also well regarded as a garden maker in his time, in whom Mirei Shigemori saw the highest combination of creative qualities and he therefore praised him highly. In an essay titled "On Tea Ceremony and the Garden," Mirei Shigemori writes: "I think the reason that Enshû was so good at making gardens is that he was a great student of Furuta Oribe's tea ceremony practices and by becoming his leading disciple, he obviously had mastered Oribe's art."[22] Here Mirei Shigemori is suggesting what many Japanese garden makers would also affirm, that a person well versed in the art of tea would also have the potential to make a good garden. Regarding his own career in tea Mirei Shigemori writes: "From the age of 15 or 16 years old I learned Fumai style tea and Ikenobô style flower arrangement."[23] His ikebana teacher, Mrs Aizawa who lived in the next village just down the road, taught him the basic techniques of the tea ceremony. At the age of 18 Mirei Shigemori built his own tea house **[038 | 039]** with the help of his talented father. "I named this tea house Tenrai-an. [...] Usually the sound of the wind was very strong, and that is where the name Tenrai came from. Tenrai is the sound the wind makes when it blows through the trees. I gave it this poetic name, thinking that this was inspiring. The tearoom is 4 and a half *tatamis* in size, has three *tokonomas* in *shin*, *gyô* and *sô* style, and a specially designed shelf. [...] When the tearoom was completed, my father gave me some inexpensive utensils to practice tea."[24] This quote perfectly expresses the sensitivity that tea experts strive for. For instance, the feeling of a place is mirrored in the name of the tea house, different levels of formality are expressed in the design of both the house and the garden, and also tea as an art is practiced regularly and is an important social event. In 1969, when he was 73, and exactly 40 years after moving away, Mirei Shigemori eventually donated the Tenrai-an tea house to his hometown Kayôchô, together with a splendid new garden (see pages 140–145).

Tea as a Way of Life

For Mirei Shigemori tea and the culture around it was more than just a hobby. He devoted such a tremendous amount of time and money to it, that it can be rightfully called a passion, if not a way of life. **[040–042 | 044–046]** His children remember that he made a bowl of tea for each of them in the morning. Followers and clients alike often mention how he made tea for everybody on a construction site, always carrying his set of tea utensils with him. And Mirei Shigemori's *hatsugama* parties, the first tea event of the year, remain legendary in Kyoto. He invited the entire local elite, sometimes 200 to 300 people to his house. Even the head priests of Kyoto's largest temples would grant him the honor of their presence. Elaborate food was served and only the best tea was available. He chose the utensils according to the year's theme and went to great trouble to borrow famous scrolls from local temples for decoration. And, of course, there were always some twists and surprises. After all, it was not only an opportunity to show off his wonderful collection of valuable utensils, but also an important moment to assert social relationships and promote his image as a true innovator based on tradition and art. Needless to say this was all very expensive. Much to the discontent of his wife, Mirei Shigemori would often go shopping for expensive tea utensils on the way home from work, sometimes spending all the money he had just received from a client for a new garden. By the end of his life he

[040 | 041 | 042] **Cleaning the *tsukubai* in his tea garden**

[038 | 039] **Tenrai-an tea house and garden**

21 Mentioned in *Kintaifu 5*, "On Tea Ceremony and the Garden," p. 1; translated by the author.
22 Ibid.
23 In *Kintaifu 22*, "My Hometown," p. 1.
24 Ibid., p. 2.

[043] Raikyû-ji's impressive *karikomi* suggests waves

[044 | 045 | 046] In his tea room: placing incense on the coals

[047] **Raikyû-ji: a garden by the famous tea master Enshû**

had amassed a great collection of very valuable items, one of them being a bamboo tea scoop by Furuta Oribe that was approximately 350 years old; definitely something out of the ordinary and worth a fortune in Japan. Perhaps, it is no surprise to learn that Reiko, Mirei Shigemori's wife, was also a licensed tea teacher. She taught Urasenke style tea and gave lessons in the family's own tea house.

Now why is all this relevant to the garden? In Mirei Shigemori's opinion, it was all interrelated through aesthetics, or simply a sense of beauty. In the previously mentioned essay he explains: "When an artist creates something, the understanding of beauty comes first. Here the comprehension of the beauty of ink art or a bowl of tea is equal to having an advanced understanding of the garden's stones and trees."[25] This is how he starts the argument with a general comparison. But then he continues to explain that there is a central action of judging and also selecting where the different arts seem to connect: "The action of making a garden starts by selecting materials like stones and trees. So consequently, if somebody does not have an educated eye, a high-quality garden is not possible. The ability to judge the quality of beauty, while making such a selection, in the long run decides the quality of the work. So a person who understands the beauty of a single bowl of tea will also understand the beauty of a garden stone, and moreover use that stone properly to make a great stone setting."

Obviously selecting the right materials, especially the stones and trees, is a very important step when making a Japanese garden, and in some cases it may be half the work. But the next phase is equally demanding, as it requires a flair for layout and arrangement, a sense of flow and movement, and last but not least an understanding of the seasons. Of course, all these can be found, and learned, in the way of tea: "In a tea ceremony, all utensils as well as the theme of the tea gatherings have to match the season. In addition, all the utensils must be appropriately arranged. And the host's gestures and proper etiquette have to be in perfect harmony. The spirit of tea exists where these main things are understood, and those who have mastered the tea ceremony at that level share an understanding of culture and have an eye for beauty. That is why Enshû's garden works are naturally outstanding."[26] **[043 | 047]**

It is this understanding of the importance of the way of tea that Mirei Shigemori pursued all his life. Hence, he continued to tell his children, his followers and anyone else interested in the arts in general, or more specifically in the Japanese garden: "Tea is the best way to cultivate one's mind."[27]

[048] ***Maccha*: hot water and the ground leaves of *Camellia sinensis***
[049] **A tea bowl made by Mirei Shigemori**

25 From *Kintaifu 5*, "On Tea Ceremony and the Garden," p. 2.
26 Ibid.
27 From an interview titled "Gardens and Me" (Tokyo: Tokyo Sôgô Shashin Senmongakô, 1971), p. 4; translated by the author.

CALLIGRAPHY

[050]

[051]

Mirei Shigemori practiced calligraphy throughout his life. His grandfather was apparently good at Samurai style calligraphy[28], and he probably first came into contact with this art during his childhood in Yoshikawa. His love of the *kanji* characters, the Japanese writing adapted from the Chinese, was such that he studied them in depth and was able to read the original Chinese texts. This was especially useful when he needed to read ancient temple records and manuscripts written in old Chinese. For him, calligraphy was an integral part of Japanese culture and was connected to tea as well as to the garden. His use of characters, or *kanjis*, on garden fences seems to be an extension of this fondness for calligraphy. Similarly, his use of a *kanji's* shape for the layout of a *karesansui* garden[29] is clearly derived from this affection (see also page 63). On my various visits to Mirei Shigemori's clients I learned that he would often give scrolls containing calligraphic writing as presents. And when they now have a chance to show them to an interested visitor, they display these treasures with great pride. The museum at Yoshikawa also has a good selection of Mirei Shigemori's scrolls from different periods. The following are a few examples from his diverse calligraphic work:

庭 **[050]** is pronounced *niwa* and is also a word for garden, but certainly more widely used than the previous one. Mirei Shigemori, being an artist, felt free to change the *kanji* character a bit and come up with his own version. He moved the lower part, which carries the meaning of "big step" out to the left, outside the part that means "house." It almost seems as if he wanted to suggest a big step outside the house. When the Japan Broadcasting Corporation (NHK) produced a documentary[30] on Mirei Shigemori in 1999, this calligraphy was the first thing they showed on the screen. The presenter Ishizawa then remarks that: "This letter [niwa] is a little different in Mirei Shigemori's handwriting." The other presenter, Ogawa, adds that: "The details are a little different but its power convinces us that it is right." And Ishizawa responds: "In Mirei Shigemori's sense, breaking out of the usual norm, this letter is the *kanji* for *niwa*."[31] This gives a good insight into how the Japanese perceive this change in the way the *kanji* is drawn.

無 **[051]** is pronounced *mu* and is usually translated as nothingness, void or emptiness. Conceptually, it is strongly linked to the *karesansui* garden where this idea plays a vital role. The *kanji*, as it appears in Mirei Shigemori's calligraphy, is again a radical simplification of the original, replicating his approach in the other arts. He used the *mu* character several times in calligraphies, and even in the name of his favorite tearoom called Muji-an at his house in Kyoto.

林泉 **[052]** is pronounced *rinsen* and is an old word for garden. The first *kanji* character stands for a grove or a small wood, while the second signifies a spring or fountain. So the image of a spring in a grove of trees may be one of the old etymological roots of the word for garden in Japanese. When Mirei Shigemori and his friend Sokei Nakano decided to found an association for the study and promotion of the Japanese garden in 1932, they called it Kyoto Rinsen Kyôkai, which translates simply as "Kyoto Garden Association." Having studied the origins of the garden in Japan thoroughly, Mirei Shigemori was aware of this old word and revived it in modern times by using it in his calligraphy and as a name for his organization.

萬華 **[053]** can be read in two ways *banka* or *mange*. This calligraphy is read in the old way from right to left. The first character means "10,000" and the second stands for "flower." So the combined meaning is many flowers or a variety of flowers. Ikebana was Mirei Shigemori's true and lasting passion and therefore it is no surprise that he would express this also in his calligraphic work. On the other hand, he hardly ever used a flowering plant in a garden. The *Mirei Shigemori Kinenkan* in Yoshikawa now owns this calligraphy too.

28 In *Kintaifu 22*, "My Hometown," p. 1: "He was very good at Samurai-style calligraphy, did *waka* and *haiku* poems, and although he was a farmer he generally had good taste."

29 The Kôsei-ji Garden in Kyoto's Kamigyô-ku is a case in point where he used the *kanji* character for heart (*kokoro*) to layout the islands in the sea of gravel. And the design for the garden of Sakyô-ku Ward Fire Department in Kyoto features, appropriately, the *kanji* for water in the form of a dry pond.

30 The documentary was part of a series called *The New Sunday Museum* and was titled "Rinsen no Hito—Shigemori Mirei." It was aired on July 18, 1999.

31 This short conversation is the introduction to the television documentary mentioned previously, "Rinsen no Hito—Shigemori Mirei."

[052]

[053]

[054]

[055]

即妙 **[054]** is pronounced *sokumyô*. This calligraphy is also read from right to left. It means "to respond quickly in a sophisticated way," a characteristic that Mirei Shigemori certainly had. This calligraphy was also donated to the *Mirei Shigemori Kinenkan* in Yoshikawa where it now is on display.

今 **[055]** is pronounced *ima* and stands for now, the present or the moment. This was one of Mirei Shigemori's favorite *kanjis* as he was a true person of the moment. In the book *Gardens—Approach to Gods* we can see how he enjoys a moment smoking a cigarette on the *engawa* of his house in Kyoto.[32] And his lifelong motto was that "every moment is a good moment," taken from the Japanese proverb "every day is a good day."[33] In 1974 he published a book titled *Every Moment is Special*, containing many of the essays he had written for the *Rinsen* journal.[34]

青龍白虎逢年門 **[056]** is read as: *seiryû byakko hô nenmon*. This calligraphy was among Mirei Shigemori's scroll collection in the *kura*. It is not usually pronounced, but any Japanese person understands the meaning of the individual characters. That the scroll is written only in *kanji* characters (that is without any of the Japanese *hiragana* or *katakana*) indicates it might originally be a Chinese phrase. In English it could be interpreted as: "The blue dragon and the white lion meet at the gate." It probably refers to the old geomantic concept of the four gods that protect the four heavenly directions, an idea that Mirei Shigemori also used for his garden designs at the Sekizô-ji Temple in Hyôgo Prefecture (see pages 126–133).

[056]

独坐 **[323]** is pronounced *dokuza* and means to sit alone (see page 171). The *Mirei Shigemori Kinenkan* (museum) in Yoshikawa now owns this calligraphy. It refers to an activity that Mirei Shigemori spent a long time doing: sitting alone in his studio and writing his manuscripts. It also is the thing one would do mostly while visiting his gardens. Sitting there, alone or in a small group, is an inherent part of the concept of the *karesansui* garden, or dry landscape garden, that Mirei Shigemori liked so much. So it is no surprise that the garden at the Zuihô-in Temple in the Daitoku-ji complex, designed by Mirei Shigemori in 1961, was called Dokuza-tei. It is the perfect place to sit alone and be impressed by amazing scenery (see pages 168–173).

The above samples are only a small selection of Mirei Shigemori's calligraphic works. However, they all have one thing in common: all are in one way or another connected to Mirei Shigemori's core interests or characteristics. He used calligraphy as one more way of expressing them. As with most things in his life, his approach to calligraphy was unconventional, abstract and modern.

32 In *Shigemori Mirei's Collection of Works, Gardens—Approach to Gods*, p. 4; the black and white picture shows Mirei Shigemori in April 1972 at the age of 76.

33 *Kokukoku kore kôkoku* means "every moment is a good moment"; the original is: *Hibi kore kôjitsu* and translates as "every day is a good day."

34 The monthly pamphlet of the Kyoto Rinsen Kyôkai (Kyoto Garden Association).

[057 | 058] Iwashimizu Hachimangû
[059] Garden at Shrine office
[060] *Hakke*: a temporary hut for the *kami*
[061] *Hakke* with offerings

RELIGION

The Shigemori family had traditionally followed Tendai Buddhism, a movement introduced directly from China in the early 9th century by Saichô (767–822). As an outgrowth of the Mahâyâna teachings, it was egalitarian in theory and stressed that all men had the potential for Buddhahood. One of its remarkable characteristics was the readiness to find a place for all religious teachings and all forms of religious life in a comprehensive view of truth.[35] This is a quality that is still very noticeable in today's Japanese society. It is not uncommon for people to visit a Shinto shrine on New Year's day, go to a Catholic school or university and have a Buddhist funeral ceremony. Few cultures have integrated so many different religions in people's everyday life. But Mirei Shigemori eventually returned to the original Japanese religious roots, to Shinto. In his essay titled "Shin-sakuteiki" he confesses: "The only thing we can trust is nature and there is no other way than to leave everything in nature's hands."[36] Primitive Shinto had embraced cults of very diverse origins, including animism, shamanism, fertility cults and the worship of nature, ancestors and heroes. Over time the distinctions between these various cults disappeared and the sun goddess Amaterasu became the chief deity for all of them, worshipped at the famous shrine in Ise.

For much of his life, Mirei Shigemori went to the Iwashimizu Hachimangû Shrine in Yawata-shi on the 27th day of each month to pay his respects to the gods **[057–058]**. The shrine is located in the south of Kyoto City and belongs to the Hachiman Shinkô (Hachiman belief). This faith is called a Shinbutstôgô, a marriage of Shinto and Buddhism. It is known for its tolerance and integrative approach to all things in life, and in that it is very close to the way Japanese people feel. In Mirei Shigemori's case, it seems that this integration of ancient Shinto beliefs suited him well, and that Hachiman Shinkô was closer to what he felt were the roots of his culture. The cult's main temple, Usa Hachimangû, is on Kyûshû's Kunisaki Hantô (Kunisaki Peninsula). The Yoshikawa Hachimangû shrine in Mirei Shigemori's hometown was built much later than the ones mentioned above, and it was this shrine that he helped to preserve as a national monument after his return from Tokyo.

When visiting the shrine Mirei Shigemori would first stop at the main hall, pay his respects and continue along the encircling wall with all its little shrines. Here he would stop and pray for good health, rain, his studies, the right personal connections, his male and female family members, and finally for personal and business success. At each minor shrine he would carry out the following procedure:

1. throw a coin into the box to attract the attention of the *kami* (god)
2. bow twice to greet the *kami*
3. say his name and where he was from
4. thank the *kami* for past help and good fortune
5. maybe make a wish (but only rarely!)
6. bow again to say goodbye
7. continue on to the next shrine or leave the temple precincts.

For certain very important occasions he would arrange a special session with the priest of the temple. In that case Mirei Shigemori would enter the central precinct and pray together with the priest. Of course there was an extra charge to get this special service. This custom of regular monthly visits on a fixed day is kept alive by Mirei Shigemori's grandson Mitusaki. It is also worth noting that Mirei Shigemori was able to do two projects at the site of the Iwashimizu Hachimangû Shrine. The first, completed in 1952, was the small, enclosed *karesansui* garden near the shrine's office **[059]**, right off the main axis of the temple, and the second, dating from 1966, is the Tori-no-niwa garden near the temple's gate. Both are a small but not unimportant by-product of his religious life.

35 From Bary, Wm. Theodore de, *Sources of Japanese Tradition* (New York: Columbia University Press, 1958), vol. 1, p. 110.

36 In *Shigemori Mirei's Collection of Works, Gardens—Approach to Gods*, p. 313.

[062 | 063 | 064 | 065 | 066] **Tôban Matsuri**

The Yoshikawa Hachimangû Tôban Matsuri

According to Mircea Eliade, emphasis should be laid on "[...] the structure of the sacred time actualized in festivals."[37] And the Japanese calendar is full of festivals, or *matsuri* as the Japanese say, and a great many of them are connected to rituals and stories of times long past. Eliade points out that, "To reintegrate the sacred time of origin is equivalent to becoming contemporary with the gods."[38] Moreover, these festivals are not only an important part of people's life, but they also structure the time of their everyday existence as it passes by. Mirei Shigemori also attended numerous festivals in his life, as there are many in Kyoto. But the most important one for him was the Yoshikawa Hachimangû Tôban *matsuri* in his hometown, Yoshikawa.

The festival officially starts on October 1 with the selection of the Tôban (son of the god), one for the north part and one for the south part of the village. The dividing line is the watershed on which the Hachimangû shrine is located. To find a Tôban, the names of eligible young men are written on a piece of paper, which is folded and then wrapped once more. The pieces of paper are then beaten with a branch until one is picked up. The boy who is chosen becomes the Tôban for the entire year. This is quite an event for the young men and a great honor for their families. Between October 19 and October 22 a *hakke* (temporary hut for the *kami*) **[060 | 061]** is built in front of the house of the new Tôban. About 30 men in each part of the town work together to create the *hakke* in their respective locations. Then on October 22 the *kami* comes to visit for five days. From then on the *hakke* is inhabited and the priest will come to welcome the *kami*. Incidentally, the body of the god is symbolized by a bundle of grass with roots. On October 27 a loud noise at each end of the village wakes everybody up at 6:00 a.m. A preselected group of ten to twelve people from each side of the village assembles at the respective houses of the two new Tôbans. Then they parade into town with the young Tôban riding high up on a horse. Once they arrive at the local shrine, the participants are seated in two separate areas marked by an oval fence, immediately east of the shrine building **[062 | 063]**. There the participants—but not the young Tôban—are given mochi and hot sake at 9:30 in the morning. With the sake cups in their hand they shout, "tôban, tachimochi, mori, kaezoe...," before draining the cup in one gô **[064]**. While this is going on, villagers come and give presents to the Tôban (most of which are given to local schools the next day). The monetary contributions, on the other hand, will help pay the large sake bill. Sake in large quantities represents a very important part of these festivals. It raises everyone's spirits and allows people to communicate more easily with each other, which is probably one of the major objectives of this kind of event in a small town like Yoshikawa. At about 10:30 a.m., the two groups move to the west side of the shrine for a purification ceremony **[065]**. The space is demarcated with bamboo, ropes and an altar. This ceremony lasts about 15 minutes after which the group moves inside the building. There foods from the sea and the mountains are offered to the gods. Four Shinto officials carry in the beautifully arranged foods and place the elevated plates on the steps of the altar. While this takes place a few people play *koto* (Japanese zither), drum and *shakuhachi* (a flute), which gives the occasion a very special atmosphere. Then at noon the two groups move back to their previous places in the oval areas for lunch. *Udon* interspersed with boiled potatoes, konnyaku, egg and white radish is served and followed by even more sake. At about 2:00 p.m. two groups of eight people each carry two *mikoshi* (portable shrines) **[066 | 067]** to a place called *otabisho* (travel-place) **[068]** roughly 500 meters from the main shrine. There the *mikoshi* are purified and the porters take a break and drink some more sake. An *okagura* (dragon dance) is performed in front of the *otabisho* before they return to the main shrine. But instead of going straight back, they weave back and forth part of the way **[069]**, and even go beyond their destination. Then they finally reach the Hachimangû shrine, race up the stairs and through the temple gate. Each *mikoshi* weighs about 240 kg but fueled by all the alcohol, the porters have no difficulty carrying the weight. The race back to the shrine is the finale and everybody runs as fast as they can. Then with two drumbeats the *matsuri* is over.

37 Mircea Eliade, *The Sacred and the Profane*, trans. Willard R. Trask (San Diego: Harcourt Brace Jovanovich, 1968), p. 88.

38 Ibid., p. 91.

[067 | 068 | 069 | 070] Tôban Matsuri

The village of Yoshikawa has approximately 800 inhabitants, therefore most people get to participate about once every fourth year **[070]**. The festival, which takes place soon after the harvest is over, certainly creates a tremendous sense of community among the people living there. Moreover, it clearly emphasizes how important these religious roots are, even now, especially with regard to the Japanese garden.

Shinto and the Origins of the Japanese Garden

The art of the Japanese garden originally developed from a variety of sources, one of the main ones being the early influences that came from China via Korea, often in the form of gardeners hired to do work for local rulers. But another very important source, which may have been even more influential, is Shinto, the native religion of ancient Japan. Since time immemorial people have worshipped the gods that surround them, who are thought to be visible in the various forms of nature. It must have been this aspect of nature worship that attracted Mirei Shigemori to the Shinto religion. That it did deeply impress him can be seen from the frequent references he makes in his essay titled "Shin-Sakuteiki."[39] **[100]** He even recognizes this very aspect of nature worship as the origin of the Japanese garden. The following quotations, all taken from the "Shin-Sakuteiki" essay, illustrate his arguments.

He begins by citing the extremely early roots of Shinto worship. "The *himorogi* used at the shrine festivals often was simply the deification of a large ancient tree" **[072]**. This has not changed much today. All over Japan we can still find these old trees marked by thick ropes made from rice-straw, which are easily recognizable as a special or holy place. He continues: "After a while these holy sites moved to the foot of the mountain and people started to treat these as the object of their belief, and dances were performed to music in front of these holy trees." Initially, therefore, old trees were the main focus of worship, but later the places of worship changed and also other elements, such as prominent rocks, were included as objects of worship **[071]**. The way of worshipping also developed and seasonal festivals appeared. These holy rocks or stones, usually natural features in the landscape, were called *iwakura* and are maybe the oldest visible root of the Japanese garden. Mirei Shigemori states: "Nature is a world made by the gods. For example, the Amatsu *iwakura*, which is only a big natural stone, was recognized by the people as a holy place." It is interesting to note that many temples in Japan are in fact built nearby or below a naturally dominant single rock or outcrop. This suggests that these were always regarded by the local population as holy places in the landscape. As Shinto developed, and eventually had to compete against Buddhism, temples were built near sites that had already been used for centuries. A case in point here is Sekizô-ji Temple in Hyôgo Prefecture, which is built directly below an impressive natural rock formation **[249]**. This is described in greater detail in Chapter "Gods Protecting the Cardinal Points: Sekizô-ji, 1972" (see pages 126–133).

The next step in Mirei Shigemori's argument is an interesting one. He writes that, "As time passed people started to bring other big stones and added them to an existing *iwakura*" **[073]**. If this is true, this would indeed mark the start of garden-making. Moreover, it is this act that continues to be the essence of garden-making in Japan to this very day: the placing of rocks, assembling them in large groups of stones in a garden, and, in effect, creating places for the gods to visit. When I read this the first time I was quite skeptical. Why would people many centuries ago relocate huge rocks to a certain place in the landscape and add them to an existing rock? But Mirei Shigemori highlights an important intermediate step that occurred at some point: the separation of the gods from nature. In Mirei Shigemori's words: "The desire to reproduce nature and create a garden-like place means that first the gods' existence must be separated from nature." And in the next sentence he gives us the reason why: "As long as gods exist in nature, people are not permitted to alter it. When people worship nature as god, people subordinate themselves to the gods' existence." So yes, people had started to intervene in nature and change it around. By doing this, the role of the gods became limited and people assumed a new

39 The "Shin-Sakuteiki" in *Shigemori Mirei's Collection of Works, Gardens—Approach to Gods* (Tokyo: Seibundô Shinkô Sha, 1976); he republished the essay in one piece, pp. 281–315. See also footnote 1, page 18

role. "Following the birth of the idea that people could be on the same level as the gods, people recognized that nature, which had been previously regarded as the sole creation of the gods, could actually be made by man." This is the start of the Japanese garden as we know it today.

Mirei Shigemori knew these roots very well. He had surveyed several hundred gardens all over the country and was aware of the different forms they had taken. One of the gardens that left a special mark in his memory is certainly Kokubun-ji in Takamatsu on the island of Shikoku **[074]**. In his very last work, the stone setting at Matsuo Taisha in Kyoto, we can see how he strived to come close to the power of these ancient stone settings. I must admit that, when I first saw it, I was not very impressed. I didn't know how to evaluate it because in my own culture we do not set stones like this or in any similar way. But now, after several years of evaluating stone settings by Mirei Shigemori and others, and having studied the ideas behind them, I do agree that the stone setting at Matsuo Taisha is probably one of his best (see pages 86–91).

[071] **Iwakura at Achi Jinja**
[072] **Matsuo Jinja**
[073] **Himorogi, Kibitsuhiku**
[074] **Kokubun-ji**

THE MATURE YEARS

[075] Matsue Ochi and Mirei Shigemori, with their son Kanto and a friend behind

Five Children with Foreign Names

On February 28, 1923 Mirei Shigemori married Matsue Ochi. He was 26 at the time and his wife, born on May 5, 1903, was only 19 years old. They had met in Tokyo where Matsue Ochi was studying at Tokyo Music College to become a pianist. Barely three months after they had gotten married, and only shortly after Matsue's twentieth birthday, their first son Kanto (完途) was born.[40] Just over three years later, when they were already living in Yoshikawa (after the earthquake), they had their second son Kôen (弘淹) in 1926.[41] Then in 1930, a year after Mirei Shigemori and his wife had moved to Kyoto, their first and only daughter Yûgo (由郷) was born.[42] Next, after a long gap of five and a half years, and only shortly before Mirei Shigemori embarked on his legendary survey project, their third son, named Geite (ゲーテ), was born in 1935.[43] Then, in 1938, their fourth and last son Bairon (貝崙) followed, while Mirei Shigemori was still in the middle of work on the *Nihon Teienshi Taikei*.[44]

All five children were given foreign names. The first son, Kanto, was named after Immanuel Kant, the famous philosopher. The second son Kôen received his name from Herman Cohen, a German philosopher of Kant's school. Yûgo, the only daughter, apparently got her name from Victor Hugo, the author of *Les Miserables*. The name of the third son, Geite, was derived from the German writer Johann Wolfgang von Goethe. And the fourth son Bairon was named after George Byron, the famous British poet. It is interesting that all these figures were famous European intellectuals and that Mirei Shigemori, who himself had adopted the name of a French painter, always used the family names of those individuals and turned them into Japanese first names. Of course, none of the children had an easy time with their unusual names and all of them had to explain countless times to others why they had such a unique first name.

The Kyoto Garden Association

Another milestone in Mirei Shigemori's more mature life was certainly the founding of the *Kyoto Rinsen Kyôkai* (Kyoto Garden Association) in 1932, for the purpose of studying old gardens. This was an activity that, according to Kawakatsu Masatarô, was not very popular yet: "At that time the study and admiration of the Japanese garden had almost been abandoned by the people, so this organization's main aim was quite new."[45] The same source continues, "Mr Nakano and Mr Shigemori decided to found an association for the study and promotion of the Japanese garden, and to confer with Dr Amanuma Shunichi, a specialist on architectural history at Kyoto University who had been Mr Nakano's teacher. Also invited were Kanshûji Tsuneo, a horticultural researcher interested in gardens, as well as Prof Sekiguchi, a garden specialist at Kyoto University. This is how *Kyôto Rinsen Kyokai* was established in 1932."[46] At first Mr Nakano was the president and Mirei Shigemori held a position resembling that of vice president, even though this position didn't exist officially; eventually, however, he became the association's leader. Kawakatsu Masatarô himself, who was also a member of *Kyoto Rinsen Kyôkai*, was in charge of stone art related to the garden. Similarly, every committee member had his special area of expertise. Up to 30 people took part in the monthly excursions. These consisted of site visits and

40 Kanto, Mirei Shigemori's oldest son, followed in his father's footsteps and became a dedicated landscape architect and writer. He spent most of his life in Tokyo where he died at the age of 69 in December 1992.

41 Kôen became a professor of photography at Tokyo College of Photography and followed his father as an ikebana artist and critic; he also wrote poetry. He was the first of Mirei Shigemori's children to pass away, in Fall 1992.

42 Yûgo, greatly supported by her father, was educated in traditional Japanese dance and eventually became a master with her own school in Kyoto. At the same time she was teaching at the famous Takarazuka Music School near Osaka. She was the only child who chose to live in Kyoto.

43 Geite went into the field of publishing and produced the only existing retrospective of his father's work: *Shigemori Mirei's Collection of Works, Gardens—Approach to Gods* (Tokyo: Seibundô Shinkô Sha, 1976). He still lives in Tokyo and was a great supporter of this research on his father.

44 Bairon was educated as a filmmaker and ultimately had his own business in Tokyo named Iwanami Audio-Visual Media Inc.; his graduation work titled "Ishibashi's garden" was a great resource for this research project as it documents a garden construction in process and relates much of his father's way of thinking.

45 In *Kintaifu 29*, "Shigemori Mirei's Personality and Achievement," p. 6.

46 Ibid.

lectures by the committee members, often followed by lively discussions. Visiting gardens in Kyoto was clearly not as popular as it is these days; Kawakatsu Masatarô recalls: "Enjoying the excursions to our hearts content, we could spend entire days at Ryôan-ji, Kinkaku-ji, Ginkaku-ji and the other temples. There were no tourists at these temples, only once in a while an admirer visited. At that time we never experienced a situation where tourist buses lined up in front and a hundred to a hundred and fifty people crowded into a garden."[47]

In 1935 Mirei Shigemori and some members of *Kyoto Rinsen Kyôkai* restored the now famous Shôden-ji garden in the north of Kyoto City. They removed various items from the *karesansui* garden and left only a 7–5–3 *karikomi*, which contrasts beautifully with the borrowed scenery of Mount Hiei in the background. In 1961 Mirei Shigemori then designed the garden at Zuihô-in, one of the temples in the Daitoku-ji complex, a great way of commemorating the thirtieth anniversary of *Kyoto Rinsen Kyôkai*. But the group not only built or restored gardens, they also continued to meet for the monthly excursions and published a regular newsletter **[076–078]**. In fact, the association is still active today and recently celebrated its seventieth anniversary in September 2002. Many members recall Mirei Shigemori and were very willing to answer questions about the old days. In the later years they apparently would often go and visit Mirei Shigemori's most recent projects, and on more than one occasion some of his clients became new members. At its peak in the 1950s and 1960s, the association had a total of about 300 members. Mirei Shigemori is said to often have encouraged his younger followers in the Kyoto Garden Association to study tea.

Starting His Own Company

In the last year of working on the survey, Mirei Shigemori took another big step in his professional life. In March 1938 he founded a company called *Nihon Teien Kenkyûsho* (Japanese Garden Research Institute). The company consisted of two departments, which were subdivided in a total of eight sections. One department was devoted to research, the other to design and construction. The research department consisted of the following three sections:

- Documentation: this section managed the information gathered during the survey, which consisted of documents such as plans, sketches, transcripts of temple records and photos; it was also in charge of publishing.
- Survey: this section undertook two kinds of surveys, either contracted by a client or initiated by the research department itself.
- Education: this section organized classes, free and invited lectures, and practical training.

The second department, concerned with design and construction, had five sections:

- Old gardens: restoration, renovation, design and construction related to old gardens.
- New gardens: design, construction and construction supervision.
- General garden projects: other activities related to garden-making.
- Design of tea houses and other Japanese traditional architecture.
- Consulting: inquiries related to any kind of gardens or tea houses.

The members of the board of directors were: Mirei Shigemori (chairman), Takuo Shimizu, Hiroo Nabeshima and Nori Fukui. Clearly, the purpose of this company was to provide services ranging from survey all the way to construction. The business address was Mirei Shigemori's home at the time.[48]

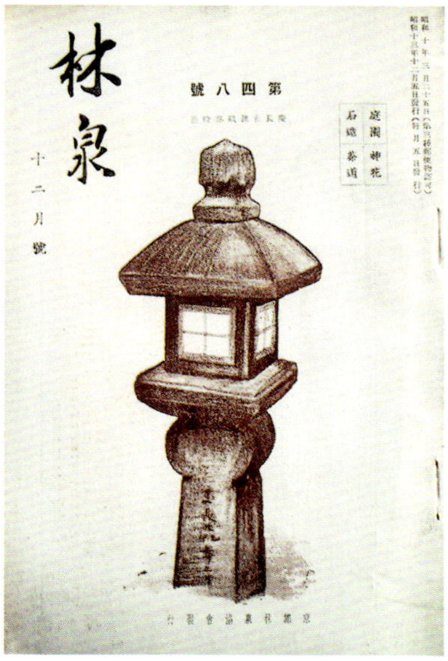

[076] Rinsen Newsletter, September 1939
[077] Rinsen Newsletter, November 1942
[078] Rinsen Newsletter, December 1938

47 Ibid.
48 Source: *Nihon Teienshi Zukan, Geppô no. 19* ("Illustrated Book on the History of the Japanese Garden," monthly newsletter no. 19); it came with volume 16 of the Survey and was published on April 25, 1938 in Tokyo by Yûkôsha. The address of the first Shigemori residence is 45 Shimoôji-chô, Yoshida, Sakyô-ku, Kyoto.

[079]

[080 | 081]

[082 | 083]

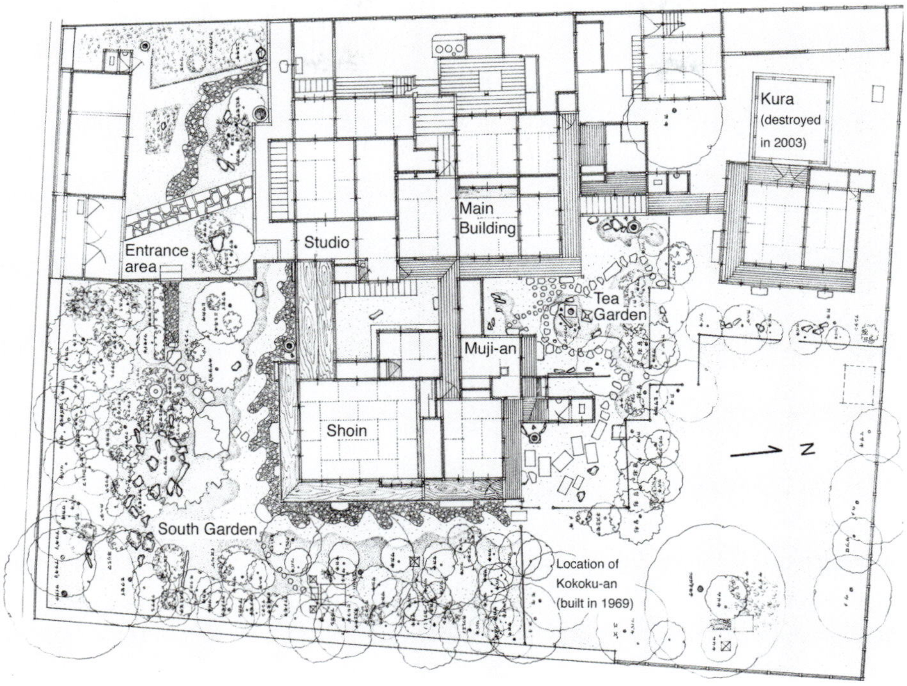

[084] **Plan of the Shigemori residence and garden**
[085] **Model to scale, including Kôkoku-an to the right**

A Residence for Life

In 1943, right in the middle of WW II and much to the surprise of his friends, Mirei Shigemori decided to buy the former house of the well-known Suzuka family that was being auctioned off **[084 | 085]**. The house was an Edo period structure built in 1789; it used to be part of the Yoshida shrine complex and was formerly the priest's house. It was here that Mirei Shigemori lived for the rest of his life.[49] In 1953 he built the Muji-an tea room, thereby making the first major extension to the house he had bought ten years earlier. In April that year he made a tea garden to go with it, shown in the center of the plan **[084]**, just to the north of the *shoin*. In 1955 he redesigned the entry area to the south of the main building and added the straight and the curving path. The garden to the south of the *shoin* was built in two stages, a first phase in 1952 and the second in 1956 **[079–081]**. It features four stone settings symbolizing the Elysian islands Hôjô, Eijû, Hôrai and Koryô, set in a sea of *Shirakawa suna*. For stones he used his favorite *aoishi* from Shikoku. Most of his writing on book manuscripts was done in the studio located between the main building and the *shoin* **[086]**. This residence still exists and has just been turned into a museum by one of Mirei Shigemori's heirs.

[086] **A special *shôji* window in Mirei Shigemori's study**

After the War

In 1948, only three years after the war was over, Mirei Shigemori became the first winner of the Kyoto Bunka-in prize, which was awarded by the Kyoto Cultural Academy. This represents an important recognition of his cultural contributions in the fields of ikebana and tea, as well as the Japanese garden. In 1949 Mirei Shigemori founded an ikebana research group called Byakutôsha at his house in Kyoto. Later, in 1950, he started publishing the ikebana art magazine called *Ikebana Geijutsu*. Both these events show how important ikebana remained throughout his life. The Byakutôsha group also met once a month, mostly at Mirei Shigemori's residence. Being a true study group, at these meetings they would actually do ikebana, critique each other's works and discuss the future of ikebana as an art. Some of the core members were Nakagawa Yukio, Sudô Masao and Kusakabe Yûsaku. Mirei Shigemori was the leader of the group and organized the monthly meetings.[50]

Even though WWII had practically put a stop to much of his garden-making, Shigemori was not inactive during this time. In fact, he wrote more than ever before and in 1949 published a record number of nine books in one single year. Then, in the early 1950s, his garden-making quickly picked back up and by 1953 he had already created 14 outdoor spaces for clients, more than in any year before the war. So when Mirei Shigemori built the garden at the Maegaki residence in 1955 (see pages 98–105), he had already progressed much further with his career as a landscape architect. In 1956 Yukio Okamoto joined the

[079] **Shigemori Residence, South Garden**
[080] **Stone setting in the South Garden**
[081] **View from the main room**
[082] **Kôkoku-an tea house**
[083] **Uniquely designed *fusuma* at Kôkoku-an**

49 The address of the second Shigemori residence is 34 Kamiôji-chô, Yoshida Sakyô-ku, Kyoto 606-8312; for appointments contact tel. +81 (0)90 8467 8988, fax +81 (0)75 761 8776.

50 A study group meeting on January 7, 1955 also lists the following people as participants: Ono, Kusuhara, Imanishi, Shimizu, Handa, Saga, Yanagida, Tanaka and others; Mirei Shigemori notes though that interest in the group already seems to be fading.

company, the gardener with whom he later built more than 130 projects over the next 19 years. Mr Okamoto eventually became Mirei Shigemori's right hand, taking over much of the on-site responsibility when building the gardens.

Isamu Noguchi and the UNESCO Garden in Paris

One of the more important events of his life was certainly the meeting with Isamu Noguchi and their resulting cooperation for the UNESCO Garden in Paris. Mirei Shigemori and Isamu Noguchi met for the first time on April 18, 1957 in Himi, on the island of Shikoku. At the time Mirei Shigemori was working on the garden of Eiichi Ochi and Isamu Noguchi came to see him there. They spent the day together looking at some gardens, most of which were Mirei Shigemori's projects, and were chauffeured around in the car belonging to the governor of Kagawa Prefecture. In the evening they were invited to dinner at the governor's residence. Isamu Noguchi was already quite famous at the time, and Mirei Shigemori was impressed by the pomp and publicity. On April 20, they went to Ueyama together trying to find stones for the Paris garden **[089 | 090]**. According to Mirei Shigemori they marked a total of about 80 stones in the quarry. On April 27, back in Kyoto, Mirei Shigemori took Isamu Noguchi to a tea ceremony in Kômyô-in and afterwards showed him his garden design at Tôfuku-ji **[092 | 094]**. Then, from May 7 to May 11, they worked together on a mock-up of the stone settings for the UNESCO Garden. On a site in the city of Tokushima, on Shikoku island, they built a trial garden for that project, setting up all the stones needed **[091]**. This is where Mirei Shigemori's advice must have been most valuable to Isamu Noguchi, as he had asked him for help with the garden project.[51] But for Mirei Shigemori the collaboration was not an easy one, as he could not work in a way that was to his liking. From this point on, Isamu Noguchi was a frequent visitor to the Shigemori residence in Kyoto, a fact that is well documented in the family album **[093]**. The two men frequently met socially and visited gardens together. Also Mirei Shigemori continued to make contacts for Isamu Noguchi and introduced him to people like the stonemason Kinzô Nishimura and others. There was even talk of Mirei Shigemori going to Paris, but he declined as he was afraid of flying. In the evening of August 8, 1958, Isamu Noguchi came to Mirei Shigemori's house to show him the pictures of the completed UNESCO Garden. Later Mirei Shigemori received various presents for his help with this project, among them a lamp designed by Isamu Noguchi **[087 | 088]**. This oval shaped paper lamp can still be admired in the Shigemori residence *shoin*. Although there were no collaborative projects after the UNESCO Garden, the meeting with Isamu Noguchi left a deep impression on Mirei Shigemori.

[087 | 088] **Two presents: a scroll and a lamp by Isamu Noguchi**

Busy Building Gardens, then Resuming Writing

The 1950s were an uneventful period in terms of publishing garden-related books. Between 1949 and 1956 Mirei Shigemori published not a single book on this topic. This is only remarkable because of the uninterrupted stream of such publications since 1933. One reason for this was that he was simply too busy building gardens. But with regard to writing, there are two ikebana-related publications in the early 1950s and Mirei Shigemori was also working hard on publishing an issue of *Ikebana Geijutsu* every month. Then in 1956 he resumed his writing of garden books and published *Japanese Gardens* with Kadokawa Shoten in Tokyo. Two years later, in 1958, Mirei Shigemori wrote the book *Gardens* together with his son Kanto, gradually getting back to publishing books on this subject. 1964 is the year in which he started to work with the photographer Haruzô Ôhashi, a collaboration that was to last for the next eleven years. The first book they worked on together was *Mirei Shigemori's Collected Works—Gardens*, published in 1964 by Heibonsha in Tokyo **[095]**. This is actually the only book Mirei Shigemori wrote that is entirely about his own work. The other publication mentioned earlier, *Mirei Shigemori's Collection of Works, Gardens—Approach to Gods*, was produced after his death by his son Geite and Saitô Tadakazu.

51 May 8, 1957 in "Excerpts from Mirei Shigemori's Diary": "Isamu Noguchi: 1957—1958."

[089 | 090] **Looking for suitable stones in Ueyama**
[091] **Working on a mock-up for the UNESCO garden**
[092 | 093] **Isamu Noguchi visits the Shigemori residence**
[094] **Visiting a garden together**

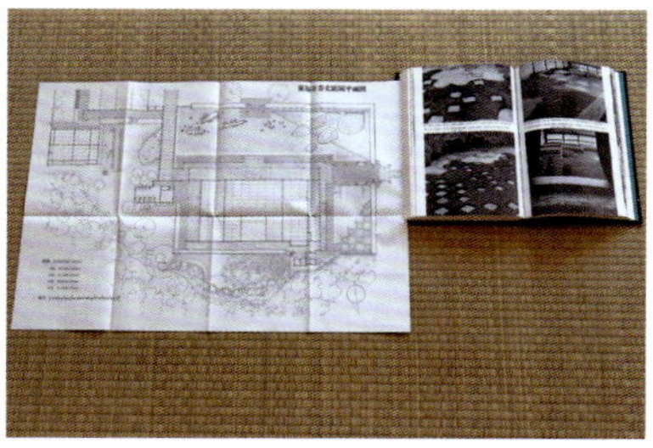

[095] ***Mirei Shigemori's Collected Works—Gardens***
[096] Japanese Garden History Survey
[097] Large foldable plans drawn to scale

Toward the End: A Second Survey

In 1969 Mirei Shigemori built the Kôkoku-an tea house at his residence in Kyoto **[082 | 083]**. It is still a structure that Mirei Shigemori's heirs proudly show to anybody who visits the residence these days. The paintings on the *fusuma* are of particular interest **[083]**, as they clearly reflect Mirei Shigemori's approach to Japanese art. The tea house also contains many nice architectural details, including custom-made door pulls.

Throughout these years Mirei Shigemori remained connected to his hometown and tried to go there for the yearly Tôban Matsuri, as described earlier. Also in 1969 he donated Tenrai-an, the tea house he had made together with his father in 1914, to the town of Yoshikawa **[038 | 039]**. A passage in *Kintaifu 22*, published in January 1974, shows how much he still liked the place he had grown up in: "There is nothing better than having a hometown. [...] My hometown was especially blessed, as the village has absolutely no pollution; whenever I looked at the sky it was clear and blue. It makes me very happy that a great place like this remains until this day."[52] These *Kintaifu* pamphlets were published together with the updated survey, and contain several unique essays about Mirei Shigemori's life.

Thirty years after the publication of the monumental *Nihon Teienshi Zukan*, Mirei Shigemori decided it was time to revise the text, redraw the plans and issue a new and extended version of his survey, now called *Nihon Teienshi Taikei* ("Japanese Garden History Survey"). The updated survey consisted of 35 volumes **[096]**, in part with color pictures by Haruzô Ôhashi and large drawings at the back of each book **[097]**. Mirei Shigemori's followers reworked many of the plans to show the current state of the gardens. The updated survey was published by Shakai Shisôsha in Tokyo between May 5, 1971 and June 1, 1976 and can be found in many libraries throughout Japan. Mirei Shigemori's son Kanto was coauthor of the work and finished the last five volumes on his own after his father died on March 12, 1975 at the age of 79 **[098 | 099]**.

Looking back on Mirei Shigemori's achievements, his friend Masatarô Kawakatsu notes: "Everything Mr Shigemori did, he did big; nobody can mimic him in that. Then the Zukan was successfully completed. Soon after that, Mr Shigemori bought his current house in Yoshida Kamiôji-chô and moved there, taking over the former house of the great Suzuka family in the Yoshida neighborhood. There are people who mistake the magnificent estate to be a temple. We all were amazed. [...] He did most things he did in this manner."[53]

52 In *Kintaifu 22*, "My Hometown," p. 2.
53 In *Kintaifu 29*, "Shigemori Mirei's Personality and Achievement," p. 7.

[098] **The family graveyard in Yoshikawa**

[099] **Mirei Shigemori's gravestone**

STRATEGY FOR RENEWAL

Since the early 20th century cities in Japan have been changing at breathtaking speed, and with them their gardens and parks. More recently, and against a background of continuing globalization, this process is increasingly accompanied by a notable loss of local identity. This is easily discernible if we visit gardens and parks in Tokyo, Osaka or other big cities where many new designs seem interchangeable, lacking any reason for being in the specific place they are. They may be modern and international, but clearly they have no local ties. It is in this context that Mirei Shigemori's designs can offer an alternative direction for a strategy for renewal, a strategy that is necessary but also needs to be more closely linked to local Japanese culture. This is without doubt a situation that many artists find themselves in when creating something within a continuously changing cultural framework, a circumstance that is, of course, equally true of the Japanese garden.

Ideally, as an artistic product, the garden is a reflection of its time as well as its place—at least this is how it used to be for much of the garden's history. So, when examining the essential problem of its creative renewal within a specific cultural context, a number of different parameters have to be considered, with the main focus in this book being placed on the conceptual and the more formal aspects.

ROOTED IN PLACE AND CULTURE

Mirei Shigemori was a person who knew his own culture very well. He was a dedicated ikebana artist, as well as a connoisseur of the tea ceremony and the related arts. He felt so rooted in his country and its culture that he never even had the desire to go abroad. Hence, the term local culture in Mirei Shigemori's case means essentially Japanese culture, with an emphasis on Kyoto, as this was the main center of his activities.

Furthermore, Mirei Shigemori understood the Japanese garden as an abstraction of an area's natural and cultural landscapes. In fact, this was not just his personal interpretation but quite a widely shared concept among traditional garden makers in Japan, as it still is today. The famous *Sakuteiki*, written as early as the Heian period (794–1185), advises that when making a garden, one should "think over the famous places of beauty throughout the land, and by making your own that which appeals to you most, design your garden with the mood of harmony, modeling after the general air of such places."[1] This strong connection to place and the local landscape used to be one of the distinct characteristics of Japanese gardens and was at least partly responsible for their unmistakable feel of atmosphere and harmony. The aesthetic experience provided was completely rooted in the natural and cultural basis of the place.

Mirei Shigemori had not only read the *Sakuteiki* but was able to learn directly from hundreds of examples when working on the survey. In his book *Gardens of Japan* (1949), he ultimately concludes: "The influence of nature is particularly strong on the garden, because [...] it is a man-made landscape, and also because it is made up of the component parts of nature, such as land, water, rocks, trees, etc. This, however, does not mean that the garden is a photographic copy of nature, for there are many in which the interpretation is symbolic, idealistic or even fantastic."[2] This is exactly where Mirei Shigemori saw numerous opportunities to renew and develop the traditional Japanese garden. In his view, there was still much more that could be done with these interpretations, since to his innovative mind many options had not yet been explored.

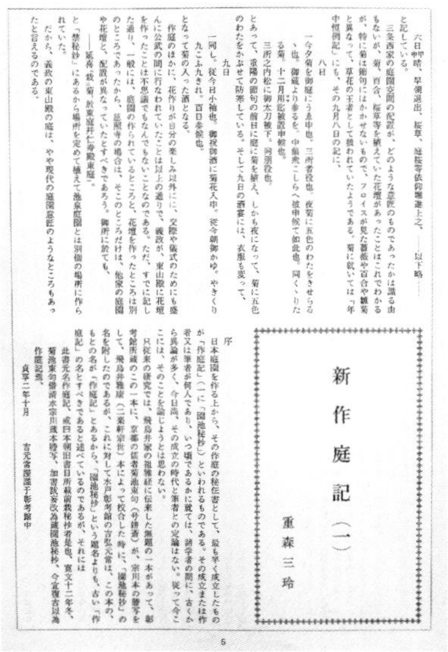
六日甲申晴、早朝退出、桜草、庭桜等依御堀進上之、——以下略——
と記している。
三条西家の庭園空間の配置が、どのような意匠のものであったかは識る由もないが、菊、百合、桜草等を植えていた花壇があったことはこれでわかるが、特に菊は欠かせないもので、フロイスが見た薔薇や百合や雛菊と異なって、草花の王者として扱われていたようである。菊に就いては「年中恒例記」にも、その九月八日の記に、
八日
一今夕菊を御庭にう点申也。三所者役也。夜菊に五色のわたをきせらるゝ也。御蔵より参るを。中臈衆こしらへ被申候て如此也。同くゝりたる菊。十二月用鉱被置申候也。
三所之内松に御太刀被下。同朋役也。
とあって、重陽の節句の前日に庭に菊を植え、しかも夜になって、菊に五色のわたをかぶせて防寒している。そして九日の酒宴には、衣服も変って、
九日
一同し。従今日小袖也。御祝御酒に菊花入申。従今朝御かゆ。やきくり九こふ九きれ。百日参候也。
となって菊の入った酒となる。
作庭のほかに、花作りが自分の楽しみ以外にに、交際や儀式のためにも盛んに公武の間に行なわれていたことは以上の通りで、義政が、東山殿に花壇を作ったことは不思議でもなんでもないことなのである。ただ、すでに記した通り、一般には、庭園の作られているところと、花壇を作ったところは別のところであったから、慈照寺の場合は、そこのところだけは、他家の庭園や花壇と、配置が異なっていたとすべきであろう。御所に於ても、
——延寿「栽菊、於東庭井仁寿殿東庭」。
と「禁秘抄」にあるから場所を定めて植えて池泉庭園とは別個の場所に作られていた。
だから、義政の東山殿の庭は、やや現代の庭園意匠のようなところもあったと言えるのである。

新作庭記（一）
重森三玲

序
日本庭園を作る上から、その作庭の秘伝書として、最も早く成立したものが「作庭記」（一に「園池秘抄」）といわれるものである。その成立または作者又は筆者が何人であり、いつ頃であるかに就ては、諸学者の間に、古くから異論が多く、今日尚、その成立の時代と筆者との定論はない。従って今ここには、そのことを論じようとは思わない。
只従来の研究では、飛鳥井家の祖雅経に伝来した無題の一本があって、彰考館所蔵のこの一本に、京都の儒者菊池東匀（号耕斎）が、宗川本の謄写をして、飛鳥井雅康（二楽軒宗世）本によって校合した時に、「園池秘抄」の名を附したのであるが、これに対して水戸彰考館の吉弘元常は、この本の、もとの名が「作庭記」とあるから、「園池秘抄」という題名よりも、古い「作庭記」の名とすべきであると述べているのであるが、それには
此書元名作庭記、或曰本朝旧書目所載前栽秘抄者是也、寛文十二年冬、菊池東匀借清水宗川蔵本謄写、加書跋妄改為蔵園池秘抄、今宜復古以為作庭記焉、
貞享二年十月　吉元常謹識于彰考館中

5

[100] The *Kintaifu* pamphlet with the first part of the "Shin-Sakuteiki" essay

Three Approaches to Designing a Garden

In 1971, after creating more than 200 gardens, Mirei Shigemori wrote an essay titled *Shin-Sakuteiki* (literally the "New Sakuteiki"), as already cited in the preface **[100]**. This was, in part, a response to and update of the 12th century essay on gardens, *Sakuteiki*, mentioned earlier, but it also served to summarize his stance toward garden-making. In this manifesto, he argues that there are three possible approaches to handling nature when making a garden:

1. Pursuing strict conservation and keeping the classic style or traditional style as they are [the traditionalist's approach]
2. Making the best use of classical or traditional styles in the modern period [the approach most congruent with Shigemori's position]
3. Completely ousting classical or traditional styles and creating something new [the modernist's approach]. [3]

For Mirei Shigemori, the first approach describes the leaning of Kyoto's many traditional gardeners, among them a good number of *iemoto*-style businesses that were strictly focused on past garden styles, rooted in the old craft and disinterested in any kind of contemporary renewal. He identified most closely with the second approach, which was based on history but bridged the past and the present. It is worth noting that he placed himself between two extremes, yet many of his conservative contemporaries would have positioned him at the modern end of the spectrum. The third approach is

1 Shigemaru Shimoyama, *Sakuteiki—The Book of Garden* (Tokyo: Town & City Planners, 1976), p. 1. This book constitutes a good early translation of the *Sakuteiki*. For a more recent and more comprehensive translation, see also Jiro Takei and Marc P. Keane, *Sakuteiki: Visions of the Japanese Garden* (Rutland: Charles E. Tuttle, 2001), p. 153. The *Sakuteiki* (作庭記) is the oldest textbook on the secrets of gardening in Japan. There is no established theory on its authorship or the date when it was compiled. It is generally said that Tachibana no Toshitsuna (1028–1094) compiled it from his rich childhood experiences and his keen observations of nature.

2 Mirei Shigemori, *Gardens of Japan* (Kyoto: Nihon Shashin Insatsu, 1949), p. 2.

3 Mirei Shigemori, "Shin-Sakuteiki," in: *Shigemori Mirei's Collection of Works, Gardens—Approach to Gods*, p. 308.

[101] *Nakashima* (central island) in the East Garden at Heian Jingû in Kyoto

where Mirei Shigemori located the true Japanese modernists, designers who had completely adopted Western style modernism and divested themselves of anything traditionally Japanese. While he did have certain sympathies for this approach, he did not consider it desirable to disassociate oneself totally from the history of a culture.

More fundamental differences between traditionalists, modernists and Shigemori become evident when we look at how all three conceptualized and used memory in a specific place. Memory here should be understood as a way of making some aspects of the past serve as a purposeful reference for acting in the present. Not surprisingly, each of these three groups differs radically in their way of conceiving memory.

Traditionalists felt that revered forms of the built cultural environment of the past should be strictly followed in the present and, consequently, the forms used by gardens of the past should also be strictly imitated. Memory, for this group, enables and legitimates the reproduction of forms invented in the past. A good example would be the gardens at Heian Jingû in Kyoto **[101 | 102]**, designed by Ogawa Jihei [4] between 1895 and 1926. This project was a landscape attached to a scaled-down reproduction of the Imperial Hall of State, as it existed in the Heian period. Ogawa designed a historicizing pond garden, primarily in the style of the Edo period. In the central and eastern parts of the gardens, Ogawa included all the typical elements of this garden type: the pine leaning into the water, the peninsula, the *nakashima*, the bridges, and the turtle and crane islands. As in many premodern pond gardens, it comprises a path circumscribing the water that presents visitors with actual or mythical views created as *shukkei*, a technique in which scenic spots or noted places are introduced on a reduced scale.[5] In this garden, none of the stereotypical elements is altered or changed in either form or meaning. If the date of its creation was unknown, it might be ascribed to the Edo period. This was precisely the goal: the more slavish the imitation the better. For traditionalists, respecting the past meant preserving its memory by recreating its forms over and over again, in the hope that it would restore the values, ethics and behavior of the past. In Japan in 1926, memory of the past acted as a bulwark against the modern world that was fast encroaching and threatening the identity of Kyoto as Japan's traditional capital.

For modernists, on the other hand, memory of the past was important in a negative way. The past was seen as an obstacle to be overcome, a tradition to be discarded, or a negative against which progress can be measured. Sutemi Horiguchi's work serves as an illustration. His Yoshikawa Residence **[103]**, built in 1930, totally abandons any reference to traditional Japanese architecture and garden. Complete with large glass windows and rooftop terraces, it reminds one more of Le Corbusier or the Bauhaus. Architectural historian David B. Stewart notes that it could easily be located on the outskirts of

4 Ogawa Jihei (1860–1933), sometimes referred to Niwashi-Ueji, is one of the two most outstanding garden makers of 20th-century Japan. Like Mirei Shigemori he made an effort to revitalize the Japanese garden, often showing an affinity for large lawn areas intersected by winding paths. One can't help but think that he must have been influenced and inspired by the English landscape gardens.

5 Not to be confused with *shakkei*, a gardening technique that utilizes scenery outside the garden not just as a background, but also as one of the essential conceptual elements of the garden itself.

[102] *Shukkei* (scenic spot) complete with a leaning pine tree

Brussels.[6] Horiguchi even included a western-style garden in front. In a very un-Japanese way the garden—its paths winding in a picturesque manner—presented a water feature on the front lawn and placed the entire composition on an axis with the center of the house. Only the perfectly clipped shrubs hint that maybe, after all, a Japanese gardener is at work. Stylistically, the house and garden turn their backs on Japanese cultural tradition. For the modernists, such traditions were a source of alienation, and traditionalists themselves were perceived as prisoners of a sacred reverence for ancient beliefs and an anachronistic way of life. Modernists saw their traditionalist counterparts as falling under the sway of moral prejudices that continued to go unquestioned or uncriticized.

Mirei Shigemori presented a far more complex approach that mediated and even synthesized these opposing views. He felt that memory of the past should inform present identity, but at the same time neither past forms nor past behavior offered a valid concept for the present or future, at least not if taken at face value. Rather, memory should be understood as a way of making the past a source for contemporary inspiration. Mirei Shigemori repeatedly asserted that by remembering the great achievements of garden art, studying them in detail, reaching an understanding of their creativeness, and striving to emulate their way of invention rather than the results achieved, garden makers could distill the most valuable inspiration for their work. Memory was thus a way of emulating the path toward the creation of ancient Japanese gardening here and now, in the present world, with all its new techniques and despite its estrangement from the ancient Japanese reverence for nature and its gods.

[103] Sutemi Horiguchi: Yoshikawa residence and garden, Tokyo 1930

6 David B. Stewart, *The Making of a Modern Japanese Architecture* (Tokyo: Kôdansha International, 1987), p. 144.

TRADITIONAL AND NEW DESIGN ELEMENTS

Mirei Shigemori succeeded in simultaneously conserving and renewing the inheritance of the Japanese garden by reusing many of its typical design elements and translating them into a more contemporary form. Fortunately, I was able to find drawings for 184 of the approximately 240 gardens that Mirei Shigemori designed. I have examined these drawings carefully in order to identify the traditional and new design elements of the Japanese garden. The 21 most commonly used elements found on these plans are listed in the two tables below, with the traditional ones first, then the ones introduced by Mirei Shigemori. (The numbers in the column indicate how often they appeared among the 184 plans.)

Amanohashidate-style landform	14	8 %
Tsukiyama-style landform	39	21 %
Kanji-shaped pond or *tsukiyama*	3	2 %
Mythical animal	5	3 %
Yarimizu-style river	12	7 %
Shakkei	~10	5 %
Tea garden features	28	15 %
Karikomi	9	5 %
Suhama	16	9 %
Shima in a real or abstracted pond	144	78 %
God-pond with an island	32	17 %
Stone setting	177	96 %
Himorogi stone arrangement	1	1 %

Count of specific traditional design elements

Among the traditional design elements in the drawings, I found at least five representations of mythical animals, such as dragons or turtles. However, as there is often no text available with the projects, it is only possible to guess the actual number of these design-specific elements. It seems very likely that more such references exist among the garden projects, but they are hard to decipher when only the plan is available. The same is true for the *shakkei* features, as borrowed scenery is often not recognizable just from the plan.

Wave line	41
Cloud shapes	17
Buddha emitting rays of light	4
Spiral stone setting	4
Wall painting	2
Fence motif	9+
Grid	4
Stripes	4

Count of specific new design elements

The new design elements that Mirei Shigemori added to the repertoire of the Japanese garden are more easily discernible from a design drawing because they are often inspired by his painter's education and are therefore more graphic. Only the fence motif is difficult to count, as not all projects have a fence detail or elevation drawing included. It seems likely that the number is higher though, as on my garden visits I found a good number of fences with a design motif had survived.

To illustrate this, the following pages contain some specific examples of traditional and new design elements that are used in Mirei Shigemori's garden works. Many of the images are taken from the design drawings, completed with or substituted by photographs where appropriate. At least two examples are presented for each design element, using the same order as in the two tables above.

Traditional Design Elements

The traditional design elements are those for which a precedent exists in a historic garden. Most, if not all of them, are widely accepted design elements in the long history of the Japanese garden.

Amanohashidate style landform

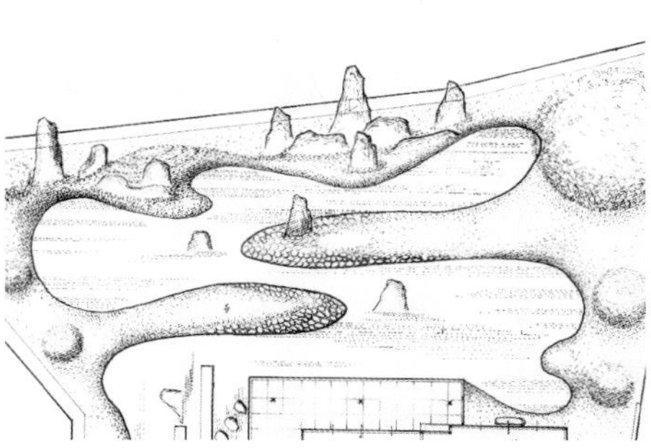

[104] A double peninsula in the garden at Kobayashi Hyakutarô, 1971.
[105] Amanohashidate peninsula with pine and stone lantern at Onohara Toshio, 1940.

***Tsukiyama* style landform in the traditional sense**

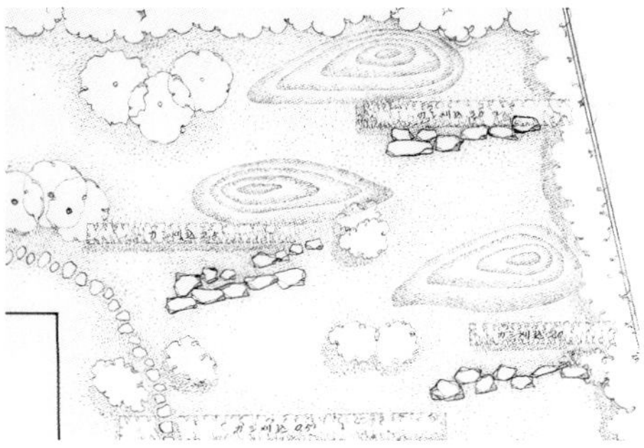

[106] Five mounds representing the five Zen sects at Tôfuku-ji, Kyoto, 1939.
[107] Three staggered *tsukiyama* mounds at Sakurai Girls High School, 1941.

Kanji*-shaped pond or *tsukiyama

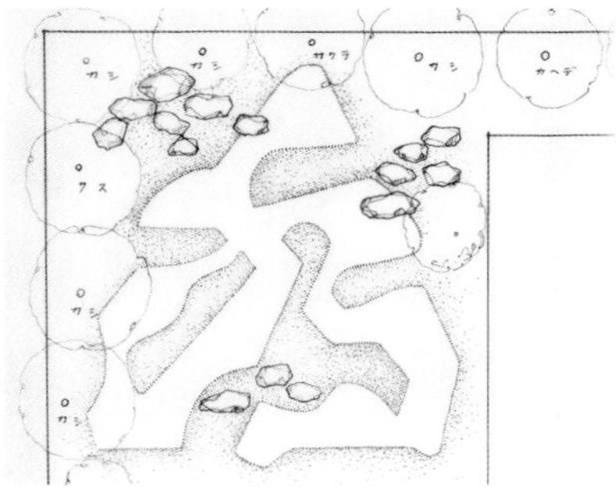

[108] The *kanji* for "water" as a dry pond at the Sakyô Ward Fire Department, 1954.
[109] The *kanji* for "heart" in the *karesansui* garden at Kôsei-ji, 1967.

Mythical animal

[110] Protecting the west direction, white tiger stone setting at Sekizô-ji, 1972.
[111] Protecting the north direction, black turtle stone setting at Sekizô-ji, 1972.

Yarimizu style river

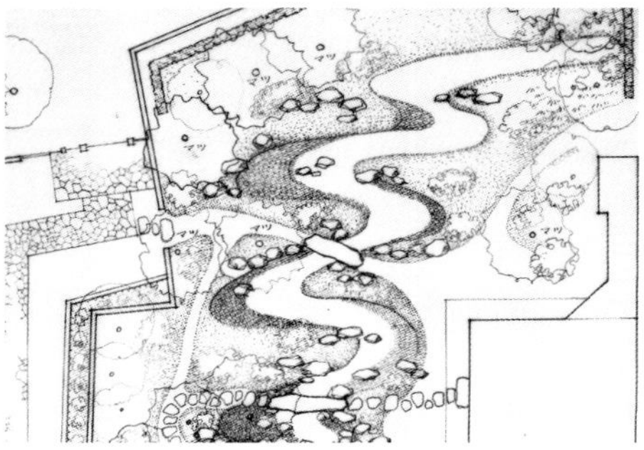

[112] Winding river design at the private residence of Mr Nomura, 1946.
[113] A *yarimizu* style river flowing towards the house of Mr Handa, 1954.

Shakkei

[114] Taking the surrounding hills into the garden of Ogura Yutaka, 1951.
[115] Borrowing a distant hill for the garden at Sumiyoshi Jinja, 1966.

Tea garden features

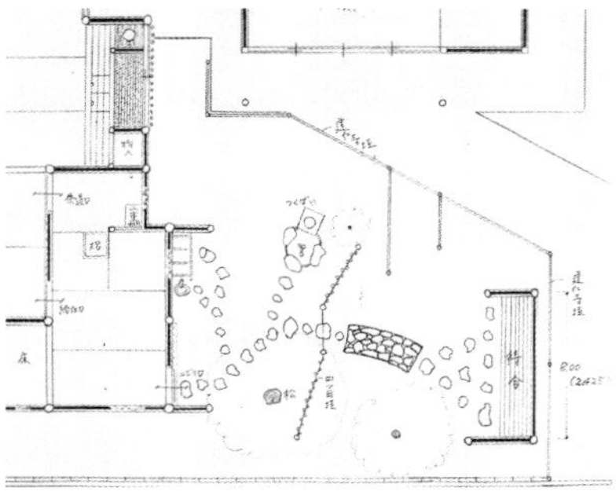
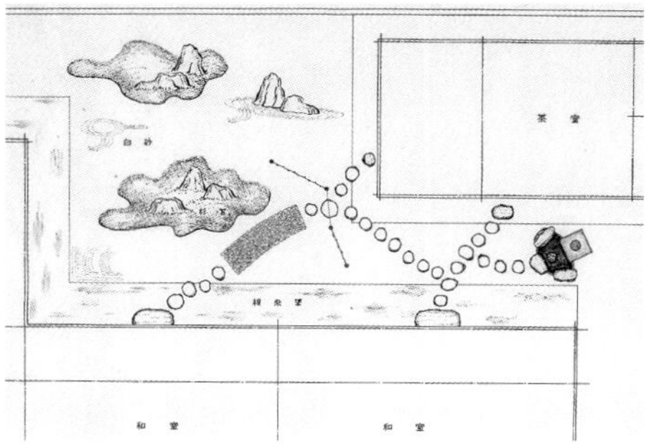

[116] A complete tea garden with waiting area at Matsuyama Sôzu, 1974.
[117] Elements of a tea garden combined with three islands at Ishii Umekazu, 1967.

Karikomi

[118] All-embracing *karikomi* in the garden at Higashiguchi Tsuruji, 1974.
[119] *Karikomi* mound with interspersed stones arrangements at Fukuchi-in, 1973.

Suhama

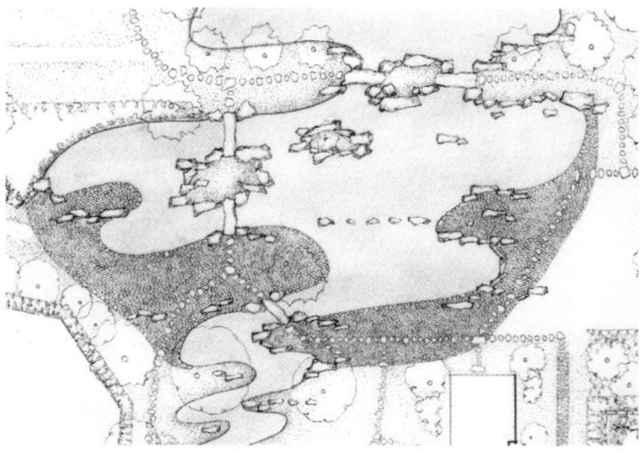
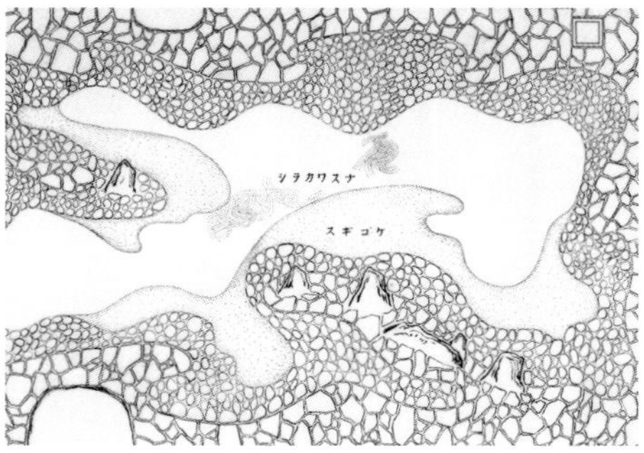

[120] An extensive *suhama* in the pond at Kumagai Kôyô-sansô, 1941.
[121] A more abstracted *suhama* at Kiyohara Seinosuke, 1965.

Shima in a real or abstracted pond

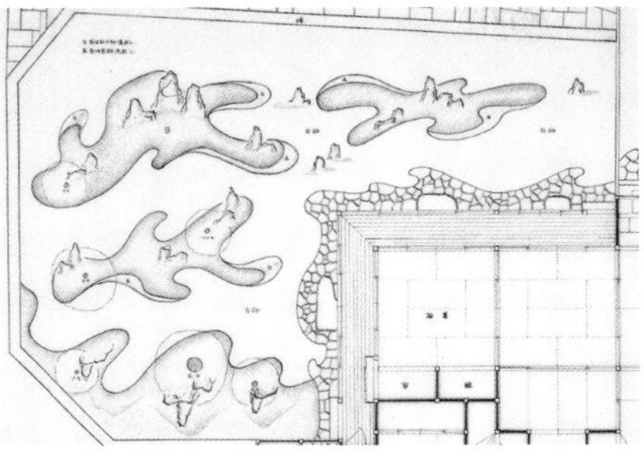

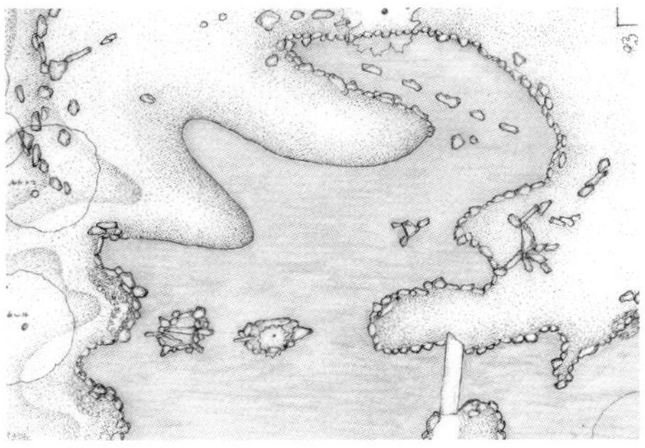

[122] Three islands in a sea of gravel at Ashida Suejirô, 1971.
[123] *Tsuru*, *kame* and other islands in the pond at Sainan-in, 1952.

Kami ike (god pond)

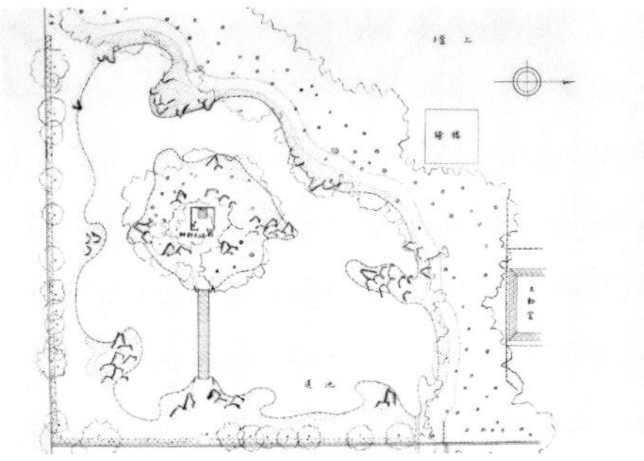

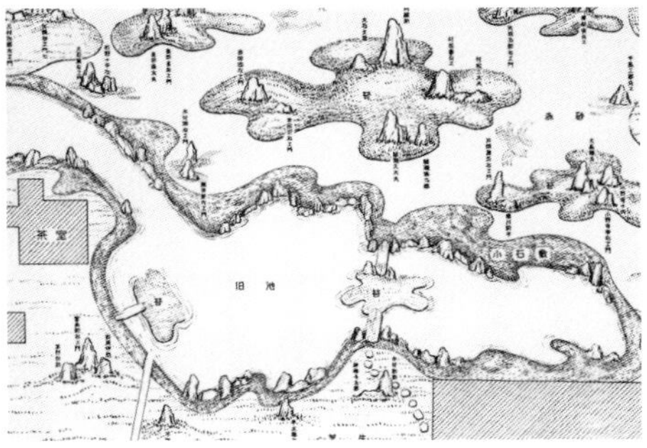

[124] An island with a small shrine in Kongôbu-ji Lotus pond, 1964.
[125] Typical *kami-ike* (god pond) scheme with two islands at Ôishi Jinja, 1967.

Stone setting

[126] Very early stone arrangement with large horizontal stones at Tôfuku-ji, 1939.
[127] Mirei Shigemori's last stone setting with *aoishi* at Matsuo Taisha, 1975.

Himorogi stone setting

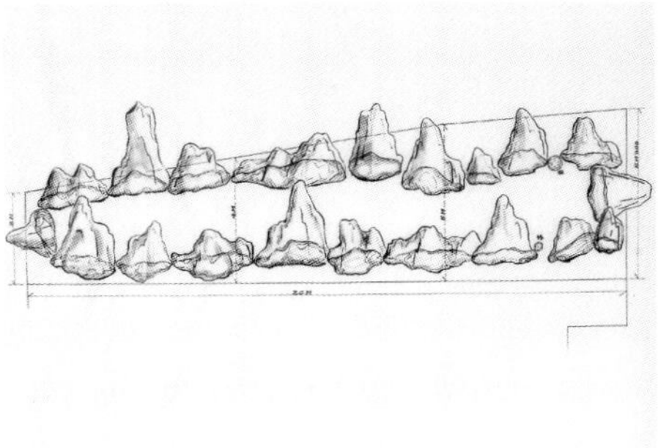

[128] The plan for the *himorogi* stone setting at Kibune Jinja, 1965.
[129] *Himorogi* stone setting with a tree for the gods to descend at Kibune Jinja, 1965.

New Design Elements

The new design elements are those for which no precedent exists in a historic garden. Most of them are new to the Japanese garden and reflect Mirei Shigemori's search for different forms of expression in a locally rooted Japanese garden culture. At the same time they provide evidence of his constant experimentation with new materials and shapes while trying to renew the Japanese garden.

Tsukiyama style landform in colored concrete

[130] **A _tsukiyama_ made from red and white concrete at Tenrai-an, 1969.**
[131] **The _hyôtan_-shaped _tsukiyama_ cast in concrete at Hôkuku Jinja, 1972.**

Wave line

[132] **Two colors of gravel and a wave line cast in red concrete at Yashima-ji, 1970.**
[133] **Paving edge along a building in the shape of waves at Okamoto Hajime, 1957.**

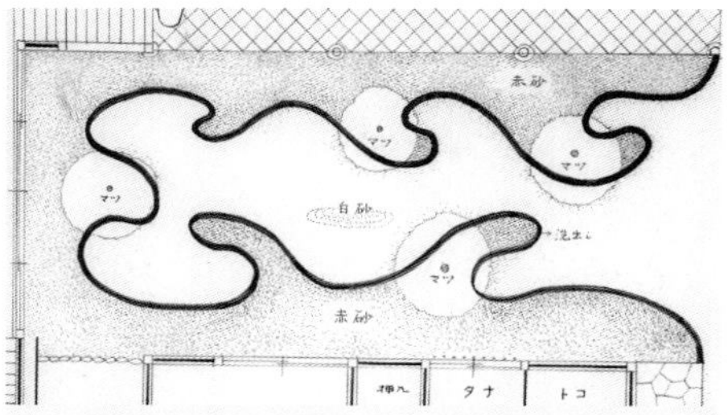

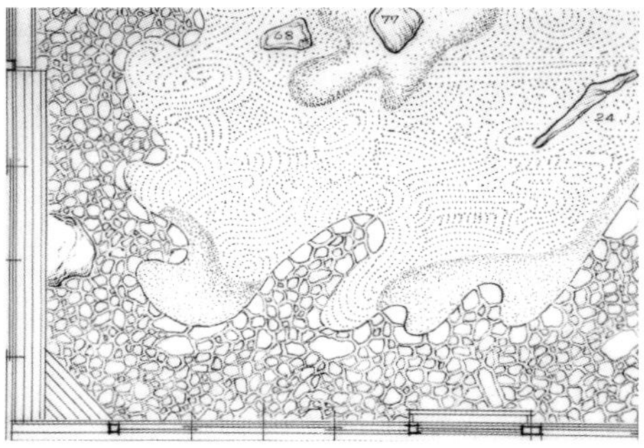

Cloud shapes

[134] **Clouds as depicted on paintings at the Nishimura Tarôemon Memorial, 1942.**
[135] **A rising dragon producing dark clouds at Ryôgin-an, 1964.**

Buddha emitting rays of light

[136] **A rising Buddha emitting rays of light above the clouds at Shôgen-ji, 1968.**
[137] **A Buddha statue as the origin of light rays at Shitennô-ji Gakuen, 1963.**

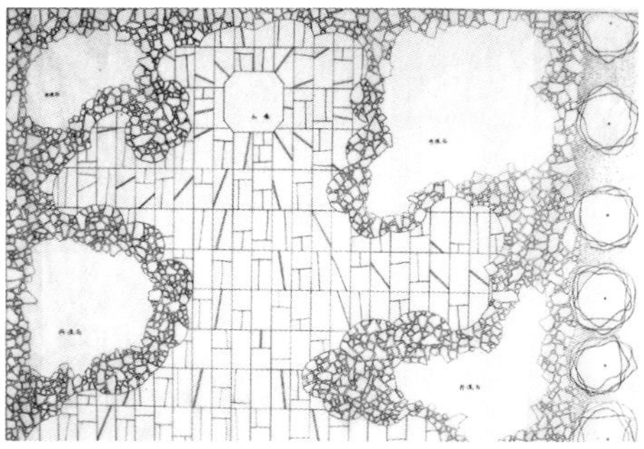

Spiral stone setting

[138] An early stone spiral at the private residence of Mr Miyaji, 1943.
[139] An ornamental stone setting in form of a spiral at Shiratori Jinja, 1952.

Wall painting

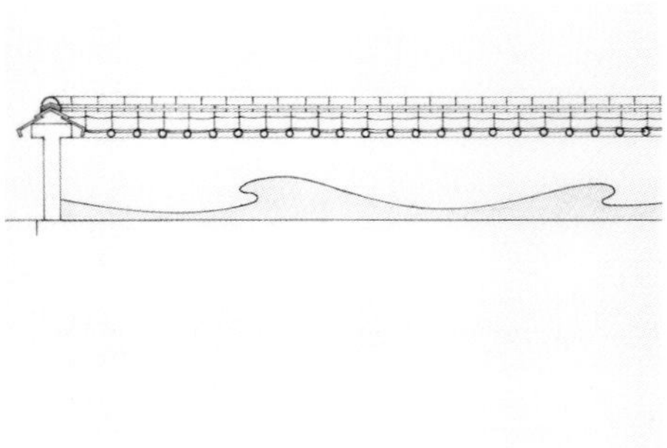

[140] The garden's landscape finds an extension on the wall at Katayama Kaoru, 1957.
[141] Black waves drawn on an earthen temple wall at Honkyû-ji, 1974.

Fence motif

[142] Four gods in *kanji* characters referring to the design concept at Sekizô-ji, 1972.
[143] Depiction of lightning on a bamboo fence at Ryôgin-an, 1964.

Grid

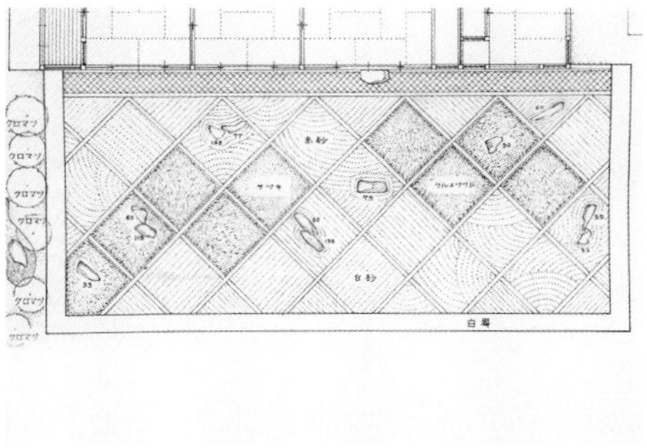

[144] The famous grid of square stones in the mossy north garden at Tôfuku-ji, 1939.
[145] A grid design filled with sand, stones and planting at Kanyô-ji, 1969.

Stripes

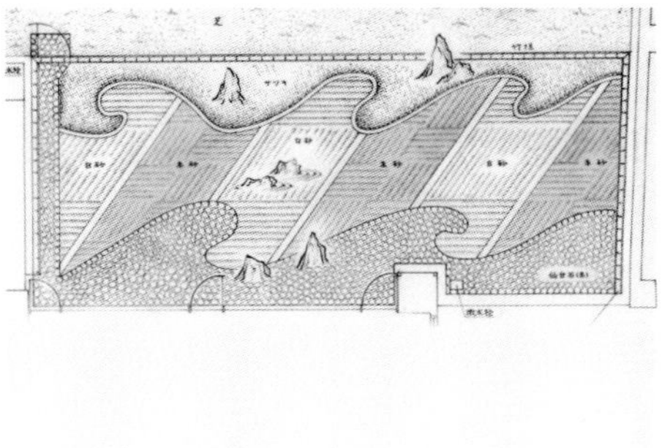

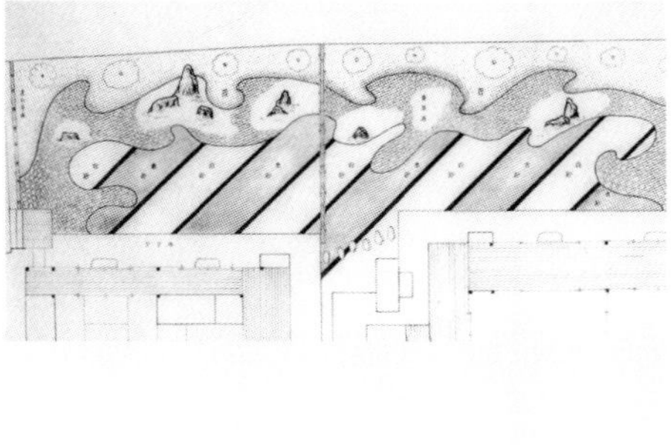

[146] Stripes of white and red sand at Shizuoka Royal Hotel Rooftop Garden, 1973
[147] Stripes of colored sand at the house of Yokoyama Hideyoshi, 1968.

THE LINES AND COLORS OF NATURE

The basis for this strategy for renewal must have been laid early on, as can be surmised from Mirei Shigemori's essays on ikebana in the early 1930s (see also pages 38–39). In one of these early essays, titled "Exploration—The Art of Flower Arrangement," he wrote, "By destroying nature, and not just physically, we must establish art. The lines and colors of art must be guided by pure creativity."[7] Here his education as a painter, his deep interest in art history and even his extensive philosophical reading become evident. This broad background provided him with a different view of ikebana and allowed him to break with the established styles. In the same essay, Mirei Shigemori then summed up his basic approach to ikebana: "It is true that in the art of flower arrangement the most important thing is to bring nature to life. But this doesn't necessarily mean bringing it alive in a realistic way. Bringing nature to life means to translate it inside myself. And in order to make it a thing of myself, all or part of nature has to be transformed: transformed from the field of nature to the field of art, emphasizing the distinction between nature and art. To bring nature to life, the lines and colors of nature are made into the lines and colors of art." Although written to explain his approach to the renewal of ikebana, this statement clearly illustrates how nature in Mirei Shigemori's view was to be transformed (or abstracted), as he would do later in many of his gardens. And naturally, for somebody educated as a painter, it is quite telling that this transformation becomes most visible in the "lines and colors."

There is one more aspect worth examining: the specific level of abstraction required by this approach. Mirei Shigemori had a very clear idea of where the designer's efforts should be directed when he suggested, that "in most cases the artistic value of the garden is proportionate to the degree of simplification carried out."[8] This indeed was an important realization for him, one that he increasingly followed in his own work, where simplification soon became synonymous with abstraction. Therefore, with regard to the proper style to be chosen for a design, Mirei Shigemori had a definite favorite in the form of the *karesansui*, or dry landscape garden, a garden style he highly valued for its level of abstraction and apparently timeless modernity. It is here that he worked hardest to develop a strategy for renewal, as the gardens in the following chapter will prove. In any case, art, also in the form of a garden, had to be contemporary and novel, otherwise it was ineffective.

[148] Sumiyoshi Jinja

7 From Mirei Shigemori, "Exploration—The Art of Flower Arrangement"; text together with flower arrangement no. 149 in: *Complete Works of Japanese Flower Arrangement Art*, vol. 6 (Kyoto: Kadô Bijutsu Kenseikai, 1930–1932).

8 Shigemori, *Gardens of Japan*, p. 36.

GARDENS

We now come to the gardens and what is the longest chapter in the book. Although they start in chronological order, the projects are presented thematically, roughly grouped into elements distilled from Mirei Shigemori's design repertoire. Some elements are visual, obvious and hence almost self-explanatory, where others might only become clear within the group of gardens they are in, or even in the wider context of the book. Naturally they can be appreciated for various different aspects, but the criteria chosen at the very least allows for some interesting comparisons and therefore enhances the overall understanding of the work.

Points, lines and planes are not only the components of many paintings, they are also part of a raster that Mirei Shigemori might well have been using when he conceived his ***karesansui*** gardens. Clearly this early embossing affected him deeply and seems to become stronger again toward the end of his career. Also variations eventually appeared, such as the planes that become mounds, while at other times it resulted in works that resist any true categorization. In this case they are often in a way traditional, but still new. All except the garden at Kasuga Taisha, the first garden presented here, were made after Mirei Shigemori conducted his large survey and they were all photographed by

THE BEGINNING

1934 **Kasuga Taisha**

春日大社

The garden at Kasuga Taisha represents Mirei Shigemori's first design for a public space, with a shrine as the client. Before this, he had only done a small number of residential gardens. After moving to Kyoto in 1929 it took him some time to get established. In February 1934 he started to work on the design for the garden at the shrine office at Kasuga Taisha. However, this project was designed without the benefits of the survey, the broad study of gardens that Mirei Shigemori undertook a few years later. For that reason, Kasuga Taisha is more a product of his early education and lets us understand how his approach to garden-making was shaped by these basic influences. It is therefore a true early work, representing his struggle to get established as a professional and find his own formal design language. The result, a modern shrine garden based on old Shinto roots, is also significant, as until then the shrine garden had not existed as a distinct style.

The shrine's new office building had been finished in 1926, but it was not until 1933 that the priest decided to approach Mirei Shigemori for a garden design. On November 4 that year Mirei Shigemori came to have a look at the site and accepted the commission. The following year, on February 3 he started to work on the garden project. In his diary he notes: "In the morning I started to work on the design of Kasuga Taisha Teien, at the shrine's office. I put a lot of effort into making a good design."[1] And then the next day he remarks that, because it is his first garden for a shrine, he "[...] will try to make it a very unique garden." On March 11 Mirei Shigemori then had a meeting with the priest to explain the garden's design and they agreed to start construction soon. He prepared the project specifications together with Junichirô Kawasaki. Construction started on April 12, 1934 and ten days later the east part of the garden was already completed. There is a second part to the garden on the northern side of the shrine office, but because of lack of funds the construction of this part was postponed. On September 21, 1934 the notorious Muroto typhoon hit Japan and this further delayed the project since it felled more than 600 trees on Kasuga Taisha's grounds alone. It was the anticipated visit of the Empress Dowager that got the project moving again in 1937. As the empress was planning to stop at Kasuga Taisha on her trip to the Kansai area and use the shrine's office for a short rest, the priest felt that the garden should be completed quickly. So he unexpectedly summoned Mirei Shigemori, who then came to the shrine with Junichirô Kawasaki on May 4, 1937. The plans had already been prepared earlier and so construction of the northern part of the garden could start immediately. But as Mirei Shigemori was busy surveying gardens in the Gôshû area,[2] this part of the garden was mainly built by Junichirô Kawasaki, naturally using the prepared plan. By May 10, the work was practically finished. Mirei Shigemori came on May 12, changed a few details and for the first time let water flow through the stream.

[149] Present-day view of the east garden

The budget for these two parts of the garden was quite small. Mirei Shigemori notes that he was limited to ¥ 600 for the east garden and ¥ 400 for the north garden.[3] In today's currency that would be about € 2,285.00 and € 1,523.00 respectively. This, of course, had to pay for all the materials as well as Junichirô Kawasaki's wages. Mirei Shigemori himself received an extra ¥ 80 for the design of the garden and for directing its construction (corresponding to approximately € 304.00 in today's currency).

Description: The temple's name was changed in 1946 from Kasuga Jinja to Kasuga Taisha. The east garden is surrounded on three sides by buildings **[150 | 152 | 153]** and can therefore be seen from three different vantage points. There is a guest room to the north, the shrine office with the waiting room to the west and some additional rooms to the south. Naturally, Mirei Shigemori's design takes advantage of this spatial arrangement. The five stones in the center can be seen from all three sides, but the rest of the stones are only visible from certain viewpoints. Regarding his design intention, he writes in his

1 Excerpt from his diary: "Kasuga Taisha: 1933–1934," February 3, 1934. Also it is interesting to note that he actually worked at the shrine's office. One reason was that he could be closer to the garden, but, more importantly, by this time Mirei Shigemori, his wife and three small children were living in a rather small house and there was no excess space for design work.

2 Gôshû is the area around Lake Biwa, located in Shiga Prefecture, immediately east of Kyoto.

3 From *Nihon Teienshi Zukan*, vol. 22, p. 49.

[150] Plan for Kasuga Taisha

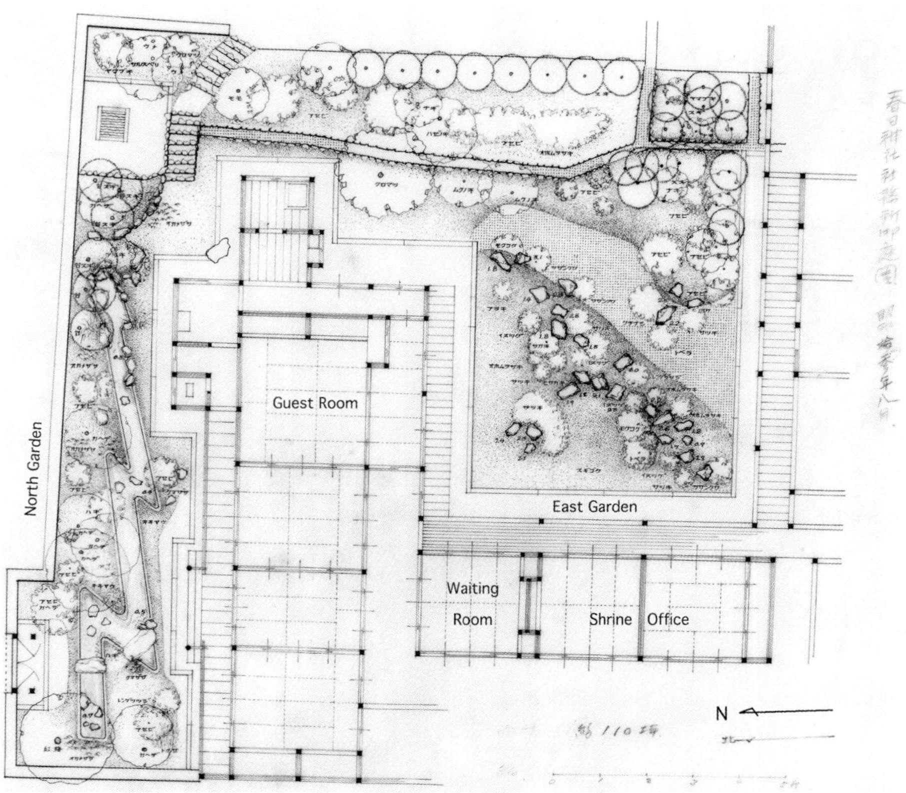

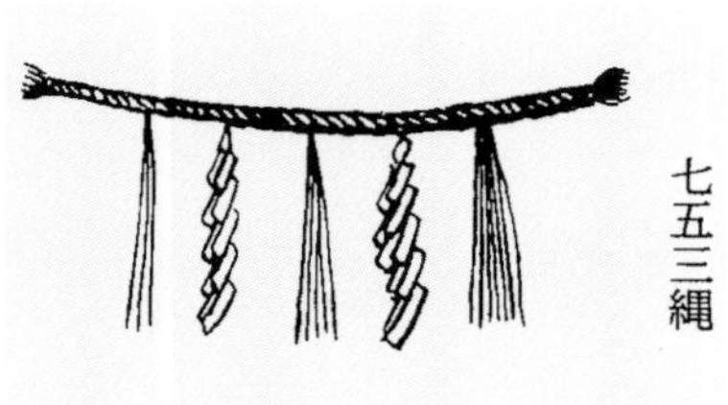

[151] *Shime-nawa*: 7–5–3 rope made from rice straw
[152] Sketch of North Garden

diary: "As it is a shrine garden, the key numbers for the design are 3–5–7. My idea is to set 25 stones here in a way that they can always be seen in groups of 7–5–3 from each of the three viewpoints."[4] But what are the key numbers 3–5–7? Mirei Shigemori here takes inspiration from the *shime-nawa*, a holy rope that marks stones and trees as deified places in Japan **[071 | 072 | 073]**.[5] He feels that this connection to very early Shinto symbolism is the key to creating a garden that is appropriate to a shrine.[6] And there are more symbolic references, but they are even less apparent. The contiguous four stones, out of the five in the very center of the garden, refer to the four initial gods at Kasuga Taisha. And the entire group of five stones then includes a god that was added later. In this way Mirei Shigemori dedicates the central stone setting to the shrine, respectively the top tiers of its gods. Then the total number of trees and stones in the east garden is 52, which refers to the 52 shrines that are under the patronage of Kasuga Taisha. All the stones are set in an upright fashion, just like the ones at an *amatsu iwasaka*.[7] But in its essence, the east part is a *karesansui* style garden, featuring the typical elements of stone, gravel and some vegetation.

The main element of the north garden is a winding stream called a *yarimizu* **[152]**, a popular garden element in the *shinden* style gardens of the Heian period. Mirei Shigemori here drew inspiration from the existing architectural features, such as the typical railing. And Kasuga Taisha was also the family shrine of the Fujiwara clan, who prospered during the Heian period.[8] Making reference to these historical circumstances, he used the *yarimizu* as a typical element from that specific period, thus displaying and reinforcing those roots. As the east garden already was in the *karesansui* style, Mirei Shigemori clearly wanted to provide some contrast and diversity in the shapes and materials. Therefore, he decided to design a lightning-shaped stream for the north garden and use real water instead of sand. In this way the two parts of the garden ended up being rather different.

4 Excerpt from his diary: "Kasuga Taisha: 1933–1934," February 3, 1934; note that Japanese traditionally start counting from right to left.

5 Some interesting research regarding *shime-nawa* has been done by Günter Nitschke, "Shime–Binding/Unbinding" in *Architectural Design*, vol. 12/1974, p. 760. According to him, a *shime-nawa* fences off and sanctifies a sacred area or object. He looks at it as a way to occupy space and mark it.

6 From *Nihon Teienshi Zukan*, vol. 22, p. 49.

7 A spiritual or holy place where the gods descend; the ancient Japanese believed that a place surrounded by rocks was inhabited by gods, thus naming it *amatsu iwasaka* (heavenly barrier) or *amatsu iwakura* (heavenly seat).

8 As the noble family of Fujiwara consolidated its grip on power during the Heian period, an aristocratic, natively inspired art and culture developed. The *yarimizu* fits that image as it refers to the heart of Japan, referring to the rivers coming from the many mountains the country has, the source for its abundance of water.

Materials and Technique: As the east garden can be seen from three different vantage points, the stone setting is designed with three faces. Mirei Shigemori used 25 stones in this garden, but only stone groups of 3–5–7 can be seen from each viewpoint. The other ten stones are always hidden by vegetation. Only the five stones in the center are visible from all three sides. The 7–5–7 stone arrangements create one line, whereas the groups of 3–5–3 stones describe the other. The two lines intersect and continue toward the respective corners of the garden, basically describing a large "X". The entire garden was planted with moss, except the western part, which was covered with white sand to reflect the heat better.

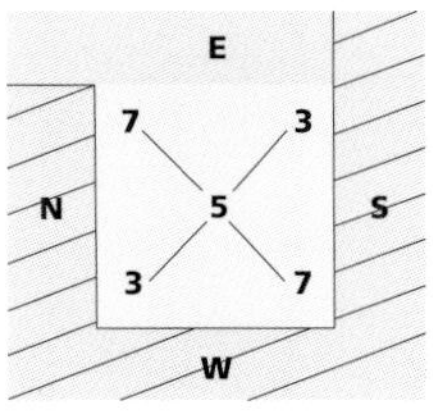

Spatial orientation of the stone arrangement. The central square outlines the garden area; the outer line indicates the proximity of the buildings as the garden is surrounded on three sides. The two crossing lines of the stone setting are 7–5–7 and 3–5–3.

In contrast to the east garden, real water is used in the stream for the north garden. The water enters the garden from the east and flows through the lightning-shaped stream as shown on the plan. The *yarimizu*'s bed is cast in concrete and becomes deeper in the lower part of the stream. There are several small stones set in the stream to give it a more natural appearance. Between the north gate and the temple entrance, two bridges cross the *yarimizu*, both made from natural stone. The following plants were used in the east garden: *Camellia sasanqua, Ilex crenata, Pittosporum tobira, Camellia species, Pieris japonica, Gardenia jasminoides, Castanea crenata, Rhododendron species, Rhododendron pulchrum, Astragalus sinicus, Aphananthe aspera, Pinus thunbergii* and *Cryptomeria japonica*. Four of the plants were selected because their name also appears in one of the shrine's subordinate names. The stones used in the east garden are all from the mountain areas of Kurama, Kibune and Tamba. The vegetation in the north garden was selected on the basis of an old poem about a place called Mount Takamado.[9] So, accordingly, we find *Acer japonica, Pieris japonica, Cryptomeria japonica, Lespedeza bicolor, Platycodon grandiflorum, Sasa veitchii, Shibataea kumasaca, Prunus mume* and *Equisetum hyemale*. These are all plants that grow well in the shady environment of a valley or, similarly, on the north side of a building in Nara.

Interpretation: The problem that Mirei Shigemori had to address was that there were hardly any gardens at shrines and, furthermore, there was no established style of garden that one could call a shrine garden. A reason for this lack of examples might have been that shrines originally simply did not have gardens. People worshipped places in nature, mainly unique rocks or old trees, marked by a *shime-nawa*, thinking that these were places visited by the gods (see also page 49). Later, as a result of the competitive situation created by the arrival of Buddhism in Japan, actual shrine buildings were built close to these natural sites. But still no garden was needed. The natural setting with the ancient holy rocks and trees was enough. But then as Buddhist temples built beautiful gardens around their buildings, the difference became more apparent. Although Shinto was a religion based on nature, it had not yet progressed to the point of surrounding itself with a more cultured version of nature, a garden. So, having been hired to design a garden for a shrine, Mirei Shigemori had to think about what a shrine garden really was, or more important, what it might look like in the 20th century. The brilliant idea that came to

9 A mountain near what we know today as the city of Nara. As it was conveniently located to the southeast of the old capital called Heijôkyô (710–794), roughly congruent with today's Nara, people went to Mt. Takamado to enjoy the cherry blossom and fall color amidst the rolling hills that surrounded the ancient city. The poem must have been written at about the same time.

[153] Sketch of East Garden

him while designing the garden for Kasuga Taisha was to take the *shime-nawa* **[151]** as his main inspiration. This rope made from rice straw is the one quintessential marks of Shinto. When it was used in ancient times to indicate those special rocks in the landscape where the gods were thought to descend, the *shime-nawa* represented the cultural layer **[071–073]**. It was the thing man added to that place. As a garden is nothing but a product of nature overlaid by culture, it seems understandable that, in the case of a Shinto shrine, one could go back to that very first manifestation of man's religious behavior and take inspiration from the shape it took at that time. This is exactly what Mirei Shigemori did and he found two ideas that he used to create shape and meaning for his garden design. One is the concept of 7–5–3 and the other is the *gohei* symbol. Both concepts can be found hanging from the rice straw rope, one in the form of rice stalks numbering 7–5–3 and the other as paper streamers: as such, they are inherent parts of Shinto.

The numbers 7–5–3 are of special significance in Japanese culture and therefore appear throughout the arts. In the garden we often see the *shichigosan ishigumi*, literally the seven–five–three stone arrangement, where 15 stones are placed in groups of seven, five and three stones each, arranged in overall harmony. This is exactly what Mirei Shigemori used in the garden at Kasuga Taisha, not only once but three times. The *gohei* is an even more commonplace symbol. The white zigzag paper streamers are everywhere, hanging from cords made of rice straw, marking deified and purified spaces or objects **[071–073]**. As a talisman against evil they are found at shrine entrances and always around trees or rocks. The *gohei* recall the brilliance of the sun and the glare of its light. And that light is what inspired the shape of the river in the north garden. But it is not merely light that the river represents, but lightning, the much stronger version that in Shinto became the symbol of the cosmic power of enlightenment.[10] A rather appropriate reference to make for the garden in front of the shrine office! This garden, small as it is, offers some valuable insights into Mirei Shigemori's design approach. Because of its complexity and detail it takes a while to analyze and understand it. The following note from Mirei Shigemori's diary shows that the design of the garden indeed required explanation and was not obvious to everybody, not even a Shinto priest: "I went to Kasuga Taisha at 5:00 p.m. As I had already said that I would come around that time, the priest was there waiting for me. I explained the design of the garden to him. It was good to have a chance to talk about my plan directly with him. Now priest Emi understands it well and we agreed to start construction on the 20th or so."[11] This means that the priest only approved the design and agreed to build it after some convincing explanations by Mirei Shigemori! But Shigemori's courage paid off as the priest liked the outcome and even decided to continue work on the north garden. Both parts of the garden still exist, but can only be visited by appointment.

10 In "The Litany of Wind and Lightning," it says: "The wind and the lightning speak to us of the visible and invisible forces that touch the physical life of the environment, sometimes to bless and sometimes to bring chaos. Lightning can make rice grow. Lightning can set a forest on fire," from Stuart D.B. Picken, *Shinto meditations for Revering the Earth* (Berkeley, CA: Stone Bridge Press, 2002), p. 76.

11 Excerpt from his diary: "Kasuga Taisha: 1933–1934," March 11, 1934.

[154] Original view to east
[155] Present-day view to east

[156] Original view of central stone setting
[157] Present-day view of central stone setting

[158] Original view from the northwest corner
[159] Present-day view from the north-west corner

[160] The original *yarimizu* with flowing water
[161] The dry *yarimizu* today

POINTS OF STONE

Mirei Shigemori modernized the Japanese garden by introducing the point as an independent geometric element. Of course points, or rather conglomerates of points, have always featured in the Japanese garden in the form of stone settings. Famous *karesansui* gardens, such as Kyoto's well-known Ryôan-ji, essentially consist of a sea of gravel with a few scattered rocks symbolizing islands. In a way they look like dots on a large canvas. Even in other gardens with different styles, the stone arrangement often has a point-like character, marking a specific spot in the scene, or a moment in the garden's landscape. Mirei Shigemori focused on the role of the point in the Japanese garden, but sometimes he changed its physical manifestation by using different shaped materials. In his first major contemporary garden, the Hassô no Niwa at Tôfuku-ji, Mirei Shigemori carried the element of the point to the extreme. He played with it in various situations and used points for many different purposes; he scaled them and simplified their form. In few, if any, of his later works is the point as obvious and diverse in appearance as here. Later in his career Mirei Shigemori was more attracted to the old idea of the *iwakura*, a point of contact, or a place in the landscape where human beings get in touch with the spiritual side of their existence. At Matsuo Taisha the stone becomes the focal point again, and it is these groups of rocks that are the central point of the garden.

1939 An Early Masterpiece: Tôfuku-ji Hôjô

東福寺方丈

The gardens at Tôfuku-ji's main hall are an early masterpiece among Mirei Shigemori's works and are now considered the epitome of the contemporary Japanese garden. The arrangement of square stones among thick green moss has achieved iconic status and inspired numerous garden makers throughout the world.

Tôfuku-ji is the main temple of the Tôfuku-ji sect of the Rinzai school of Zen Buddhism. Michiie Kujô, grandson of the chief adviser to Emperor Kujô Kanezane, is said to have founded the temple on July 21, 1239. The temple's name was derived from the names of two nearby temples in what is now Nara Prefecture: *Tô* is taken from Tôdai-ji and *fuku* is from Kôfuku-ji. Apparently the Kujô clan sold their house and all their property in order to build this temple! On August 23, 1938, head priest Sonoisan Saidô contacted Mirei Shigemori and asked him to prepare a master plan for the improvement of the general scenery at Tôfuku-ji over the next century or so.[12] Shigemori started immediately by surveying the entire Tôfuku-ji temple complex. The surroundings of the *hôjô* were particularly unsightly, so eventually the priest asked Shigemori for a garden design that would improve conditions there. The latter noted the details of this conversation as follows:

Priest: "It is good for the spiritual richness of a temple when it doesn't have enough money. But it is time for me, as head priest, to think about having a garden here at the main hall."

Shigemori: "There is no better place for a garden than the area around the *hôjô*. If I were to make a garden here, my work would live forever at this temple. I would even pay to be asked to do a project here or simply donate a garden design."

Priest: "I appreciate that very much, and you shall be the one I ask. So please accept our request to make a garden here, and we in return will regularly pray for your soul, now and forever.[13] And we shall not interfere with your work at all, so you may do whatever you deem appropriate."

Shigemori: "All right, I will put all my energy into creating a garden here. But I will not accept any requests for changes."

Priest: "In that case, before you start, I have one thing I need to tell you. In our Zen sect, nothing is allowed to go to waste. So I would like to ask you, if possible, to reuse the paving stones piled up over there at the gate."

[162] Stone setting symbolizing Hôjô island

Next page:
[163] Visualization of the executed version of the garden's design

12 The impetus for this was a project for the enhancement of the natural landscape of the Higashiyama area, the hills east of Kyoto where Tôfuku-ji is located. Initiated in 1936 by the Forestry Agency of the national government, the project covered all 36 nationally owned hills in the Higashiyama area, from Mt. Hiei in the north all the way to Mt. Inari in Fushimi-ku, south of Kyoto.

13 Temples in Japan usually charge rather a large amount of money to provide this kind of service, so this was quite an unusual offer.

[163]

[164] Overview of the South Garden with the main gate

[165] Detail of Eijû island stone setting

[166] Five *tsukiyama* symbolizing Kyoto's five Zen sects

[167] Clipped azaleas symbolizing rice fields

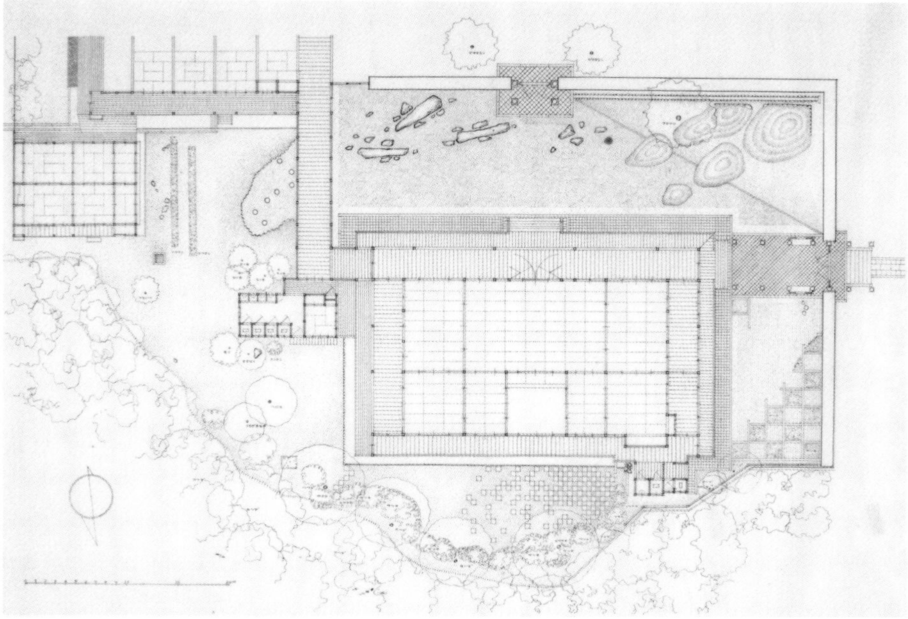

[168] Plan of Tôfuku-ji's Hassô no Niwa

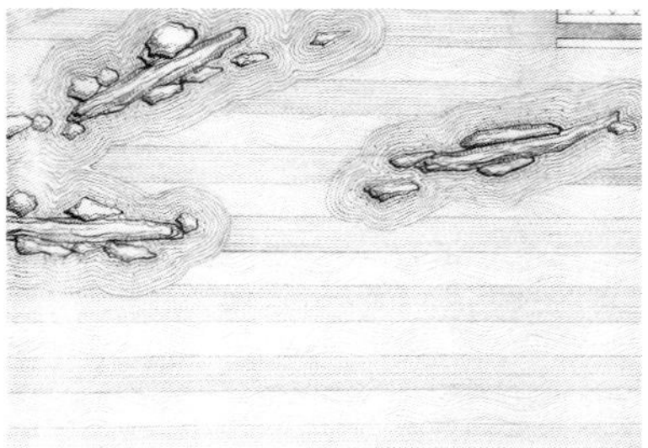

[169] The *tsukiyama* are the bridging element
[170] Rice fields in the landscape
[171] Islands of stone in a sea of raked gravel

Shigemori: "I am already aware of that and I shall include those in my proposal. Including discarded materials is always part of my garden-making, but I would like to ask you to leave how to reuse them up to me."
Priest: "Today is a great day for Tôfuku-ji. There is nothing more to say."[14]
Shigemori was not yet famous at the time, indeed he was probably as poor as the temple. But he realized what a great opportunity it was to make a garden at such a noted place and therefore decided to work for free. No doubt he was also attracted by the promise of freedom with regard to design. Construction of the Tôfuku-ji garden started on June 27, 1939, and everything was finished by November 11 of the same year.

Description: The gardens at Tôfuku-ji's main hall consist of four more or less independent parts. As you approach the *hôjô*, the first garden to appear on the left is the south garden **[164]**. There are four stone settings representing the islands of the immortals and, further west, five moss-covered mounds, symbolizing the five Zen sects of Kyoto. From east to west, the stone settings symbolize the islands Hôjô, Hôrai and Eijû **[165]**, and the group immediately west of the gate represents the Koryô islands.[15] A straight diagonal line from the northwest corner of the garden to the gate divides the area of moss from the white sand and gives quite a modern accent to the garden's layout **[166]**. Two of the mounds extend into the sea, and one is an island completely surrounded by the ocean of sand.

Continue clockwise around the building and you arrive at the west garden, featuring a layout inspired by the look of rice fields in a landscape **[167]**. The design is simple: recycled stone curbs describe a checkerboard grid pattern filled with white sand and shaped azaleas for contrast in color, texture and three-dimensional variation. These days, moss also covers most of the southern half of this part of the garden. Just around the corner, to the north of the *hôjô*, you then find the famed grid of stone plates sitting in moss **[174]**. After a semicircular space with azaleas and maples on its fringe, the grid starts in the southwest corner and fades out toward the northeast. It is small and enclosed with fresh green moss, the perfect contrast to the wide and dry south garden. As he promised the priest, Mirei Shigemori reused the square stones of the former entrance path here. The minimal design harmonizes exceptionally well with the varied backdrop.

On the way back to the entrance, you pass the east garden, situated to the east of the covered corridor **[172]**. Separated from the main garden by this elevated walkway, it features a Big Dipper stone arrangement, reusing the foundation stones of the former toilet building. The constellation design is appropriately set in a cloud-shaped area of white sand.

Mirei Shigemori named the entire garden Hassô no Niwa (八相の庭), meaning "Garden of Eight Views," a reference to the eight views he had created around the *hôjô*. The four stone settings (Hôjô, Hôrai, Eijû and Koryô) count for a view each, and the five

14 From *Nihon Teien Rekiran Jiten* ("Japanese Garden History Dictionary"), Tokyo: Tôkyodô Shuppan, 1974, p. 418.

15 Hôjô, Hôrai, Eijû and Koryô are sacred islands recorded in ancient Chinese philosophy and they play an important role in the cult of immortality. They represent imaginary islands in the East China Sea and are said to be where the immortals dwell. These islands are often depicted in Japanese gardens.

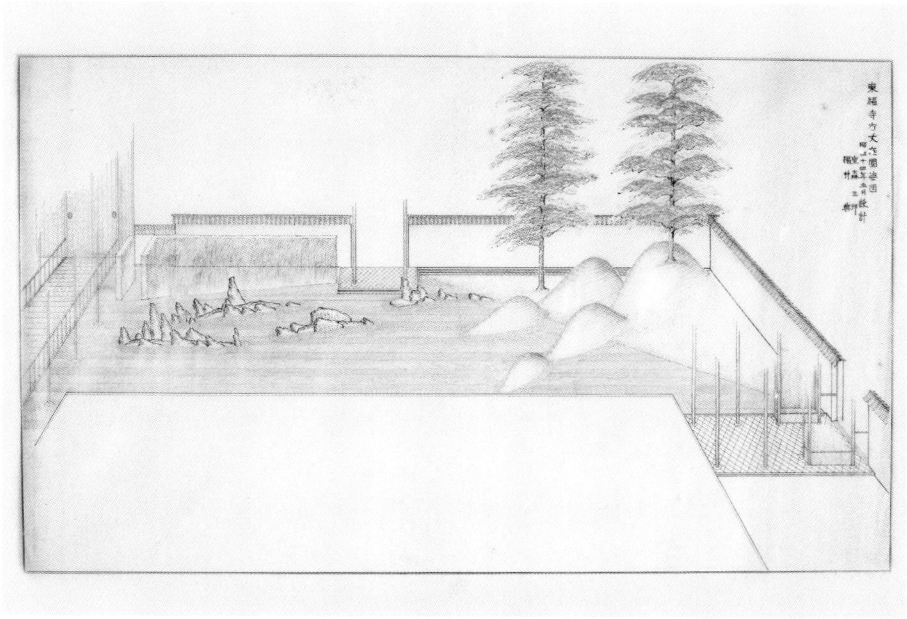

Left page:
[172] **Big Dipper stone arrangement in the East Garden**

[173] **Preliminary design drawing for the South Garden**

mounds (*gozan*) count as one, as do the grid of the north garden (*ichimatsu*), the rice fields (*seiden*) and the Big Dipper (*hokuto shichisei*). Most people seem to walk around in clockwise fashion and will therefore experience the garden in the order described here.

Interpretation: His first major contemporary garden design, the Hassô no Niwa at Tôfuku-ji expressed Mirei Shigemori's stated intention to create a modern Japanese garden—a goal he was to pursue for the rest of his life. In this early work, the points of the grid fading toward the east are a modern artistic expression and have no parallel among ancient Japanese gardens. Shigemori himself notes: "The technique I used made it a contemporary garden, and my main goal was timeless modernity."[16] He had first seen this grid pattern on the sliding doors of Kyoto's Katsura Rikyû and in the tea houses of Shûgakuin Rikyû, both famous garden and building complexes built in the 17th century.[17] The fact that this formal language now reappeared in the buildings and paintings of Modernism confirmed its timelessness and seemed to qualify the motif as eternally modern. Besides the isolation of the point as a design element, it is its reduction to the simplest possible form that characterizes its use at Tôfuku-ji gardens. Furthermore Mirei Shigemori experiments with several dot- or point-like elements, scaling them and simplifying their form. Incorporated thematically into the designs, these elements speckle the garden's various planes; in fact, some of them look more like drops of ink on a canvas than elements of an actual garden.[18] In few if any of Shigemori's later works is the point-like element as obvious and at the same time as diverse in appearance as it is here.

Next page:
[174] **The famous fading grid of stone plates on a plane of moss**

16 From *Nihon Teienshi Taikei* ("Japanese Garden History Survey"), vol. 27 (Tokyo: Shakai Shisôsha, 1971–76), p. 121.

17 Katsura Rikyû, built in 1653, and Shûgakuin Rikyû, completed in 1659, were both estates belonging to noblemen of the time and they already prominently feature the grid motif that is so modern in the eyes of Westerners. Although on both estates the pattern is used indoors on *fusuma*, it is an artistic expression of its time and one that Mirei Shigemori observed closely. It is interesting to note that neither of these gardens was all that famous at the time.

18 On April 7, 1936 Shigemori wrote an article for the *Japan Times* titled "Rittaiteki Kaiga to shite no Nihon Teien" ("The Japanese Garden as a Three-dimensional Painting"); this is noted in his diary for that year.

[174]

1975 **Close to the Gods: Matsuo Taisha**

松尾大社

The garden at Matsuo Taisha is Mirei Shigemori's last work, and its stone setting is considered by many to be one of his very best. With this work he returned to the very roots of the Japanese garden, creating an *iwakura*, a place for the Shinto gods to come and visit.

An enormous stone near the top of Mount Matsuo, just behind Matsuo Taisha, marks the origin of the shrine. This *iwakura* is where the shrine was located in ancient times, before it was moved down to its current location in A.D. 701. With the move of the capital to Kyoto in 794, the shrine gained in importance and eventually became one of the 21 grand shrines of Japan. The shrine complex's oldest building, the inner shrine, dates back to 1397 and is now designated as an important cultural asset. These days the shrine's clientele consists of many *miso* paste manufacturers and sake brewers, who come here to pray for the success of their businesses.

In October 1973 the new treasure house and a new building for ceremonies were finished, both distinctly modern structures made from concrete. Already in 1971 Mirei Shigemori had been selected as the designer for the adjacent new gardens. The plan was finished on May 14, 1974, and construction started two weeks later. Due to the garden designer's declining health, the project took almost one year to complete. The last part of the work was then supervised by his son Kanto after Mirei Shigemori passed away on March 12, 1975.

[176] Schematic plan of the Jôko no Niwa

[177] Sizable *aoishi* are part of the place's magic feel

Description: The entire Matsuo Taisha gardens consist of four independent parts, only two of which are covered in this book: the Garden of the Winding Stream and the Prehistoric Garden. The first, called Kyokusui no Niwa (曲水の庭), features a winding stream that enters the garden in the southwest corner and leaves it in the north. The banks are covered with flat blue stones and the bottom of the shallow river with gravel **[179 | 181]**. The backdrop is an impressive *karikomi*, a large mound of azaleas roughly in the shape of a turtle, symbolizing hope for a long life **[178]**. At the same time it refers to Mount Matsuo located behind the shrine, because from a distance it has a very similar form. Stone settings are spread throughout the garden and form a stark contrast to the smooth *karikomi*. The entire eastern section of the garden is paved and accessible to visitors who can cross the stream via two stone bridges.

The second part of this garden is named Jôko no Niwa (上古の庭), which translates as "Prehistoric Garden" and refers to the style chosen by the designer, not the time of its construction **[182 | 183]**. Located on a steep slope next to the new treasure house, the garden features a massive stone setting that alludes to the ancient *iwakura*, the origin of not only this particular shrine, but more broadly the Shinto religion as a whole.[19] The farther up the hill the garden goes the more dramatic the stone setting becomes **[175]**. At the top, rocks weighing between five and eight tons are placed at various angles and distances, creating a very powerful movement. Hence the highest point of the *iwakura* is so dynamic that the stones seem poised to fly away at any minute. All of the stones are *aoishi*[20] from Shikoku,

Left page:

[175] Powerful stone settings in Jôko no Niwa

19 Shinto, literally "the way of the gods," is the indigenous faith of the Japanese people and is as old as Japan itself. It was originally an amorphous mix of nature worship, fertility cults, divination techniques, hero worship and shamanism. Today it remains Japan's major religion in addition to Buddhism. Shinto gods are called *kami*. They are sacred spirits that take the form of objects in nature, as well as embodying concepts important to human life, such as wind, rain, mountains, trees, rivers and fertility. Humans become *kami* after they die, at which time they are revered by their families as ancestral *kami*. The *kami* of extraordinary people are even enshrined at some shrines. An altar, the *kamidana* (godshelf), is given a central place in many homes. The Sun Goddess Amaterasu is considered Shinto's most important *kami*. Shinto is an optimistic faith; humans are thought to be fundamentally good, and evil is believed to be caused by evil spirits. Consequently, the purpose of most Shinto rituals is to keep away evil spirits by purification, prayers and offerings to the *kami*.
Shinto shrines are places of worship and the homes of *kami*. Most shrines celebrate festivals (*matsuri*) regularly in order to show the *kami* the outside world. But ancient Shinto did not bother to erect shrines until the 3rd and 4th centuries. The introduction of Buddhism in the 6th century was followed by a few initial conflicts, but the two religions were soon able to coexist harmoniously and even complement each other.

20 Aoishi (青石) is a general term for the blue-green colored stones that are often used in the Japanese garden. In most cases they are green schist and according to their area of production they are called Kishû Aoishi, Awa Aoishi, Iyo Aoishi, etc. Aoishi is a metamorphic rock and naturally occurs in a vein from Tokyo to Wakayama, Shikoku, and on to Kyûshû.

[178]

[179]

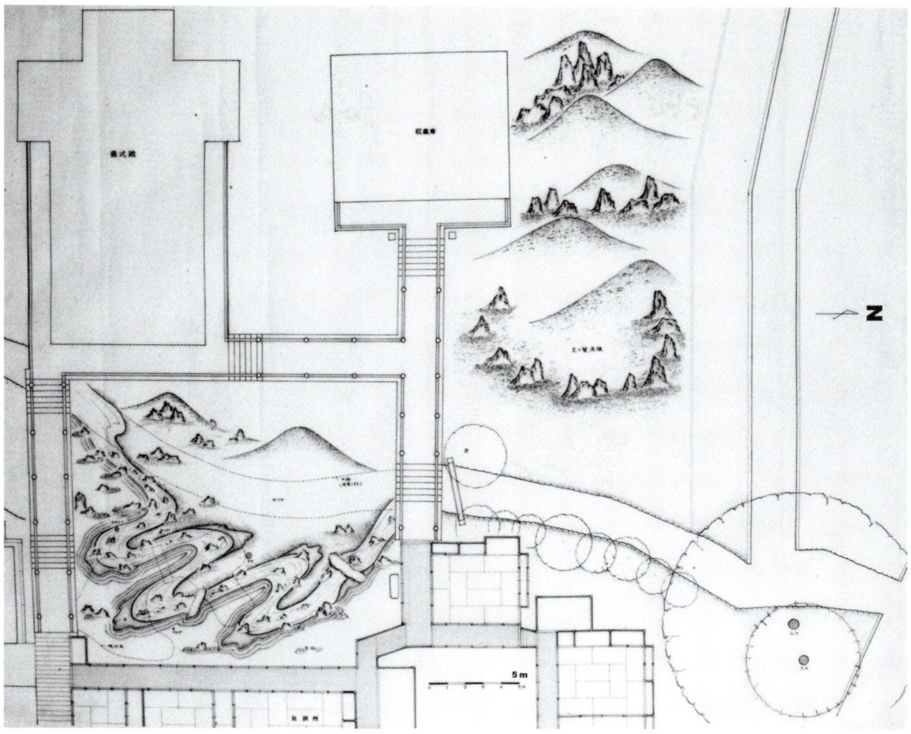

[180] **Schematic plan showing both parts of the garden**

Mirei Shigemori's absolute favorite for stone arrangements. A low bamboo that is commonly found on rocky mountain ridges covers the ground.

Interpretation: Mirei Shigemori only used real water in a few of his gardens, usually preferring the abstracted version of the white sand plane. But the little stream flowing down Mount Matsuo just south of the new buildings must have been too tempting to ignore. Mirei Shigemori integrated the available water in a *yarimizu* design, a winding-stream element already popular in gardens from the Heian period (794–1185). The *karikomi* as a backdrop is also a comparatively infrequent design element among Shigemori's gardens, even though he had used it just two years earlier at Fukuchi-in. Together these two elements create a unique and untypical garden, at least when compared with what Shigemori had created in the past 45 years. Unlike Buddhist temples, shrines had long existed in Japan without a designed garden around them. Initially the *iwakura* was worshipped in its natural setting. The rock itself and its surroundings were sometimes cleared of vegetation, and there is some evidence that here and there, stones might have been added, but hardly more that that. Around the time that Buddhism came to Japan, Shinto too started to build shrines near or on the sites that had been worshipped for centuries. But in contrast to the Buddhist temples, few Shinto shrines ever had anything close to what we would call a garden near their buildings. Mirei Shigemori noticed this early on in his career and always remarked that the shrine garden as a style still needed to be created.[21] This historical background is what motivated him to create what he called a "Prehistoric Garden" at Matsuo Taisha, and it is the *iwakura* behind the current shrine that then inspired his stone setting. In a way he returned to what he saw as the origin of the Japanese garden, especially the *karesansui* garden that so fascinated him, and brought it back into the garden right next to the new buildings of the shrine, thereby making the garden's ancient roots visible again.

According to Mirei Shigemori, to place stones as he did here at Matsuo Taisha is to take on the role of the gods: "To set the stones of an *iwakura*, the garden maker should be of the same mentality as the gods, otherwise it can never become a true *iwakura*. But it is impossible to actually become identical to the gods. So what this is all really about is how close a garden maker can get to the gods and how pure his mind can become. That is easy to say but very difficult to do."[22] While working on the stone arrangement at Matsuo Taisha, Mirei Shigemori emptied his mind as best as he could and let himself be guided by the voice of the gods. The result is a divine piece of stone-arrangement art.

[181] **Gravel and stone on the banks of the winding stream**

Left page:

[178] **Winding stream with a turtle-shaped *karikomi* in the background**

[179] **Overview of Kyokusui no Niwa with Mount Matsuo in the background**

21 As early as 1934 Mirei Shigemori was commissioned to design the Shamusho garden for Kasuga Taisha in Nara, his first large shrine garden project. In volume 22 of *Nihon Teienshi Zukan*, he describes the garden and mentions how he struggled to come up with a design that would be related to a Shinto shrine.

22 From *Nihon Teienshi Taikei*, vol. 33, p. 93.

[182] The top part of the stone setting is most dramatic

[183] Overview of the stone arrangement as seen from the bottom of the hill

Right page:
[184] Winding stream in Kyokusui no Niwa

LINES IN CONCRETE

Mirei Shigemori modernized the Japanese garden by introducing geometric elements, such as hard lines made from stone or concrete. This is significant because, before then, anything unnatural or too man-made looking, like a simple geometric shape, for example, would have been avoided at all costs in the naturalistic pond gardens, as well as in gardens built around tea houses. The *karesansui* garden, on the other hand, is full of lines, curves and circles raked into the sand. But they are impermanent and soft, and only the continuous work of man keeps them visible. Mirei Shigemori used this as his starting point. He was looking for a way to introduce the element of the line in a stronger and possibly permanent fashion. This is one of the main reasons why he created hard lines made from stone and concrete.

The following pages illustrate a few projects that highlight Mirei Shigemori's use of the line element. Since we can find straight lines as well as curved lines in his work, both types will be discussed using suitable examples. By 1955 he had completed about 80 projects and published 56 books. He was, by any standard, an established professional and scholar. And he was beginning to be well known. Also, as he got closer to the peak of his career, he started to experiment more. Actually, in Mirei Shigemori's case, the majority of his really unique and creative works were built in the last twelve years of his life.

1953 Unusual Lines in a Castle Garden: Kishiwada-jô

岸和田城

Mirei Shigemori's layout suggests the castle's old fortification walls and at the same time stages a battle scene from Chinese mythology. The garden's location on the site of a military castle is what inspired Shigemori to use his stone settings to refer to Zhuge Liang's eight-fold battlecamp formation. Stylistically the garden presents a *karesansui* design that slopes up toward the middle, where the stone setting representing the general's Central Camp is the focus of attention.

The castle was built in its current location in 1615 when Koide Harima-no-kami Hidemasa took up residence in the area as its ruler. Soon after Okabe Minô-no-kami Nobukatsu came to power in 1640, he built a moat and a stone wall around the castle. From then on, Kishiwada Castle developed together with the castle town. After the Meiji Restoration in 1868, the government abolished the old feudal domains and reorganized Japan into new geopolitical units called prefectures. Eventually Mr Okabe, Kishiwada Castle's last owner, donated the property to the city. In early spring 1953 Fukumoto Tarô, Osaka's mayor, proposed the construction of a garden at the castle. On June 30, he asked Mirei Shigemori to prepare a design proposal for the garden. The plans were finished by July 27, and work on the garden started on October 13. Prince Takamatsu visited the site once during construction on November 16, an important day for everybody involved. Work progressed quickly and the garden was completed by December 20. The castle tower, which had been destroyed by lightning in 1827, was finally rebuilt the following year, in 1954.

Description: The site is enclosed by an impressive stone wall, dating from the Momoyama period (1568–1600), and at 1,650 square meters is comparatively large. The only access to this man-made island is from the northwest via a bridge across the moat. The castle tower is located to the southeast, opposite the entrance. Writing about his design intention, Shigemori notes: "Castles are supposed to last for ever, and the garden attached to such a castle should be designed in the same spirit. This is what I was most concerned about; hence, I made a garden from stone. But I was also inspired by the fact that this is the garden of a fortress, for it is located in the heart of the castle grounds. So in designing the garden's layout as an abstraction of the old fortification system I am referring to the organization of the site during the Muromachi period."[1] It seems that durability and the potential for abstraction were the main reasons Mirei Shigemori chose the *karesansui* style for this garden design. The sharp-angled lines of low walls in the sand, depicting the layout of the old moats, is the image a bird would have seen some 300 years ago from high up in the sky.

[186] Kishiwada Castle seen from the far end of the garden

Left page:
[185] Points and lines in a plane of gravel

1 In *Nihon Teien Rekiran Jiten*, pp. 108 and 110.

[187] The garden as seen from the castle's top floor

[188] View of the central stone setting with the castle wall in the back

[189] Stone setting symbolizing the Phoenix camp

[190] **Names of the stone settings, counterclockwise, starting with the 2 stones in front: Snake, Heaven, Tiger, Earth, Phoenix, Wind, Dragon, Cloud; Central Camp in the middle**

Concerning the stone arrangements in the garden, Mirei Shigemori continues: "I designed the arrangement of the stone settings with respect to the eight-fold battle-camp formation adopted by Zhuge Liang. It has a main camp in the center with eight subcamps surrounding it. These were called Heaven **[195]**, Earth, Wind, Cloud, Dragon, Tiger, Phoenix **[189]**, and Snake."[2] The names of these historical camps, originally related to Chinese mythology, are what Mirei Shigemori used as the chief inspiration for his stone settings in the garden. In addition to the eight peripheral camps, there is the general's Central Camp **[185 | 188]**, depicted by the main stone setting in the middle of the garden. It is composed of several large upright stones and can be viewed from all sides. The peripheral stone settings each consist of between two and nine stones, depending on their theme. The Camp of the Dragon stone setting in the south part, for example, uses nine stones to represent a dragon rising up to heaven through black clouds. The Camp of the Snake stone setting in the east part, on the other hand, consists of only two stones representing a long snake. Incidentally, the stones are Mirei Shigemori's favorite *aoishi*, in this case from Okinoshima, a small island near Shikoku.

The Central Camp stone setting sits on the highest level in the center of the garden **[190]**. The Camp of the Tiger and the Camp of the Wind are located below on the middle level, and the rest of the camps are on the lowest level. The jagged lines marking the edges of the three different levels meet at various angles and create a variety of shapes. Sometimes they are almost parallel and elsewhere they form triangles or even diamond-shaped spaces. Each level is 30 centimeters higher than the one below, sloping up as it approaches the center **[194]**. Unlike most other *karesansui* gardens, this castle garden can be appreciated from any viewpoint; the scene naturally changes as you walk around the edge of the garden. The design can also be enjoyed from the top floor of the castle tower, which offers a commanding view of the garden and the surrounding urban landscape. Another distinctive feature is based on Shigemori's notion that people should be able to walk on the wall lines and thereby approach the center without stepping on the sand. He notes: "If you walk on the outer line, you can jump to the next inner line when the two get close. And then, finally, you can step onto the innermost line and get even closer to the center." Not only did he think people should enter the garden, he even thought of it as a space for events: "I planned for the possibility of using this garden as an exhibition space and even as a theater. And as the city was planning a library in the castle tower, I thought the garden might also be used as an outdoor reading space. So even though the design of this garden seems very simple, it in fact allows many different uses."[3] This is how the garden at Kishiwada Castle became the first *karesansui* garden in Japan to be used as an exhibition and performance space. Two years after the garden's opening, a number of metal sculptures were displayed during an outdoor exhibition.[4]

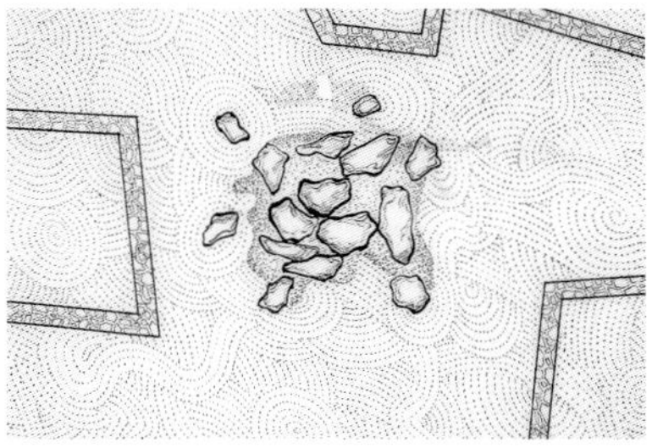

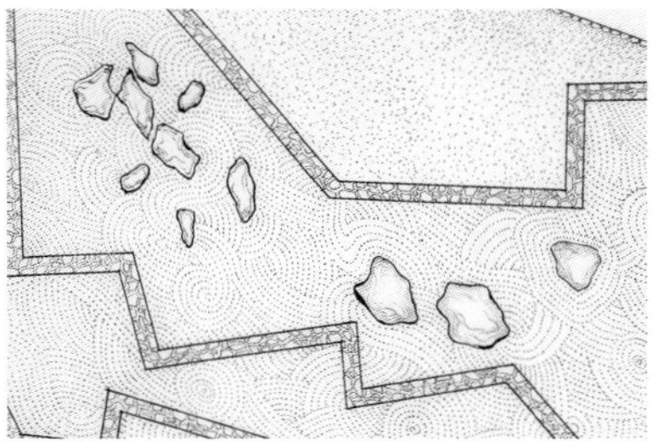

[191] **In the middle is the captain's Central Camp**

[192] **Phoenix camp to the left, Earth camp on the right side (3 stones)**

2 Zhuge Liang, in Japan known as Shokatsuryô Kômei, was a famous Chinese tactician of the 2nd century AD; his famous eight-battlecamp formation is a defensive formation, not an offensive one.

3 From *Nihon Teienshi Taikei*, vol. 29, p. 35.

4 From October 22 to 24, 1955, an outdoor exhibition of modern art by the Byakutôsha group was held at Kishiwada Castle.

[193]

[194]

And during that same event Yûgo Shigemori, Mirei Shigemori's only daughter, gave a traditional Japanese dance performance on the garden stage. Mirei Shigemori produced his daughter's performance, and who would have guessed that the theme of the dance was the straight and the curved line!

[193] **The Camp of the Tiger seen from the path leading to the castle's entrance**
[194] **Three different planes stepping up towards the middle of the garden**

Interpretation: Without a doubt, the stone settings are an important part of this garden, but the angled lines are really the main feature. They represent a revolutionary addition to the traditional vocabulary of the *karesansui* style garden, which for centuries had been made from sand and rocks alone. The linear walls were built in stone, first and foremost to make them last: lines raked in sand fade away rather fast as a result of wind and weather, but these lines will remain as long as the concrete holds the stones in place. However, when designing this garden, Mirei Shigemori did not have only longevity in mind. He was also striving to create his own contemporary Japanese garden. In his words: "As you can see on the plan, the garden is composed of three stone lines, which are angling back and forth. I used the old layout of the fortress as a reference and transferred it into a modern artistic expression. My main idea was to create a layout that referred to the original Kishiwada Castle, seen from an aerial view; something that had never been done so far."[5] Being just a contemporary garden was not quite enough; it had to be new as well. And looking at the result, we have to say that a *karesansui* garden like this had never been seen before in Japan.

However, there is still another aspect to the folded angular lines in the garden at Kishiwada Castle. Shigemori had a vision of the future, in which people would see gardens and landscapes more often from the air. He explains: "People in the future will probably appreciate the garden in ways that differ from those used presently. This garden is supposed to last for more than a thousand years, so it is not good enough to think about how people in today's world will appreciate such a garden. Technology will develop and people will be using planes and helicopters more frequently, in which case the garden will often be seen from above, high up in the sky."[6] Admittedly, this is rather a rare aspect to take into account when designing a Japanese garden, but in the case of the garden at Kishiwada Castle, it is a clear argument for the use of the strong line. Mere planes of gravel and points of stone would not have been easily detectable from up in the air. It must be one of the ironies of history that, 40 years after its establishment, this garden is just a stone's throw away from the new Kansai Airport built on a man-made island in Osaka Bay.

[195] **This upwards-pointing stone setting symbolizes heaven**

5 From *Nihon Teienshi Taikei*, vol. 29, p. 35.
6 In *Nihon Teien Rekiran Jiten*, p. 108.

1955 **The Wave Appears: Maegaki Residence**

前垣壽男氏邸

Although still relatively early in his career, the Maegaki garden features one of Mirei Shigemori's first true inventions that later became his trademark: the undulating line **[196]** symbolizing the coast, the beach or simply waves. It was here that he used it for the first time, creating, at his first attempt, one of the most flamboyant lines he was ever to design. Furthermore, the Maegaki garden also represents a typical residential garden design by Mirei Shigemori, a type of which he did many, and a style that made him very successful among his clients, people who wanted something contemporary and out of the ordinary.

Mr Toshizô Maegaki owned a sake brewery named Kamoizumi in Saijô-chô, part of the Kamo-gun area in Hiroshima Prefecture. The town is situated in the Chûgoku highlands, an area famous for the beauty of its natural scenery. The good quality of the local spring water and the rice grown here make for a flourishing brewing industry. Brewery owners in Japan are usually quite wealthy and often have a broad range of interests. Therefore local brewers are usually among the better-educated people in town and well aware of culture. This way they supposedly are able to have interesting conversations with their clients and eventually sell more sake. Mr Maegaki was apparently such a person, and due to his wide range of interests, he collected and owned many excellent artifacts.[7] Mr Kuwata from Fukuyama introduced Mirei Shigemori to Mr Maegaki. He was a close friend of Mirei Shigemori and a relative of Mr Maegaki. The Maegaki family tea house had just been finished at the time and it needed a garden to go with it. So on November 4, 1955, Mirei Shigemori visited the site together with Mr Kuwata, whom he had met on the way. At 1:00 p.m. they arrived at Saijô station and headed straight to Mr. Maegaki's residence. Because in Japan hardly any serious business is done without first having had a cup of tea or even a meal together, they were invited to lunch with the owner and his family. Then they went to a mountainous site that the Maegakis owned, about 8 kilometers away, to look around for possible stones for the new garden. But at first they did not find anything suitable there, so the gardeners returned later and searched more thoroughly. After this, both visitors were invited to stay at the Maegaki's house for dinner and to spend the night. They all had dinner together and apparently a very interesting conversation. Mirei Shigemori returned to Kyoto the next day.[8]

Description: This residential garden in *karesansui* style consists of the following three parts: the south garden, the Courtyard Garden and the front garden **[197]**. The entrance from the street is located to the north of the property and access to the door is through the front garden. The South Garden is the largest part and is contained by a *kura* located to the south of it, which is visible in the background **[204]**. It extends along a corridor of *shoin* rooms, creating a U-shaped space that stretches into the center of the building. According to Mirei Shigemori, the garden is designed in Hôrai style, inspired by the ancient Chinese cult of immortality. So the stone composition in the center represents the mythical Mount Hôrai as well as a dry waterfall.[9] The stone settings to both sides describe imaginary islands in the East China Sea, inspired by the rolling hills that supposedly surround this famous mythical mountain. In front of the Mount Hôrai stone arrangement, Mirei Shigemori created two peninsulas that reach into the space from the east and the west, while their tips overlap in the center of the garden. The inspiration for this came from the ancient *Sakuteiki*. He explains: "Working on this design, I remembered that there were examples of mist-shaped center islands in the *Sakuteiki* from the Kamakura period. Originally that referred to islands, but I used the idea for the peninsulas."[10] When creating a landscape resembling the Inland Sea, the image of islands and mist is actually quite compelling. Also, depending on the viewpoint, this garden layout creates quite a bit

Left page:
[196] The undulating line and the boat stone

7 The writer was able to visit the brewery and the garden in 2001. As in the winemaking industry, sake brewers try to present themselves and their beverage as a cultural product. By surrounding themselves with the necessary objects, and this is also where the garden plays a role, they are creating an atmosphere of distinction. Old Mr Toshizô Maegaki has passed away, but his wife and the younger generation still keep the place up.

8 The last paragraph is based on excerpts from his diary: "Mr. Maegaki: 1955," November 4th.

9 In *Nihon Teienshi Taikei*, vol. 28, p. 77.

10 Ibid.

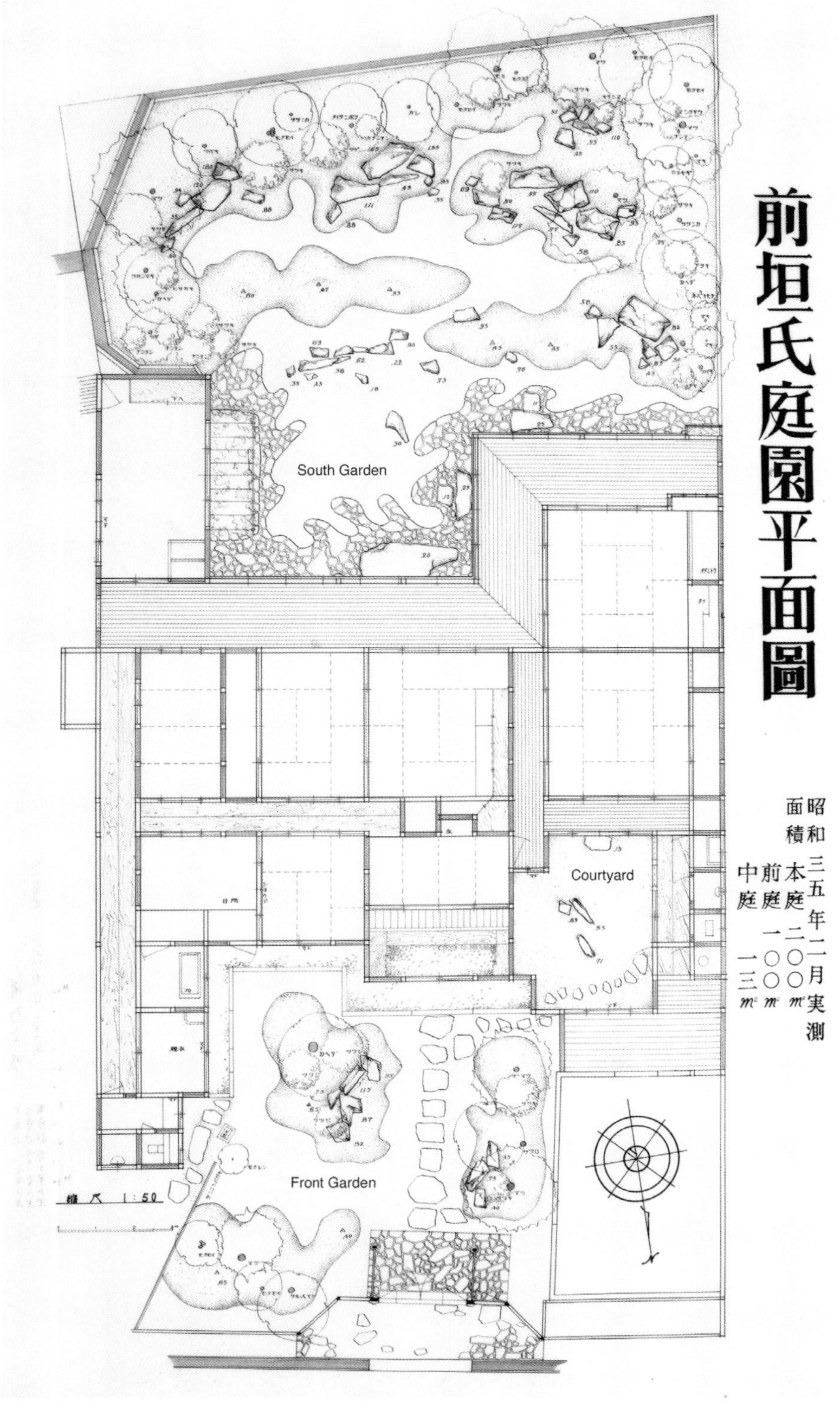

[197] **Plan of the Maegaki residence and garden**

[198] **Sketch of the South Garden with stone settings labeled as discussed in the text**

of depth. In front of these two peninsulas is an area covered with white sand, creating an open space right in front of the house. This reinforces the image of the landscapes of the Inland Sea. In the overall context, the paving stones of red *kurama-ishi* under the eaves are an abstraction of the coastline.

The Courtyard Garden **[200 | 201]**, only 10 square meters in size, is also designed in the *karesansui* style, but has no vegetation at all. It is a very simple, dynamic garden with only three rocks and white sand. In the front garden, the stepping-stones are arranged in a straight line facing the entrance with low *tsukiyama* mounds on both sides, the one to the west featuring a group of three and the other to the east a group of five rocks. Connecting to the overall theme of the Inland Sea landscape, most of the entrance area is covered in white sand and raked with lines. Screened from the street by a 3-meter high wall, the front garden here is a completely private space.

While we look at the technical aspects of the stone setting of the South Garden in more depth, it is helpful to refer to image 198, which shows a sketch of the South Garden. The stone arrangements depicted in the image are marked with letters A to H, which are also used in the following text. The most dominant stone (A), a tall and wide rock in the center of the arrangement, depicts Mount Hôrai and is at the same time the *Mizuochi-ishi*, often a leaning stone that the (imagined) water runs down **[207]**. Mirei Shigemori slightly inclined it toward the right so it looks a bit more dramatic. Another similarly inclined upright stone is placed to the right of the previous one. Then there is a smaller mountain-shaped stone to the left, in front of the main stone, and an even smaller rock with a sharp top stands on the far left. Right in front of the *Mizuochi-ishi*, just about in the center of the group, Mirei Shigemori placed the lying *Daiza-seki*, a base or foundation stone, usually with a horizontal appearance. Then, to the far right of the stone composition, there are two small rocks for balance. This is a complete Mount Hôrai style stone arrangement with seven rocks and it represents the main formation in this garden. On the back other peninsula, further to the right of Mount Hôrai, are nine stones arranged in a group (B) **[206]**. In front of the tallest stone, a sharp-pointed rock is placed leaning forward in the center of the group. Then an upright and a low mountain-shaped stone are set further to the left. To the right of the group stands a larger, slightly pointed but more horizontal stone, with a small vertical one in front of its left corner. These are the stones to the front of the group, but there is a second line of rocks behind them. And then further back, toward the far right corner of the garden, is another small group of five stones. The latter are most likely the stones reused from the old garden. On the far left, next to the two round-shaped *karikomi*, a group of four rather upright stones and one horizontal rock, all of different sizes, are placed erratically as a backdrop (C). Then, again on the opposite side, in the northwest corner of the garden, is another group of stones. Designed to be the point from which the peninsula extends out, this is a rather diverse formation consisting of six rocks (D).

In front of stone settings A, B and C are the two long peninsulas that reach into the space from east and west. They are modeled after a mountain ridge, with curved lines inspired by the coastline. Like the *tsukiyama* in the back and the front gardens, they are covered with moss. As there are hardly any rocks on them, the moss is really the main characteristic of the two peninsulas; there is only one upright stone in the center of the right peninsula. The space in between, where the two peninsulas overlap, is covered with white sand. There are a few rock island-type stones placed in an upright fashion (E), a technique called *Risseki*, which literally translates as "standing-stone technique." In front of the two peninsulas, slightly left of the center of the garden, is a *Sanzon* style stone arrangement (F) **[208 | 209]**. Resembling the Buddhist Trinity, this triad stone setting contains three Buddhas, the main figure in the center flanked by two attendants. A larger horizontal stone is placed among the upright ones, and two small upright stones are close to its left corner. Further to the right, two tall stones are set upright (G) and another small horizontal stone is placed between them and the *Sanzon* style group **[209]**. This is a very unique composition by Mirei Shigemori and was probably invented by him. If we look at the entire scene, it becomes clear how this stone arrangement really is the centerpiece of the garden. The boat-shaped stone (H) is then placed in the middle of the white sand **[210]**, a little closer to the building, but it faces the group described above. This stone

[199] Front Garden with stepping-stones leading to the entrance
[200] Stone setting in the small Court yard Garden

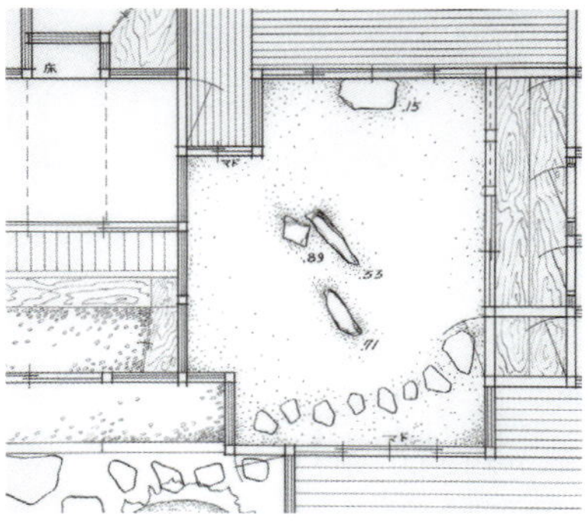

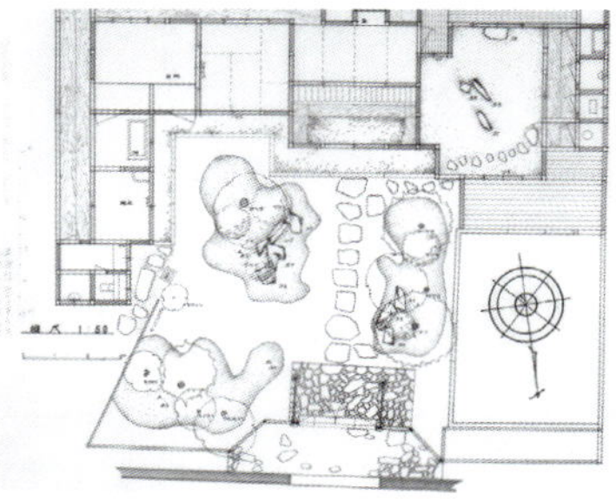

[201] Courtyard Garden detail as indicated in the plan
[202] Detail of the Front Garden as shown in the plan
[203] An early sketch for the design of the South Garden

[204] The house and garden are well interconnected; the *kura* is visible in the back

[205] View parallel to the main stone setting and the peninsulas

[206] A scenic view: a pine tree leaning over a group of stones

signifies a ship on its way to the islands of the immortals, and it therefore complements the whole composition of a Hôrai style garden.

The main characteristic of this garden is, of course, the stone settings. The *tsukiyama* mounds, the peninsulas and the vegetation are supporting features. With regard to the stone arrangement, Mount Hôrai (A) is the main character and the stone settings to both sides are supporting characters (B and C). Also the central stone setting (F to G), despite its uniqueness, is one of the supporting characters here. Furthermore, there is always a main stone and several supporting stones within each of the stone arrangements.

As the stone selection was limited to the local granite, Mirei Shigemori had to work with what he could find in the area—an interesting challenge for any garden maker. He chose well-shaped and powerful stones, many of them with sharp edges. The gardeners dug up the stones while Mirei Shigemori was absent. About a third of the stones used were from the previous garden, although Mirei Shigemori did not like them: "They were less powerful and absolutely not to my taste. It was difficult to integrate those stones, so I used them in rather inconspicuous places."[11] The vegetation from the former garden was also salvaged. Within three days the gardeners had transplanted *Pinus thunbergii, Quercus dentate, Podocarpus macrophyllus, Aucuba japonica, Acer palmatum, Ternstroemia gymnanthera, Osmanthus fragrans, Rhododendron indicum, Rhododendron japonicum* and *Ilex crenata*. Through careful maintenance, their shapes were adapted over the next few years to fit into the new garden better. The moss was ordered from a nursery in the Gôshû area, in Shiga Prefecture, and the white sand, as always, is the famous *Shirakawa suna* from Kyoto. The red stones for the paving are *Kurama ishi* from the Tamba area, just north of Kyoto city. Red mortar was used in between the paving stones, a detail that Mirei Shigemori was particularly fond of.

Interpretation: The garden for the Maegaki family embodies the quintessence of a residential project designed by Mirei Shigemori. In addition, it represents a great leap forward in his formal design vocabulary, as it marks the creation of the undulating line built in stone **[196]**. To gain a better understanding of Mirei Shigemori's point of departure, it is helpful to take into account some of what he has to say about the character and design of today's residential gardens and his own approach to such a situation. On pages 80 and 81 of volume 28 of the *Nihon Teienshi Taikei*, he presents the following thoughts: "Gardens are made in various kinds of places: shrines, temples, residences, restaurants or hotels, government offices, schools, museums, banks, companies etc. However, quite a lot of them are actually residential gardens, and most of them are neither old nor artistic. In contrast, the gardens at shrines or temples are usually relatively old and they have been rather well preserved. And often they are even considered to be art. In comparison, the new gardens at restaurants or hotels are seldom at that level. Many gardens have been built in the recent boom, but I have trouble finding any outstanding ones among them." So far, this is his analysis of the current state of affairs. Then he goes on to give us the reasons why he thinks this situation exists: "People tend to think that anybody can make a garden, without any education or original ideas. A lack of insight on the part of the owner, and knowledge on behalf of the garden maker, provides for many tasteless gardens. The garden makers think a few stone arrangements and some trees are the only things needed to make a garden. This doesn't do much for the cultivation of garden art." This constitutes a direct critique of the work of many of his fellow garden makers, as well as their clients. It is a remarkable statement in the context of a society like Japan, where such criticism is usually only made behind closed doors. Then, Mirei Shigemori continues to explain why he thinks residential gardens are of special importance here: "At a residential house, the people living with the garden look at it every morning and evening, so it should be a sophisticated and inspiring sight. If this is the case they can absorb civilizing information every day. Residential gardens should be top quality cultural products, but what is being built at the moment is unfortunately the opposite." These thoughts set the scene for the design he made at the Maegaki's house.

[207] **The Mount Horai stone setting marks the center of the garden (A)**
[208] **A very dynamic combination of upright and flat stones (F)**

11 In *Nihon Teienshi Taikei*, vol. 28, p. 78.

[209]

[210]

The spatial concept of the garden is quite simple and basically determined by the location of the house. A front garden is situated between the street side entrance and the main door. Then a little courtyard garden occupies the space between the storehouse and the rest of the residence. And finally the south garden is laid out in front of the most important rooms of the house, letting in the winter sun and providing some shade in the summer. Moreover, this is also the sequence followed by a visitor to the house. You first enter a relatively calm space, and then you walk past the very simple and reduced courtyard, and finally you arrive at a rather dramatic and vivid landscape scene. We could say that in terms of level of intensity, it starts somewhere around the middle mark, falls to a low and then ends on a high. But then there is a whole range of conceptual ideas that give form to the garden. Since the garden is located not far from Japan's Inland Sea, Mirei Shigemori takes this commanding landscape as the major inspiration for the design of the garden. He essentially creates a miniaturized version of it, complete with references to its individual elements, such as the sea, its islands and the varied coastline. And, in addition, there is a layer of symbolism from other places and landscapes. This is, for example, where Mount Hôrai, the island of the immortals, comes into the concept; also the Buddhist trinity stone setting, or the so-called rock islands. Then, with the long and narrow shape of his peninsulas, he makes reference to one of the most famous landscapes in Japan called Amanohashidate, learning from renowned examples, such as the garden at Katsura Rikyû in Kyoto.[12]

So basically we are looking at an imaginary landscape of a house situated on the coast, connected to other mythical and real places by way of symbols or garden elements. In its built form this concept then translates into earth mounds and rock formations, supported by vegetation and a sea of white gravel.

In addition, this garden reveals a design feature that Mirei Shigemori had been working on for a while, at least there are small hints of it in a number of his earlier works. However, it is here, in the Maegaki's garden, that one of his key design elements was born: the undulating line carved in rock **[196]**. In his diary he notes on the subject of this design element: "The design under the eaves was inspired by the tidal beach, and this is the first use of it among my designs."[13] It is not the very first curving line used in one of his gardens, but it is the first time he built it from stone and furthermore in a very lively, even flamboyant form. Moreover, as in many *karesansui gardens*, this one also works on different scales. Depending on the point of view we choose, the undulating edge represents the coastline seen from high up in the sky, or when close up it becomes the waves washing onto the beach.

In Japan most gardens are given names, and in Mirei Shigemori's case there is also a concept behind the name of his garden. He called this one Jusen-tei (寿泉庭), taking the first *kanji* character of the owner's given name, which can also be pronounced as *ju*, and adding *sen*, which signifies well or spring. Together it comes to mean the "Garden of the Lucky Well," quite an appropriate name for a brewer's garden, I suppose.[14]

[209] The boat on its way to distant Mount Horai

[210] Dramatic Inland Sea landscape and the boat stone

[211] This stone was a present from Ms Maegaki's parents when she joined the new family

12 Amanohashidate is considered to be one of the three most scenic places in Japan. It is located on the Tango Peninsula in the north of Kyoto Prefecture at the Japan Sea; the peninsula is 3.6 kilometers long, less than 189 meters wide and covered with about 8,000 twisted pine trees. The Japanese name translates as "Bridge to Heaven." The garden at Katsura Rikyû features a miniature version, including a stone lantern that has become quite famous.

13 See December 24, 1955 in excerpts from his diary: Mr Maegaki: 1955.

14 Jusen-tei (寿泉庭), literally "happy-spring-garden." The first *kanji* character can also be pronounced *toshi* and was taken from the owner's name: Toshizô Maekgaki. The second *kanji* character *sen*, is now used to denote well or spring, but in old times also meant garden: for example *rinsen* (林泉), literally "forest-spring," is an old word for garden. The last *kanji* character, pronounced as *tei*, translates simply as "garden."

1963 Clouds Mirrored in the Ocean: Kôzen-ji

興禅寺

Kôzen-ji is a Zen temple located on the Kiso-Yamanaka plateau, 1200 meters above sea level. So not only is this place closer to the world of the gods, but due to the high altitude even the sky feels different. Drawing inspiration from these characteristics, in 1963 Mirei Shigemori designed a *karesansui* garden here that features a sea of clouds contrasted by a 7–5–3 stone arrangement **[215]**. The outline of the clouds is drawn in the gravel by a narrow line made of white concrete. And appropriately the garden was named Kanun no Niwa, or the "Garden for Appreciating Clouds."

Part of the Rinzai Zen sect, this temple in the town of Kiso-Fukushima (Nagano Prefecture) lies on the upper Kiso River in a mountainous region near Mount Ontake and it is the largest in that area. In 1434 Kisoshikibu Nobumichi, the twelfth generation head of the Kiso family clan from this area, built the temple in memory of Kiso Yoshinaka, who was a famous warrior from the Kamakura period. Kisoshikibu Nobumichi then asked priest Daika to become head of the temple. There is still a pagoda in the precincts of the temple which is a memorial to Kiso Yoshinaka. Later Sakyô Daifu Yoshimoto devoted himself to this temple. When his younger brother, Yoshimasa, became the priest in charge he built the imperial envoy gate. On April 20, 1641 a fire destroyed the original building built by Kisoshikibu Nobumichi. In 1645 the efforts of the priests Kegaku and Shuya led to the rebuilding of the Buddhist sanctum, and the Kannon hall was completed with the help of Yamamura Yoshitoyo, a famous local magistrate. Later, in 1654, they also built the mountain gate. Then in 1656 a bell was placed on the property. However, on December 24, 1906, a fire again destroyed all the buildings on the grounds. In 1912 the main hall was once more rebuilt and this time lasted until May 12, 1927 when the third fire occurred. Again everything was destroyed. Little by little, the temple was rebuilt once more and in 1962 the living quarters were the last building to be completed. It was in 1963 that the current priest, Matsuyama Hôzan, asked Mirei Shigemori to work on the front garden, and the latter soon produced a design for it **[217]**. The construction of the new garden was completed the same year.

Description: The front garden is about 990 square meters in size and has a perfectly rectangular shape. It lies in front of a rather modern temple building, with a black and white checkerboard patterned patio located in between **[213]**. On the south, east and north sides it is delineated by an earthen wall **[214–216]**. Since Kôzen-ji is a Zen temple of the Rinzai sect, a *karesansui* garden here seems rather appropriate. Mirei Shigemori designed it as a 7–5–3 style dry landscape garden, using only stones without any vegetation, hence creating a true *karesansui* garden just like Kyoto's famous Ryôan-ji. Regarding his design approach he notes: "From the beginning I had the following theme in mind: a garden depicting a sea of clouds. Naturally I didn't want to just copy the garden at the Ryôan-ji temple, this would not have been very artistic of me. So, consequently, I did my best to develop my own concept of a sea of clouds in this garden."[15] Mirei Shigemori decided to depict this concept by using white concrete lines in the sand representing the clouds **[212]**. He says: "I used a two-dimensional technique [like drawing] for a garden which has three dimensions. Something I have never before seen done in a Japanese garden. But to bring something pictorial into the garden is part of the appeal of this composition."[16]

[213] Patio with black and white checkerboard pattern in front of the garden

This garden is Mirei Shigemori's very first design of a *karesansui* garden featuring a sea of clouds on top of water, contrasting it with 15 stones set in a 7–5–3 style stone composition **[217]**. The inspiration for the garden's theme is its location on the upper Kiso River, at an altitude of 1200 meters. When one looks out from the garden into the landscape, the sky indeed is very clear and apparent. This duality of the enclosed space, mirroring the sky and the backdrop, becomes the main attraction of the garden. The stones then represent the peaks of mountains in a sea of clouds. And, more generally, being a Zen temple, the garden expresses the ideas of existence and nothingness, coexisting in the same space. At the opening ceremony Mirei Shigemori apparently presented several possible names for the garden to the priest, who then chose to name it Kanun no

Left page:
[212] Clouds mirrored in the ocean

15 In *Nihon Teien Rekiran Jiten*, p. 159.
16 Ibid.

[214] An earthen wall frames the sea of clouds

[215] Five stones out of the 7–5–3-stone arrangement

[216] The garden lies in front of a rather modern temple building

[217] **Plan of the cloud pattern at Kôzen-ji**

Niwa (看雲の庭), or the "Garden for Appreciating Clouds." In the meantime the white concrete lines have fallen into disrepair in certain parts of the garden, due to the impact of frost. Naturally, they need to be repaired to preserve the image and content of the garden. Branches of pine trees along the outside of the earth walls have recently been guided into the garden on wooden posts. This breaks the harshness of the garden a little, but most likely it is not what Mirei Shigemori had in mind for this composition. Also the view of the surrounding hills has been impacted by the growth of the town. Many houses can be seen, which is a problem that nowadays affects many gardens that borrow parts of the scenery around them.

Interpretation: As the above citation well illustrates, Mirei Shigemori's model when designing this garden was the famous Ryôan-ji Temple in Kyoto itself. But at the same time he was trying very hard to create something unique and different from that well-known Kyoto example. For the very first time in his career, and for that matter in the history of the Japanese garden, he added the line made of concrete as its own independent element to a *karesansui* garden. He formed it, at first rather thin and in white concrete, 8 to 10 centimeters wide and reaching 5 to 6 centimeters out of the ground. This was a design element that was soon to be further enlarged. So finally a fine line had been added to the points of stone and the planes of gravel. To the eyes of a painter, this was an ideal composition, as the contrasting set now seemed complete and in perfect harmony. Furthermore, the issue of the impermanence of the raked lines was also partly solved. There was now a guiding line in place, which was supposed to remain for eternity. Of course, the gravel area still needs to be raked periodically, but the main theme stays in place.

[218] **Unique raking patterns are to be found throughout this garden**

1966 Waves Washing Ashore: Sumiyoshi Jinja

住吉神社

According to Mirei Shigemori, the shrine garden did not yet exist as a distinct style. Therefore, he selected the *karesansui* style, with its design rooted in the ancient Shinto *iwakura*, as the most appropriate form for this garden. Using an undulating concrete line Shigemori introduced the wave to the ocean of sand, thus giving the garden an unmistakable contemporary accent.

In 1081 a spirit was brought to Suminoe from Sumiyoshi Taisha in Osaka, and the local community built Sumiyoshi Jinja as its place of worship. The shrine was restored once in 1467. Matsudaira Yasunobu, who governed the area at that time, dedicated a bell to the shrine.[17] The tower for it still exists, and a replica of the original bell has recently been installed. Other than that, only the shrine, dating from before the Meiji Restoration (1868), and the main hall remain to this day. The latter is a fine piece of architecture from the Edo period (1600–1868) and was originally the shrine's guesthouse. It is currently used as the office. Masao Nonoguchi, head of the Shrine Association in the 1960s, worked hard to maintain the shrine and wanted to see it flourish again. That is why in March 1966 Mirei Shigemori was formally asked to make a garden at Sumiyoshi Taisha. Shigemori directed the construction in person and completed the work by July of that year.[18] Today the widow of the former priest keeps the building and the garden up, with the help of the shrine's supporters. The white sand is weeded and the raked pattern redrawn every year for the Minaduki Festival at the end of July.

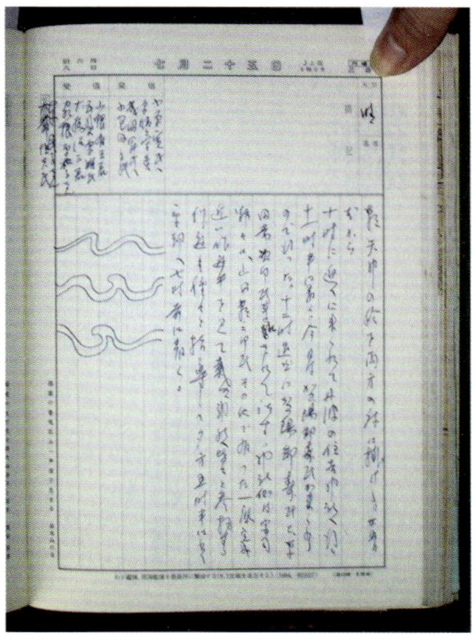

[220] **The basic idea as it was first sketched in the diary**

Description: The garden is located to the north of the main building and was for a long time enclosed by trees. In recent years much of the vegetation has been removed, opening up a view to the surrounding landscape **[226]**. The garden's shape is a perfect rectangle, with earthen walls to the east and the north, and a bamboo fence on the west side. The god enshrined in Sumiyoshi Jinja is the *kami* of the sea. This inspired Mirei Shigemori to depict a seaside landscape in the garden, despite its location amid the hills of Hyôgo Prefecture. He drew three winding lines on a plane of gravel and contrasted them with 15 stones. The lines are made of white concrete and symbolize waves washing up to the beach. The closer they get to the building, the imagined shore, the more undulating they become **[221]**. In the ocean of white sand, brought in from Kyoto, Mirei Shigemori designed small islands of moss, mostly adjacent to one of the lines. The stones, set in a 7–5–3 combination, are his favorite *aoishi* from Shikoku **[222]**. Between the waves is a small but relatively elongated stone, floating alone in the sand, representing a boat en route to the islands of the immortals **[226]**. On the west side of the garden, where there is no earthen wall, Mirei Shigemori created a bamboo fence with a theme also connected to the beach scene. The original design depicted a fisherman's net hung up to dry, albeit in a rather abstract fashion **[115 | 225]**. Unfortunately, this unusual fence has recently been replaced by a much simpler version.

Interpretation: Even in the 1960s there were few shrines with a distinctive garden, so Mirei Shigemori was very interested in working on such a project and further exploring the possibilities for a more defined shrine garden style. Well aware that the tradition of the early *karesansui* garden, which Zen had adopted, was deeply rooted in ancient Shinto, he felt it would be well suited to a contemporary shrine garden design.[19] And since the idea of a seaside scene was in such strong thematic and aesthetic contrast to the hilly landscape surrounding the shrine, only the *karesansui* style, Mirei Shigemori realized, would allow the garden to achieve the degree of abstraction needed to make the contrast work. When he arranged the stones as islands in a sea of sand, he referred

Left page:
[219] **Waves in an ocean of sand washing round islands of stone**

17 The fact that a bell tower was built on the property of the shrine, indicates that Buddhism and Shinto were peacefully coexisting at the time; it was in fact not until the Meiji Restoration (1868) that they were separated.

18 Mirei Shigemori had sketched the undulating line in his diary on July 25, 1966.

19 He had manifested this already in one of his earliest designs, that of the garden for Kasuga Taisha, deriving the 7–5–3 stone settings from the ancient *iwakura* and its overall organization from the *shime-nawa*, a rope made from rice straw that signifies the place where a *kami* descends to earth.

[221]

[222]

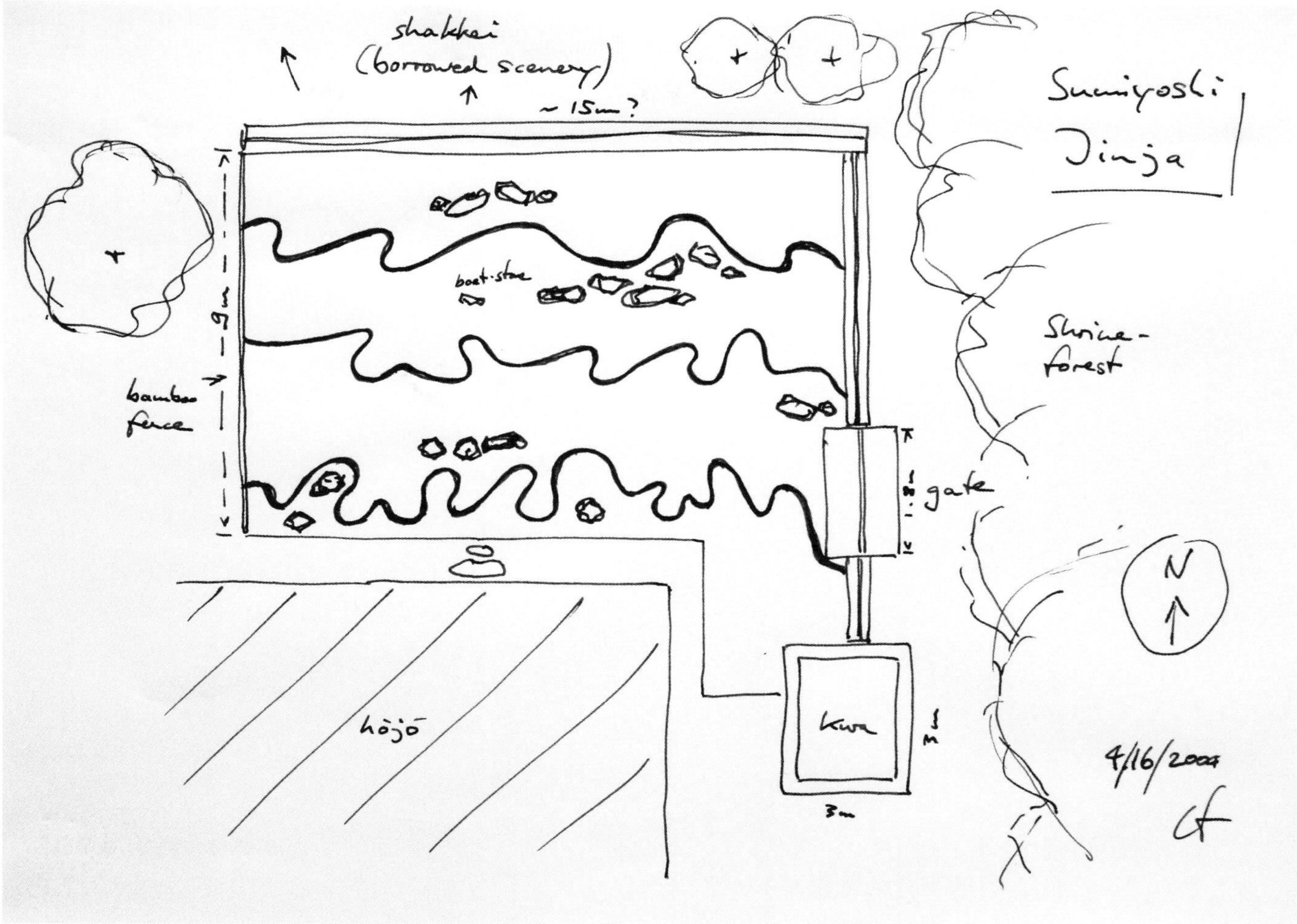

to the Taoist idea of the islands of the immortals. But at the same time they stand for the original Shinto concept of the *iwakura*, a purified and godly rock. By establishing this connection between the god of the sea and the *kami* of the *iwakura*, he could validate the coexistence of both religions, Buddhism and Shinto, a tradition that Sumiyoshi Jinja had followed over much of the past 900 years. Clearly this garden features the boldest line design among all of Mirei Shigemori's works.[20] In no other garden did he create an independent line with such vigor and vividness: three waves made from white concrete, getting stronger and more coiled as they wash up to the shore. The result is a very unique shrine garden, with a design that was flamboyant but at the same time well rooted in time and place.

[221] Three waves washing ashore
[222] Single stones with a lot of character (aoishi)

[223] A rough sketch of the garden layout (by the author)

[224] Early photograph showing perfect islands of moss
[225] The original fence depicted a fisherman's net hung up to dry

Next page:
[226] Overview of the enclosed garden with the boat stone between the second and third wave

20 Sumiyoshi Jinja is chronologically the third of Shigemori's projects to contain a line or lines. He used a rather thin line to depict the outline of clouds at Kôzen-ji in Kiso-Fukushima, and then more dramatic lines for a cloud design at Tôfuku-ji's Ryôgin-an in Kyoto. This is the first use by Mirei Shigemori of lines depicting waves.

[226]

PLANES OF GRAVEL AND SAND

Gravel is often used in a traditional dry landscape garden, but it is almost always of a light gray color, with the most commonly used type being the famous *Shirakawa suna* from Kyoto. This had been the custom since the beginning of the *karesansui* garden and thus so far nobody had dared to question it. But for the renewal of this garden style, the idea of using more than just one color was groundbreaking, as it opened up numerous new possibilities for experimentation. It is also worth pointing out that Mirei Shigemori was already 68 years old when he used differently colored planes of gravel in a Japanese garden for the first time. However, it was one of his major contributions toward its renewal.

The plane is the clearest and simplest topography there is. It is this abstract simplicity, enhanced by color, that suited Mirei Shigemori well in his garden-making. There are two levels of planes that need to be mentioned here. One is the large rectangle that so many Japanese gardens consist of and which has become a classic mark of the *karesansui* garden: a plane often bordered by walls, usually on three of the four sides. Seen through the eyes of a painter, Kandinsky describes it with the following words: "The schematic basic plane is bounded by two horizontal and two vertical lines, and is thereby set off as an individual thing in the realm of its surrounding."[1] Consequently, the material used always emphasizes this notion. The second kind of plane, then, is a subset of the previous one, delineated by lines or other elements that cut it away from the larger plane. These partial planes are usually the product of a distinct edge, often a straight or curved line, and an inner area that is sometimes a different color. We can find both of these types among Mirei Shigemori's garden works, and the latter one might even be unique to his gardens. With regard to color, for centuries tones of gray had been the standard in the Japanese garden, at least when it came to planes of gravel, usually symbolizing lakes or oceans. Why not use black and red sand and add a layer of meaning and complexity to the garden? By doing so, the plainness of the past was replaced with a bit of modern colorfulness. Maybe it really needed the eyes of a painter to see this possibility for the contemporary Japanese garden.

1964 The Chanting Dragon's Hermitage: Ryôgin-an

龍吟庵

Ryôgin-an, although part of the Tôfuki-ji Temple complex located just 1.5 kilometers southwest of Kyoto Station, is little known, even to those interested in the Japanese garden. One reason might be that, except for a single week in November, it is usually not open to visitors. Another reason could be that it does not comply with any of the typical clichés. Hence, Ryôgin-an Hôjô Teien is one of the most unique *karesansui* style gardens to be found at a temple in Japan, and as such may be something for the more advanced connoisseur of this style.

The main hall at Ryôgin-an is one of the oldest remaining structures of this kind in Japan and certainly an outstanding piece of *hôjô* architecture. This explains why the building was declared a national treasure and extensively restored in 1960. The work took two years to complete, but the splendor of the old structure has survived as most of it was fortunately preserved. However, the space around the temple buildings was still in disorder and desperately needed work: the original garden had been built in around 1287 and much of it had since vanished. So priest Furuta Yoshihiro decided to ask Mirei Shigemori to restore the gardens to their original magnificence. But Ryôgin-an was a poor temple and could not afford to build the designs that the latter proposed, so a sponsor was needed for the project. Mirei Shigemori visited his friend Onohara Toshio in Nishinomiya City, for whom he had made a garden 25 years previously. On November 7, 1964 Mr Onohara agreed to donate ¥ 1 million toward the cost of the project, about ¥ 1,705,000 (€ 11,375.00) in today's currency. Grateful for this generous contribution, priest Furuta immediately went to Mr Onohara's house to express his gratitude in person. Right after this Mirei Shigemori started to produce the drawings for the garden. The construction of the garden began on December 2 and everything was completed by December 27. Mirei Shigemori supervised the construction in person. The contractor was Mr Yukio Okamoto from Yamashina, with a crew of seven people. They all must

[228] Dark clouds in the gravel and thundermarks on the fence

Left page:
[227] The head of the rising dragon amid black clouds

1 Wassily Kandinsky, *Point and Line to Plane* (New York: Dover Publications, 1979), p. 115.

[229] The scene described in the legend of Daimyô Kokushi

[230] Three wolves attacking (3 right stones)

[231] The child (middle) protected by a dog on either side

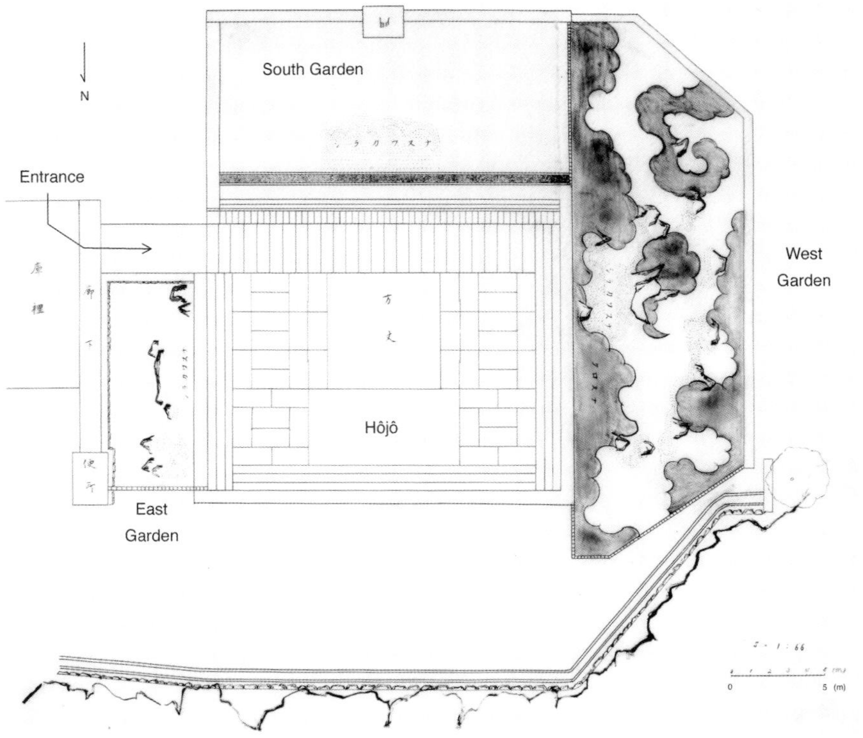

[232] Plan for three gardens at Ryôgin-an

[233] Child and wolves
[234] Three wolves

have worked very hard as, calculating a regular Japanese six-day working week, the garden was built in just 23 days! Quite fast for a garden this size.

Description: Among the plans discovered in Mirei Shigemori's storage house was a detailed drawing of the design for Ryôgin-an **[232]**, produced on November 22, ten days before the start of construction. It is not completely congruent with the actual built version, but gives a very good account of the initial design idea as well as the overall layout. As one enters the temple and then turns left to go to the *hôjô*, the first part of the garden, which appears on the right, is the courtyard of the East Garden. Here, in between the priest's living quarters and the *hôjô*, is a small enclosed garden with nine stones set on a plane of red sand **[229]**. The design is based on the legend of Daimyô Kokushi who, having been abandoned in the forest as a child, was guarded by two powerful dogs when he was attacked by packs of wolves. The 16 *tsubo* (52.8 square meters) of the rectangular space are covered with red sand from Kurama, just north of Kyoto. A longish stone is placed in the center of the space, reflecting the feverish child lying on the ground **[231]**. Near the child's head and feet, a white and a black stone symbolize the dogs that protected him. To the north and the south is a group of three stones each representing the attacking wolves **[230]**. One of them seems poised to leap at a dog (Wolf 1), whereas the middle one is obviously fleeing from the dog's assault (Wolf 2). This special stone arrangement is quite vibrant and shows the scene in full motion. It is a free, yet extravagant and even playful composition. The bamboo fence at the north end of this garden refers to the place in the mountains where Daimyô Kokushi was abandoned **[229]**. It is an abstract painting and shows a treeless mountain, thereby emphasizing the sad circumstances of the legend.

Continuing along the southern side of the building, a vast empty space covered in white sand lies to the left **[235]**. The main gate, used only for ceremonial purposes, is located at the center of the south-facing wall. On its west side, a bamboo fence featuring lightning marks announces further action to the approaching visitor.

Next, as we are about to pass the fence and actually enter the West Garden, the rising dragon comes into view for the first time **[238]**. This part of the garden elaborates on the meaning of the temple's name, Ryôgin-an (龍吟庵), which can be literally translated as the "Chanting Dragon's Hermitage." An earth wall encloses 70 *tsubo* (231 square meters) of newly leveled ground immediately to the west of the *hôjô*. The southwest and northwest corners were cut off in a triangle shape, resulting in a garden that is similar in shape to a flat *hakama* **[232]**, a traditional Japanese formal skirt for men. The new earth

The Legend of Daimyô Kokushi:
Ryôgin-an was originally the home of Museki Fumon Daimyô Kokushi, who had been born in Shinshu Hoshina and later founded the famous Nanzen-ji Temple. The following legend about his upbringing is related here as it inspired the design of Ryôgin-an's East Garden. Daimyô Kokushi's mother dreamt that one morning, as the sun rose to the east of the summit of Mount Fuji, she drank its rays and became pregnant. No wonder Daimyô Kokushi was such an abnormal child. He had triangular eyes whose pupils were unusually close to each other. His ears described a twofold loop. He was a very badly behaved boy, and at the age of seven his mother decided to give him to his uncle Jakuen who would take care of him. At that time his uncle was the priest at Shoen-ji Temple in Echigo Urahara-gun, today part of Niigata Prefecture. But he, too, was unable to control the child and sent him on to Shinshu Aida in Nagano Prefecture. It was there that the child caught a contagious disease and was abandoned in the mountains. But Jakuen was worried and wanted to go and check on the child. When he got to the mountains he saw a black and a white dog sitting next to the child, and it looked as if they were keeping guard over the boy. Suddenly a pack of wolves appeared and tried to attack the child, but the two dogs defended Daimyô Kokushi and wounded or killed several of the wolves. The next day an even bigger pack of wolves came, but again the two dogs killed most of them. So Jakuen realized that, having survived all this, the child must be a very special human being. He brought the boy to priest Shakuen in Serada who then raised Daimyô Kokushi to become one of his disciples. And subsequently Tôfuku-ji's priest Hirakijama Seiichi even trained him to become the *sansei*, the third generation priest at that famous Kyoto temple. This was where the retired Emperor Kameyama became one of Daimyô Kokushi's followers. And it was Kameyama who eventually built Ryôgin-an as a home for Daimyô Kokushi. However, shortly after moving there, Daimyô Kokushi became seriously ill, and it was Kameyama himself who took care of the priest at Ryôgin-an. According to the legend, this is where Daimyô Kokushi then died on December 12, 1291, at the age of 80.

[235] The South Garden with the main gate

[236] Lightning on the fence announces the action to come

[237] **Conceptual drawing for this garden's design**

wall runs north to south and then around the corner to the east. Bamboo fences close the garden off toward the east, as well as to the north.

The central feature of the garden is a dragon creating black clouds, while rising up from the sea toward the sky **[227 | 240]**. Even the bamboo fences are designed to echo this theme. The fence separating the South Garden shows the abstract design of lightning mentioned earlier **[236]**, whereas the fence on the north side features an abstract thunder mark design **[239]**. The rectangular marks suggest that the rising dragon not only causes black clouds but also produces a thundering sound. Here Mirei Shigemori creates a unique supporting effect. In the end, just about everything in and around this part of the garden is an abstraction of the main theme, the dragon rising from the sea, creating black clouds, lightning and thunder. And it all starts to make sense from the very moment that you see the dragon.

Here, as in many of his projects, Mirei Shigemori used blue stone from Awa for the stone settings. He placed the dragon's head just to the southeast of the garden's center, with a body spiraling counterclockwise around it, surrounded by a sea of sand **[240]**. The dragon eventually extends his tail all the way to the southeast corner of the garden. The aligned stones are an abstraction of the dragon's back, depicting the parts of its body that one would see above the waterline **[241]**. Mirei Shigemori points out an interesting effect of this stone setting: "When the visitors look at this dragon's head, standing at the southwest corner of the *hôjô*, and then walk to the north, never taking their eyes off the dragon's head, the creature seems to actually be moving in the sea." [2] This is rather remarkable, as the temple's pamphlet proudly points out **[243–248]**. The entire ground plane of the West Garden is covered with a pattern of dark clouds, all made with just two colors of sand. Mirei Shigemori obviously needed a device to ensure that the black and white sand would not mix, so in between the two he used the concrete line again, marking the border between the two colors of gravel **[242]**. After a longer search, the black sand was, eventually, located in Wakasa, Fukui Prefecture, near the northern border of Kyoto Prefecture. The white sand is the often-used *Shirakawa suna* from Kyoto. The forms and materials clearly emphasize the notion of the rising dragon. The stones representing the animal's body are hard and full of edges. The lines of the clouds, on the other hand, are soft and round, while the thunder and lightning marks are sharp and pointed. All these details differ from most other *karesansui* gardens.

[238] **The first glimpse of the rising dragon**
[239] **Fence with thundermarks at the back of the garden**

Next page:
[240] **Dragon producing black clouds while rising from the ocean**

Interpretation: At Ryôgin-an Mirei Shigemori used different colors of gravel in a *karesansui* temple garden for the first time, thereby creating three distinctly different planes: a red plane, a white one, and a black and white one. Using the legend of the priest's childhood as the theme for the East Garden, he told the story of Daimyô Kokushi and the origin of this temple through the stone settings of this garden. Knowing the story, the legend brings an interesting dimension to the space of the garden, and it really seems as

2 From *Nihon Teienshi Taikei*, vol. 29, p. 108.

[240]

[241] The dragon's back sticking out of the ocean

[242] Lines of gray concrete divide the two different colors of gravel

if the dogs and wolves are actually there fighting. With its aggressiveness, the plane's red color accentuates this impression as it suggests intensity, and even violence. This part of the garden would certainly feel much calmer on a light gray colored plane made with the ordinary *Shirakawa suna*. But with the red sand, the result is a rather dynamic *karesansui* garden. Furthermore, it is in effect a contemporary garden, not only because of the color of the sand Mirei Shigemori decided to use, but also because he managed to infuse the stones with real life and drama.

The South Garden then allows the viewer to quieten down and rest. One can enter the *hôjô's* main room from here and worship. The vast empty plane of white sand in front suggests nothing but an expanse of water and throws the visitor back on his own thoughts, mirrored in his mind and reflected by the sea. But, in fact, this is only a void between two spaces full of action. Finally, the West Garden is the most elaborate yet in terms of planes. Mirei Shigemori outlined the clouds with a dark concrete line, and then filled them in with gravel of a similar color, creating two separate planes of color. The result is a monochrome image with black and white sand, or really a lighter and a darker gray tone. This composition is very pictorial, a large painting made of sand, with the dragon sticking out as a three-dimensional stone sculpture. Moreover, it is a painting depicting an abstract scene rather than a natural landscape, as is so often the case. But not only did Mirei Shigemori use the ground plane to paint on, he also utilized the fences as a canvas. It is a truly unique idea to use those areas to depict lightning and thunder in conjunction with the garden's central theme, and it probably required the eyes of a painter to see these opportunities. The outcome is a kind of animated *karesansui* scene, and as such certainly the first one in the history of the traditional Japanese garden.

[243–248] The dragon is moving—or maybe the observer?

1972 Gods Protecting the Cardinal Points: Sekizô-ji

石像寺

For two reasons, Sekizô-ji represents a milestone in the development of the *karesansui* garden. First, it does not imitate or recall a mythical landscape or a painting of such a landscape, and second, it uses four colors of gravel instead of one. In this garden Mirei Shigemori deliberately tested the limits of what a dry landscape garden could be in 20th century Japan.

The fact that the old name of the temple is Iwakura-ji, together with the large *iwakura* visible on the hillside behind the site **[249–251]**, suggests that this location has been a place of worship for a very long time. The recorded history says that Sekizô-ji[3] had originally been built in the forest behind the current building, but that it had burned down and been rebuilt in 1644 by the priest Tôseki at the current location. The *iwakura*, as the name implies, is a rock that the ancient Japanese people admired as a god or as the site of a god's immanence. It was believed that the *kami* descended at certain times of the year on this stone outcrop, thus connecting this locale to the world of the gods. But, at some stage in the 20th century, people forgot all about the *iwakura* behind the temple; the trees grew, and little by little the stone outcrop was hidden. In 1971 supporters of the temple began to discuss making a garden in front of the main hall. Masao Nonoguchi, who owned a brewery in the nearby town of Tanba Taki, introduced Mirei Shigemori's work to the temple's priest.[4] At about the same time, the trees that had grown up around the *iwakura* were removed and the entire stone outcrop was suddenly revealed. On July 6, 1971, Mirei Shigemori was officially commissioned to design a new garden for Sekizô-ji. He drew up a project plan on September 25, but construction did not start until March of the following year, as the requisite fundraising took some time. On March 22 and 23 Shigemori was on site for the placement of the four stone arrangements. Construction was completed on May 14, 1972, resulting in the first garden in Japan ever to be based on the concept of *shishin sôô*.[5]

Description: Inspired by the newly revealed *iwakura* **[249]**, Mirei Shigemori decided to make a garden for the gods, basing it on the ancient Chinese concept of *shishin sôô*, the four gods who protect the four heavenly directions.[6] The four gods, represented by four stone settings, chase each other counterclockwise around a circle in front of the main hall **[256]**. Each stone setting is associated with one of the four directions:

- East is symbolized by the dragon and is associated with the color blue **[259]**. The dragon also represents the element of wood and is considered the earth guardian. In the east square of the garden are long stones placed to suggest the blue dragon with surrounding blue sand.
- South is symbolized by the phoenix and is associated with the color red **[255]**. The phoenix also represents the fire element and is considered a guardian against it. In the south square a red phoenix stone setting is spreading its wings in a plane of red sand.

[250] The stone outcrop can be seen from afar

[251] An ancient painting recorded the temple's history

Left page:

[249] The ancient *iwakura* marks the origin of this temple

3 The current name Sekizô-ji is written 石像寺 but had been changed from 石蔵寺, which was read as Iwakura-ji, referring to the *iwakura* on the hill. The first character 石 means "stone" or "rock" and is usually read as *seki* or as *iwa*. The character 蔵 in the middle of the old name signifies "storage" and can be pronounced *zô* as well as *kura*, like in the word iwakura. The Chinese characters used in the old name could thus also be read as Sekizô-ji. Then, at one point, the middle character was changed to 像, meaning "statue" and read as *zô*, which then excluded the old reading of *kura*; hence, from this point on the temple was called Sekizô-ji, which literally translates as "Rock Statue Temple."

4 Masao Nonoguchi was also head of the followers at Sumiyoshi Jinja where Mirei Shigemori built a garden in 1966.

5 Shishin sôô (四神相応) is the name of a concept for a site layout based on the ancient Taoist idea that a land area is protected by the following four gods: *seiryû* (青竜), the blue dragon; *byakko* (白虎), the white tiger; *suzaku* (朱雀), the red phoenix; and *genbu* (玄武), the black tortoise. This is a geomantic concept, already seen on paintings in ancient tombs, that eventually became part of Feng Shui. The layout of the ancient Chinese capital of Xian, as well as that of Kyoto, is based on this concept.

6 This concept ties in with ancient Asian astrology, as Gill Hale explains: "Chinese astrologers identified 28 constellations which, when divided into groups of seven, became the Blue Dragon, White Tiger, Black Tortoise and Red Phoenix. Collectively known as the 28 Lunar Mansions and used in conjunction with the 365.25 divisions of the compass, they enabled ancient astronomers to predict eclipses and locate the exact position of the sun in relation to the moon." From Gill Hale, *The Feng Shui Garden* (Singapore: Asiapac Books, 1998), pp. 54 and 55.

[252] The entrance to the garden is on axis with the temple building

[253] The paths to the side connect slightly off-center

[254] The temple's main hall with the priest's residence to the right

[255] The fence encloses the garden but enhances the view

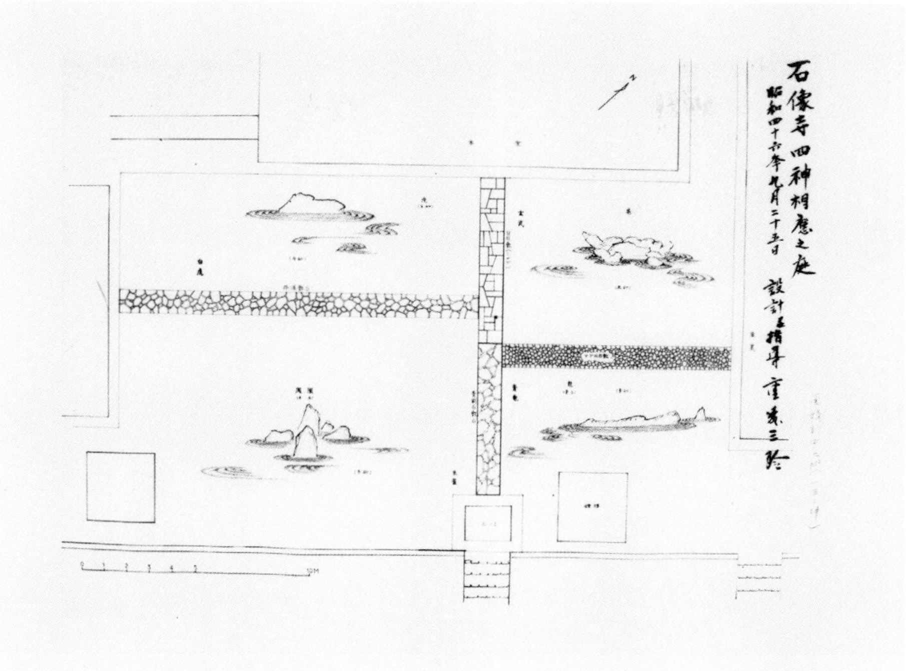

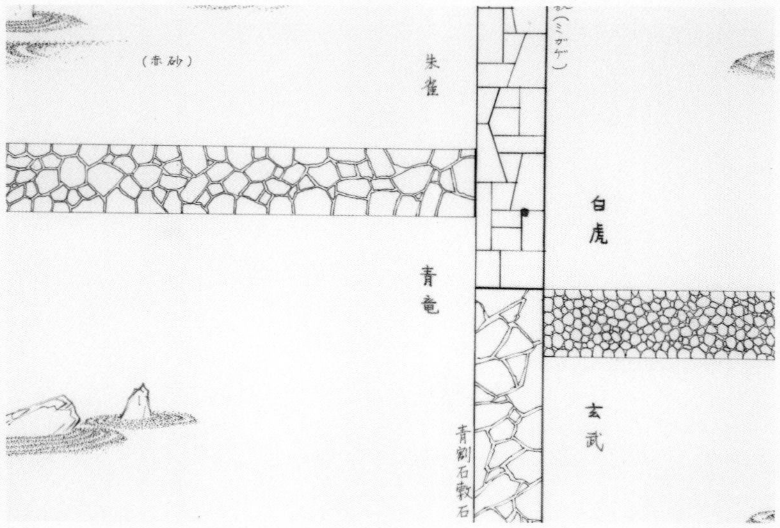

[256] Plan of Sekizô-ji
[257] The four sectors are detailed in different ways

- West is symbolized by the tiger and is associated with the color white **[261]**. The tiger also represents the element of metal and is considered the wind guardian. In the west square the stone setting imitates a white tiger with a bed of white sand around it.
- North is symbolized by the tortoise and is associated with the color black **[260]**. The tortoise also represents the water element and is considered the water guardian. In the north square a black tortoise stone setting is placed amid a plane of black sand.

Taking all four quarters together, we are looking at a 4–2–5–7 stone arrangement. The idea is that the *kami* first descends from the *iwakura* to the black tortoise (north), as it is geographically the closest. Then it continues to the white tiger (west) and on to the red phoenix (south). Next the god jumps from the phoenix to the blue dragon (north), and in the end all four gods perform a dance while facing each other around the circle. The system of paths in the garden cuts the plane in front of the main hall into four sectors **[257 | 262]**, of which the northern and the eastern are the smallest. One path leads straight from the gate toward the main hall. About halfway, and slightly off center, two more paths branch away in the direction of the two smaller buildings on each side of the main hall. As you face the garden while standing in front of the main hall, you can see Chinese characters that read as *shishin* (四神) visible on the bamboo fence to the right, just behind the red phoenix **[263]**. Meaning the "four gods," the graphic refers directly to the garden's main theme. To the left of the gate, and continuing on around the corner from the little bell tower, the bamboo fence features the Chinese character pronounced *seki* (石), the first *kanji* of the temple's name Sekizô-ji (石像寺), a reference to the temple's origin at the *iwakura* high up behind the building.

Left page:
[258] View across from the red phoenix to the white tiger

[259] The blue dragon right next to the bell tower

[260] The black tortoise is swimming westward

[261] The white tiger chasing westward

Left page:
[262] Different materials and colors characterize each of the four sectors

[263] On the fence the *kanji* meaning four gods hints at the theme of the garden

Interpretation: The garden at Sekizô-ji essentially consists of a single large plane defined by the buildings surrounding it on three sides and the fence that marks its southeastern border. It is further divided into four subplanes, as suggested by the concept of *shishin sôô*. Each subplane is dominated by a stone setting that acts as its focal point. Not only are the four gods designed with regard to their assigned direction, but their designated color is then applied to the rocks, the gravel and the paving stones. Each of the stone settings thus appears in a plane of gravel whose color is determined by *shishin sôô*. Choosing *shishin sôô* as the basis for the garden prompted Mirei Shigemori to create four different planes of color in a *karesansui* garden and even to have them all raked differently. This is a remarkable and significant design innovation marking the first time in the history of the Japanese garden that a garden maker used four different colors of gravel in a single dry landscape garden.

Here, as he did at the garden at Tenrai-an, discussed in the following chapter, Shigemori uses the bamboo fence as an additional plane to draw on **[263]**. This time he includes a reference to the garden's main theme as well as a link to its origin. Both are obvious statements for those who know the meaning of this garden, but for everyone else they serve as an aid for a better understanding of the place. This is also the first instance that writing or a font is literally used in the Japanese garden as an ornament on a fence, and its purpose is to add further layers of meaning to the garden space. The *karesansui* plane offers the ideal platform for the *shishin sôô* idea. In no other style of Japanese garden would a design with this theme have come out so clearly. But Mirei Shigemori had another good reason to make a *karesansui* garden here: his quest for a new style of temple garden is another aspect of his enduring commitment to the contemporary garden. He notes: "This garden is not a *karesansui* garden just because there is no water in it. It depicts the ancient faith in gods in a contemporary design appropriate for modern times. As such it departs from the concept of the conventional *karesansui* garden, which usually imitates natural landscapes. Therefore, Shishin Sôô no Niwa should really be seen as a new type of *karesansui* garden."[7] Once more the *karesansui* garden's great potential for abstraction led Mirei Shigemori to experiment with stone and gravel; the result is a distinctive use of geometry and color, this time in the garden of a temple in the Japanese countryside.

[264–267] The different paving materials are linked to the colors of each sector

7 From *Nihon Teienshi Taikei*, vol.33, p. 45.

1969 A Kimono Inspires a Garden: Yûrin no Niwa

友琳の庭

Originally designed for the building of the *Association of Kimono Manufacturers* in Kyoto, the layout of the garden refers to a local kimono famous for its colorful *noshi* bundle design. *Noshi* are auspicious strips of dried fish or seaweed that are tied in a bundle as a symbol of good luck and unlimited happiness. The garden was saved from destruction and recently rebuilt in Mirei Shigemori's hometown.

Relocating buildings and gardens is not uncommon in Japan, but among the gardens in this book Yûrin no Niwa is the only one to have had two homes. The garden's history began in April 1968 when the *Association of Kimono Manufacturers* in Kyoto decided to build an exhibition hall and hired an architect named Tomiie to work out a plan. In August of the same year the Matsui Kensetsu Construction Company won the contract to construct the building, and on August 23 a ceremony was held to mark the start of work. While construction was underway, some of the association's board members visited Mirei Shigemori and asked him for a design for the garden. Shigemori drew up a proposal, which he presented to the association. He got the commission and finished his drawings by the end of the year. Construction of the garden was completed on March 29, 1969, and this was followed by a big inaugural celebration the next day. Thirty years later, in December 1999, the exhibition hall was slated for demolition to make way for a new apartment building. Iwamoto Toshio, a gardener and one of Shigemori's later students, rescued most of the garden's materials. More than 80 truckloads of stone and rock were stored in Okayama until a new location for the garden was found. As chance would have it, Mirei Shigemori's hometown, now part of Kibichûô-chô, was building a new town hall. Not surprisingly the town took this as an opportunity to bring home a garden designed by one of its most prominent native sons. The new building was thus designed to accommodate the shape of Shigemori's garden, and during construction the salvaged pieces of stone were assembled on a nearby trial site. Iwamoto Toshio and his team finished the second incarnation of Yûrin no Niwa on October 4, 2002. For the official opening on November 10, Saitô Tadakazu came and gave a lecture. A former employee of Mirei Shigemori, Saitô had been in charge of the garden's first construction 34 years earlier in Kyoto.

Description: This courtyard in a pond-garden style consists of a square and an adjacent rectangular space at the conjunction of which is a covered corridor **[271 | 274]**. Where, in Kyoto, the stepping-stones connected the exhibition hall with lecture rooms and offices across the pond, in the new setting the stones are a shortcut from the offices to the library and the maintenance facilities. Originally the garden covered 410 square meters; the second version is just slightly larger. Mirei Shigemori makes the following statement regarding his design intention: "When I designed this garden I wanted to create something that felt very modern and that was completely out of the ordinary."[8] Since his client was a very artistic group of craftsmen, it was the right moment to create a highly inventive and abstract garden. No wonder the outcome is colorful and, of course, modern.

A pond, whose design is based on a kimono pattern, dominates the center of this space **[272]**. The shallow water nicely highlights the red stones from Tanba and the blue ones from the island of Shikoku. The triangular area in the southwest corner is a *karesansui* garden, and so are most of the northern and western sections of the courtyard. Some of the blue stones set on pebble-covered mounds in the pond naturally represent islands in the ocean. Two narrow white lines made of cut stone extend out of the pond all the way into the paving in the eastern part of the garden, thereby making a secure connection between the dry and wet areas. The *tsukiyama* in the southwest corner is planted with a large pine tree and covered with moss, as is the longish peninsula in the northern section that represents the famous landscape of Amanohashidate **[271 | 273]**.[9] Shigemori designed this garden to be admired from any corner of the site, as well as from above.

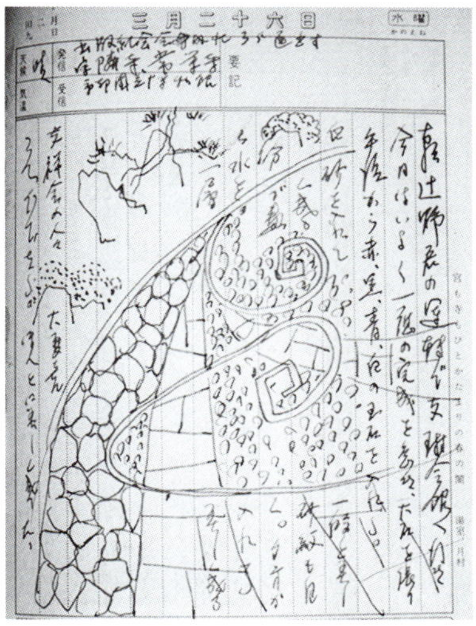

[269] The basic idea as it was first sketched in the diary

[270] A *tsukiyama* with a hard and a soft side

Left page:

[268] A kimono pattern transferred to a garden of water and stone

8 From *Nihon Teienshi Taikei*, vol. 30, p. 79.

9 Amanohashidate is located on the Tango Peninsula in northern Kyoto Prefecture, on the Japan Sea, and is considered one of the three most scenic places in Japan. The peninsula is 3.6 kilometers long, less then 189 meters wide, and covered with about 8,000 twisted pine trees. The Japanese name translates into "Bridge to Heaven."

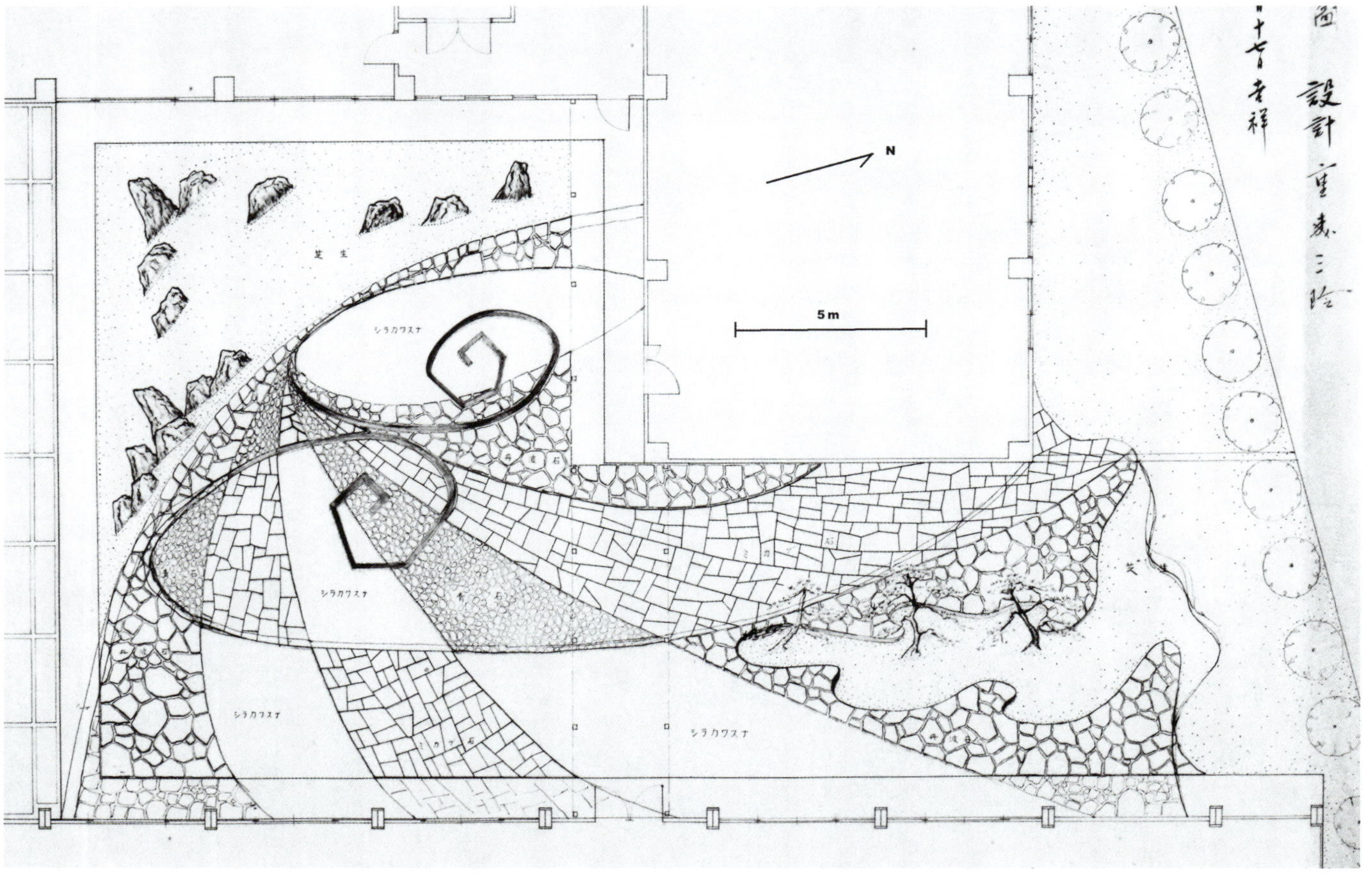

[271]

[272]

[271] **Original plan of Yûrin no Niwa**
[272] **Overview of the garden as seen from the second floor of the building**

Interpretation: The garden's main feature is a pond inspired by the design of a *noshi*[10] bundle on a famous 18th century kimono. This piece of clothing still exists; it is classified as an *Important Cultural Property* and symbolizes the high level of craftsmanship reached by silk dyeing in Kyoto. The spirals of thin white lines represent the ribbons that hold the bundle together; the wider, colorful paving symbolizes the *noshi* strips. The pattern successfully occupies the ground plane, an effect much used in recent Western landscape architecture, for example in the works of Peter Walker.

By referencing this famous kimono, Mirei Shigemori gave the garden a strong local connection, one to which all the members of the Association of Kimono Manufacturers could relate. Taking one of the client's main icons as an inspiration for his garden was a very shrewd move and must have helped considerably with getting this very abstract design approved and actually built. The garden's name is composed of the first syllable of *Yûzensai*, the man who developed the silk-dyeing technique, and the second syllable of *Kôrin*, a famous painter said to have inspired *Yûzensai's* textile designs. Mirei Shigemori saw these avant-garde kimono patterns, among them the *noshi* bundle design, as a collaborative work of *Yûzensai* and *Kôrin*, hence the name. The association's members liked the idea so much that they not only agreed to call the garden Yûrin no Niwa, but even decided to name the entire complex the Yûrin Exhibition Hall.

[273] ***Tsukiyama* planted with pine trees in the narrow part of the courtyard**
[274] **Covered stepping-stone walkway from the offices to the library**

Next page:
[275] **View across the courtyard as seen from the offices**

10 Originally *noshi* referred to a bundle of dried abalone strips, wrapped in red and white paper and attached to gifts to symbolize a wish for good luck and lasting happiness. These days a noshi is usually just a longish, thin, fan-shaped strip attached to a present.
Kimono with *noshi* bundle design. 18th century, Yûzen dyeing, tie-dyeing, embroidery and gold-foil. Important Cultural Property. Yuzenshi-kai, Kyoto.

[275]

MOUNDS AND MOUNTAINS

Terrain or shaped ground has always been one of the mainstays of the Japanese garden. In fact, the term *tsukiyama* is so essential to the subject that making an earthen hill in olden times was basically synonymous to making a garden (*Tsukiyama Teizôden*). Moreover, if we include the spiritual aspect the mountains stand for, much of what the garden in Japan is all about comes together in this very element. Therefore, it should not come as a surprise that Mirei Shigemori was very fond of this old design element, the *tsukiyama*, and played with it throughout his career. It is in the gardens at Tenrai-an and Hôkoku Jinja where he takes it to the extreme, but in many others we can find interesting fragments of the same idea, as illustrated in the following pages by the Ashida Residence and also Fukuchi-in. The scheme is simple: he continues to use the volume but changes the material, which now becomes concrete, sometimes even with added color. In the realm of the Japanese garden, this was equal to a small revolution. Therefore, it is not surprising that many criticized this adaptation as being un-Japanese, while others thought it was amazing and modern. For Mirei Shigemori, it was just another way of pushing the limits of what a Japanese garden could be in the 20th century.

1969 — Pushing the Limits of the Tea Garden: Tenrai-an

天籟庵

In 1969 Mirei Shigemori gave the tea house he had built as a young boy together with his father to the town of Kayô-chô. The new location called for a few adjustments as well as a new garden, all of which was included in this gift to his hometown. Waves and sandbanks, inspired by the neighboring shrine dedicated to the god of the sea, are the theme of Shigemori's avant-garde tea garden design.

The history of this site really begins when Mirei Shigemori took up the study of the tea ceremony at the age of 15. He soon wished to have his own tea house, which he designed and built at the age of 18 with the help of his father, a gifted amateur carpenter. For the tea house's dedication he invited his tea teacher, Mrs Aizawa, as the main guest. Shigemori made frequent use of the tea house until 1929, when he decided to move to Kyoto.

By 1968 the house of Mirei Shigemori's childhood had deteriorated so much that it needed to be demolished, but the adjacent tea house was still in reasonably good shape and was saved. Mr Nishitani, an old friend, suggested that Mirei Shigemori donate the tea house to the town of Kayô-chô. A suitable piece of land was soon found between the village shrine and the town hall. The relocation of the structure required the addition of a *mizuya*, a space for preparing the tea utensils, as well as a waiting area for the guests. As the town did not have the money to pay for all this, Mirei Shigemori had no choice but to cover the cost himself. On March 29, 1968 he submitted a design proposal to the town, but construction did not start until August 15 of the following year. By the middle of September 1969 the stepping stones were already in place and the tea

Left page:
[276] On the way to the tea house, the visitor stops here to wash his hands at the *chôzubachi*

[277] Tenrai-an is now situated east of the town hall, adjacent to the local shrine

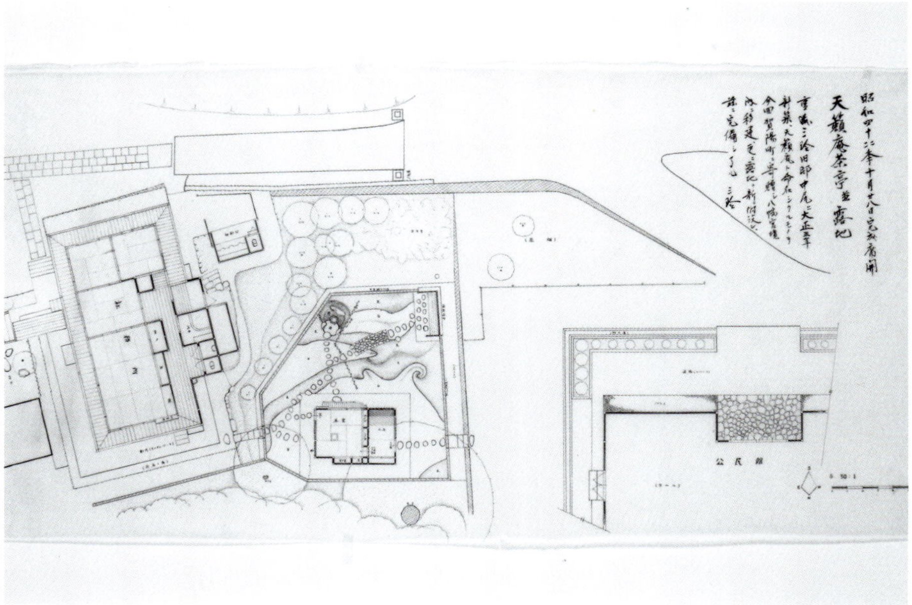

[278] The view as one enters the garden, with the waiting area to the right side

[279] The first syllable of the garden's name is hidden in the pattern of the surrounding bamboo fence

[280] Coming from the waiting area, the middle gate marks the entrance to the inner part of the tea garden

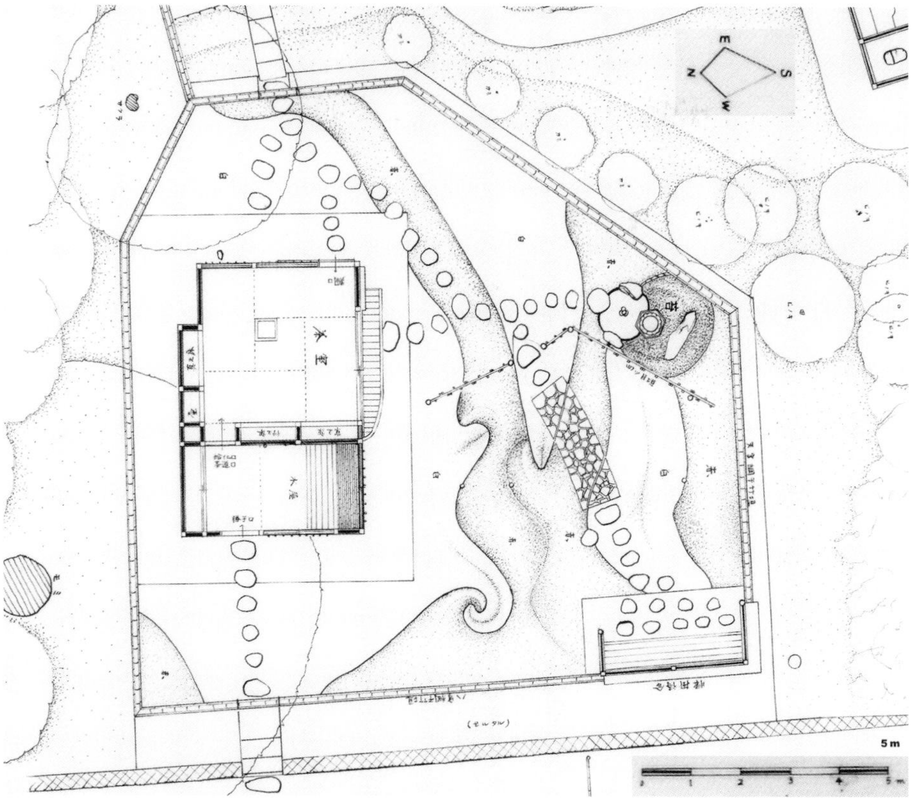

[281] Plan of the Tenrai-an tea garden

house was half finished. On October 13 the red and white sand for the *tsukiyama* was prepared and most of the construction was finished by October 20, 1969. The opening tea ceremony was held on October 28 and 29, with more than 300 people attending.

Description: The garden is located on the property of the Yoshikawa Hachimangû Shrine, which is dedicated to the god of the sea. It is the shrine deity that inspired Mirei Shigemori to design a garden representing ocean waves and sandbanks, which are suggested abstractly using red and white concrete. The wave of white concrete originates near the tea house and subsequently turns into a spiral shape, jutting out into the ocean **[278 | 282]**. Most of the red concrete is mounded, just as natural sandbanks are in the sea. Further out, the waves widen and stretch all the way from east to west. Thus, as one looks from the tea house into the distance, the waves and the sandbanks seem to fold into each other. The tea house itself sits on a rectangular platform of red concrete, connected by stepping-stones to the waiting area and eventually to the entrance. A visitor walking up to the tea house passes though the middle gate **[280]** at a bamboo fence before entering the hut through a small, low door. The tea house itself is in the center of the northern section of the property and faces south, while the waiting area is in the southwest corner and faces east. Worked into the fence pattern **[279]** is the Chinese character for "sky" or "heaven" (天), pronounced *ten*, the first syllable of the tea garden's name, Tenrai-an.

[282] A spiral jutting out into the sea, symbolizing the dynamics of water and sand in the ocean

Interpretation: The traditional tea garden in Japan is a calm, rather green space with a lot of planting, ideally suggesting an austere hermitage deep in the mountains, hidden away in a dark valley. But in Mirei Shigemori's view, anybody could create a tea garden of this kind, and certainly many exist all over Japan. As a man devoted to making contemporary gardens, he resolved to create a tea garden without using a single plant, and, what is more, he decided to make it using colored concrete. Mirei Shigemori at first gives two very practical reasons for what is probably his most extreme tea garden design: "At the northwest corner of this garden is a big old fir tree whose leaves are too small to be kept out of the sand, and this really makes it impossible to use sand in this garden. Furthermore, there is no one to take care of the moss. This is when I realized that the only design that would work in these conditions is a very abstract tea garden, not the ordinary kind."[1] Obviously, over the years Mirei Shigemori had grown skilled at selling his avant-garde ideas using very practical arguments, knowing that this tactic would get him much further than philosophical discussions. But in the case of Tenrai-an, he was in a very comfortable position anyway, since he was virtually his own client. Paying all of the costs clearly gave him the freedom to design the garden the way he wanted to.

1 *Nihon Teienshi Taikei*, vol. 28, p. 154.

[284] The garden is entered through a small gate on the western side, opposite the door leading to the *mizuya*

Moreover, since he knew that the local government would keep the garden in good condition, Mirei Shigemori was confident that his work would be well preserved for the future. So he decided to push his ideas to the limits and attempt something that he would not be able to do elsewhere. His tea garden, in reality, is less of a garden and more of a walk-on sculpture. It is somehow reminiscent of some of Isamu Noguchi's later works, many of which are similarly sculpted landscapes.[2]

Mirei Shigemori created a provocative design like the one at Tenrai-an primarily because of his conviction that also the Japanese tea garden needed to be modernized: "Tea houses and tea gardens should not just remain traditional. Tea itself is an aesthetic microcosm of all art, and it always continues to develop and be connected to the changes in our own daily lives."[3] So, in practice, this garden is a built statement advocating the continuous renewal of Japanese garden art, and especially that of the tea garden.

Left page:
[283] This *chôzubachi* is in fact a precious octagonal base stone from a Kamakura period stone lantern

2 An important event in Shigemori's adult life was his meeting with Isamu Noguchi and their resulting cooperation on the UNESCO garden in Paris. On April 18, 1957 Shigemori and Noguchi met for the first time in Himi on the island of Shikoku. Their relationship developed over the course of the UNESCO garden project, and Noguchi remained a frequent visitor to the Shigemori residence thereafter. The Tenrai-an garden was built twelve years later.

3 From *Nihon Teienshi Taikei*, vol. 28, p. 156.

1971 Tide and Islands: Ashida Residence

芦田末次郎氏邸

Mirei Shigemori worked on many residential gardens over the course of his life. Over time he developed a standard repertoire that appealed to clients who wanted something out of the ordinary, possibly something more modern. Some of these clients developed into real patrons. One of these was Mr Ashida. He owned (and still owns) a beautiful, traditional house and wanted to have a contemporary garden with it. When he hired Mirei Shigemori to design it, he knew what he was going to get.

Mr Ashida is a well-established businessman in the Osaka area and he owns a splendid Meiji period house that is now protected by the prefecture as a historical landmark. But Mr Ashida wanted a modern garden with his traditional house and he was looking around for a designer when a friend, Mr Kubo, invited him to see a new garden that had just been completed by Mirei Shigemori. What he saw was new and interesting, and he decided that this was the kind of garden he wanted, too. So Mr Ashida asked his friend Mr Kubo to introduce him to Mirei Shigemori. First, however, he had to become a member of the Kyoto Garden Association and go to Kyoto in person to ask the master for a garden design. It was important to establish a good relationship with Mirei Shigemori because he chose his clients more carefully now that he was famous, and preferred to make gardens for well-placed and culturally interested owners. In addition, he was very much concerned with a client's personal connections. Mirei Shigemori would research his client's background, evaluate the architecture of their house and the history of the site. In fact, if the architecture, for example, was not up to Mirei Shigemori's standard, he would refuse to make a garden there. After Mr Ashida had tried to invite him for about one month, Mirei Shigemori finally came to see the site. With him he brought his wife, Reiko, his right-hand man, Mr Saitô, and one additional helper. While the client was talking to Mirei Shigemori and his wife, the other two surveyed the site. The size of the garden would then determine the price. In 1971 Mirei Shigemori was already very well known and would therefore have charged about ¥ 80,000 per *tsubo* (€ 848.00 per square meter in today's money). His late works would even cost up to ¥ 130,000 per *tsubo* (€ 1379.00 per square meter in today's money). This price would have included the design, materials and construction. On top of this, the workers usually had to be given board and lodging for the time of the construction. When it came to the financial aspects of the project, Mirei Shigemori would let his wife do the talking. Mr Ashida still recalls her as a rather tough negotiator. Their first agreement only concerned the construction of the garden. The earthen wall was added to the project later, as it had initially not been included. Then, a year later, the client also asked Mirei Shigemori to build a new gatehouse and redo the entrance area. So eventually the project stretched over two years. As a first step in the construction of the garden, the *kura* was moved to make space for the new garden. Before, much of the space had been a *hiroba*, which is the traditional area in front of a

Left page:
[285] Japan's Inland Sea, with many islands covered with pine trees and sand washed ashore by the sea

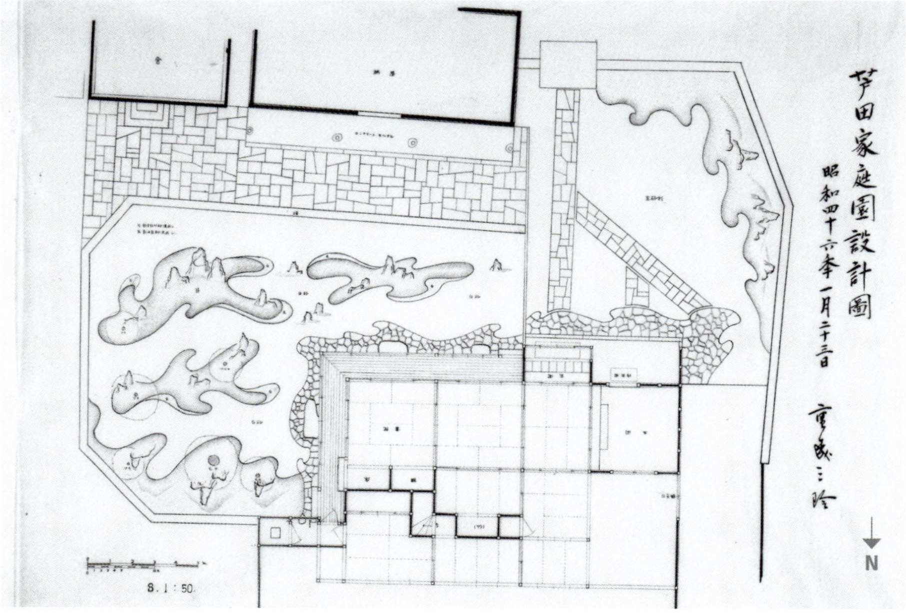

[286] Plan of the Ashida residence

[287] Overview of the garden from its eastern corner

[288] An undulating paving edge makes the transition from house to garden

[289] **The Ashida residence is now a protected historic landmark of Osaka Prefecture**

Japanese farmhouse used for drying rice. Just a few weeks after the negotiations ended, the gardeners came to clean up and start construction.

Description: The house is a beautiful and well-kept two-story wooden structure **[287 | 289]**. On two sides the property is adjacent to rice fields, in what is without doubt a very privileged setting considering its proximity to Osaka. The core of the garden lies to the south and east of the *shoin*, the main room of the house **[286]**. Two stores, one wooden the other earthen, border the property to the south, with an elaborate granite path between the two buildings and the garden. The main access to the house is through the gate in the southwest corner of the property. From there a path leads up to the entrance and branches off in three directions before reaching the house **[289 | 290]**, thereby serving the main entrance, the second entrance and the back door. A bamboo fence screens the view from the entrance area into the main garden. The central part of the garden is an L-shaped space designed to be viewed exclusively from the house and the *engawa* that follows it along the sides adjacent to the garden. To the north, east and south, a white not very tall earth wall contains the space and creates a certain intimacy. The theme here is once again the *Setonaikai*, the Inland Sea, which in this case is in fact the local landscape as it lies just a few kilometers away. Three islands with many inlets, bays and beaches dominate the seascape **[286 | 296]**. Pine trees and stone settings accentuate the hilly islands and structure the space of the garden **[293]**.

The stone settings appear to be laid out along three lines. At the same time they all face the virtual viewer sitting on the tatami mat in the main room. This is apparently also the spot from which Mirei Shigemori directed the setting of the stones. Furthermore, a number of specific views are created, designed to be enjoyed from the best seats in the *shoin* while having a bowl of *maccha* **[294]**. Seen from the inside, the doors, some of which have glass windows, beautifully frame the scenery on the outside, no matter whether they are open or closed **[295]**. In some cases, this reminds one of a triptych or other paintings hung in a series. The detail that catches every visitor's attention is, of course, the edges of the islands, some of which are sculpted in red and white concrete **[293]**. According to Mirei Shigemori, this symbolizes sand washed up by the sea, a place that Westerners would most likely call a beach. Whatever the proposed meaning, these artistic interventions create a good focal point down near the gravel plane.

The undulating line describes not only the shape of the islands in the garden, but also delineates the paving beside the house **[288]**. But apparently, there were not enough stones to continue this into the entrance area, as shown on the plan. Therefore, the line beside the house is straight, and maybe it is better this way. Usually Mirei Shigemori did not like anything to remain from previous stages of the garden, but in this case the client insisted; therefore a large *Ilex rotunda* (round leaf holly) survives and now nicely shades the northeastern corner of the garden **[296]**. However, it did not create enough shade and the moss that was initially planted on the mounds has not survived. So, in spite of the notorious humidity, the sun here is strong and the soft moss that everybody liked had to be replaced with the sturdier *Ophiopogon japonica* or *Tamaryu* (a lilyturf).

[290 | 291 | 292] **Paths, pavings and materials are elaborate and beautifully detailed**

Left page:
[293] Islands with tidal beaches sculpted in red and white concrete

[294] The beautiful view from the best seat in the room

[295] The *shôji* and glass windows frame the scenery on the outside

Interpretation: Mirei Shigemori was always experimenting and trying new things and in this project he carried the idea of using concrete and color in the traditional setting of a Japanese house and garden to a new level. The low, softly sculpted concrete volumes contrast interestingly with the planted mounds, adding to them rather than remaining separate forms. Moreover, the two colors harmonize well with the greens and grays of the vegetation and stones. The shape is amorphous and echoes the language of the *tsukiyama*, perfectly contrasting with the rough edges of the natural rocks in the garden. In addition, Mirei Shigemori here shows a new interest in nature's dynamic processes, by depicting a beach, a mass of sand moved by the tides. This is by no means a new element in the Japanese garden, as pebbled beaches have been built for many centuries in gardens to protect the shore of a pond and enhance the view; one of the most beautiful examples can still be admired at the Kyoto Imperial Palace. But, as so often, Mirei Shigemori plays with the element and the concept behind it: he twists it and turns it, and out comes something quite different. So here the *suhama* still stands for a beach but instead it has morphed into a sculptural element of its own. This is a perfect example of how he took inspiration from the cultural heritage buried in the many traditional gardens he had seen. Having discovered the element of the tidal beach, it was sure to return, although in a slightly different form; in fact, it was included in the garden of the Kitano Bijutsukan which is examined later in this book (see pages 184–189). Among the many residential gardens that Mirei Shigemori created, the garden at the Ashida Residence remains as a real treasure. The owner still admires the garden as well as its creator, and he keeps the place in perfect shape and is determined to pass it on to his children.

Next page:
[296] The island landscape as seen from the southern wall

[296]

1972 Toyotomi Hideyoshi's Emblem as *Tsukiyama*: Hôkoku Jinja

豊国神社

Hôkoku Jinja was built in memory of Toyotomi Hideyoshi, so the gourd, which is the famous warrior's trademark, offered itself as a memorable and recognizable garden motif **[297]**. Combining a large *tsukiyama* of red concrete and powerful stone settings, the garden offers a new interpretation of the *karesansui* style and as such is a milestone in Mirei Shigemori's work.

Toyotomi Hideyoshi, the great Japanese general who united Japan, died at Fushimi Castle, south of Kyoto, at the age of 62 in 1598. That same year Hôkoku Jinja was founded in his memory. The warrior's soul became a god after his death and is enshrined at Hôkoku Jinja as Hôkoku Daimyô Jin. When the rule of Hideyoshi's clan ended in 1618, the Tokugawa clan took over and destroyed Fushimi Castle and with it Hôkoku Jinja. It was not until after the Meiji Restoration in 1868 that the shrine was rebuilt in Fushimi. In 1964 it was moved to its current location within the grounds of Osaka Castle. At first the shrine had no garden, but in 1972 the Kyoto Garden Association offered to donate a garden to commemorate the association's 40th anniversary.[4] Mirei Shigemori was put in charge of the project and presented his design drawing on June 3, 1972. Because the proposed garden was within the precincts of Osaka Castle, a registered historical site, both the city and the prefectural governments needed to support the project in order to get a building permit for the garden from the Agency for Cultural Affairs in Tokyo. Lobbying and fundraising also took time, but by August 12 the permit was granted. Garden construction finally started on October 8. The garden was finished by November 12, and on December 13 an opening ceremony was held. Kyoto Garden Association members had sponsored most of the ten-million-yen construction budget.

Left page:
[297] The gourd is the emblem of the famous warrior Toyotomi Hideyoshi

Description: The garden is shaped like a large rectangle situated immediately east of the shrine building. A large metal gate marks the entrance at the southwestern corner of the garden, and this leads to an elevated platform along its southern end **[298]**. It is from here that the garden should really be enjoyed. The scene is dominated by a large gourd-shaped[5] *tsukiyama* made from reddish brown concrete **[302]**. The gourd's mouth is near the southwestern corner of the gravel area, and from there the gourd stretches diagonally to the northeastern part of the garden, covering about 40 percent of its surface. The gourd itself is interlaced with nine smaller gourd-shaped mounds **[299]**, which are slightly elevated and covered in moss. Six more similarly shaped islands are spread over the sea of gravel, all but one of which, a small concrete island **[303]**, are covered in moss. All together there are 15 small islands in addition to the large concrete gourd-shaped *tsukiyama*.

This scheme of a large gourd with smaller gourd-shaped islands is then overlaid with a 3–5–7 stone setting **[301]**. In the south, a group of three stones is placed right in front of the viewing platform, with one rock sticking directly into the gravel and no moss surrounding its base **[306]**. Covering the middle ground is a group of five, all of which sit on an earth mound on top of the concrete gourd. The last group of seven contains the tallest stones and occupies the back of the garden **[300 | 302]**. One stone is on an island to the west of the main gourd. Then immediately east of that island is a triad setting, featuring stones that are 3.2, 2.9 and 2.5 meters tall. Finally, there is a single two-stone group and two single-stone settings. There are no plants inside the garden except the mix of moss and grass covering the mounds, although many trees along the perimeter have grown so large that some of their branches actually reach into the garden.

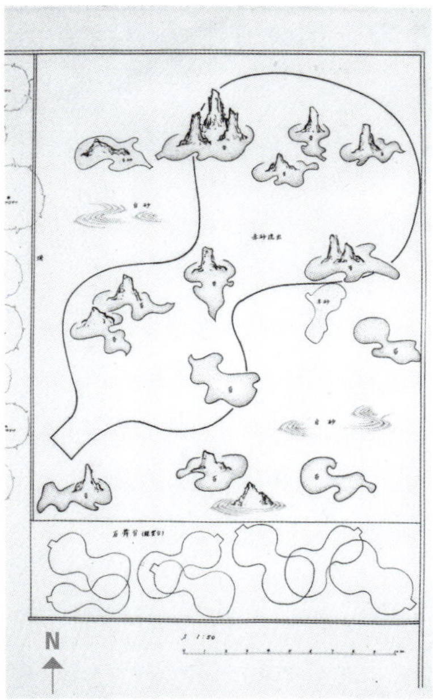

[298] The shrine as seen from the garden's viewing platform
[299] Plan of Hôkoku Jinja (viewing platform at the bottom)

4 For its thirtieth anniversary the *Kyoto Garden Association* had already donated the garden at Zuihô-in in the Daitoku-ji complex in Kyoto.

5 Gourds remind every Japanese person of Toyotomi Hideyoshi, who was a leading warrior appointed by the emperor as his shogun in charge of conquering barbarian territories and is to this day remembered as the unifier of Japan. So what is the connection between this warrior and the gourd? As Hideyoshi rode on a horse with his mounted followers, one of his infantrymen would walk ahead of him, carrying a banner with the seal of the leader. Hideyoshi liked gourds, so he hung a big gourd upside down at the tip of the banner-pole. To this he would add a small gourd every time he won a battle. This cluster came to be called *Sennari-byôtan*, which literally means "one thousand gourds growing on a tree." It eventually became a symbol for Hideyoshi's great success and remains a powerful sign to this day.

[300] The gourd-shaped *tsukiyama* is made of colored concrete, but contains many carved out green areas

[301] View from on top of the *tsukiyama* at the back of the garden

[302] Powerful upright stone settings staged in several groups on the *tsukiyama*

[303] The large gourd shape is accompanied by some smaller ones

[304] **This section well illustrates the staging of the 3–5–7-stone setting on top of the *tsukiyama***

The terrace or viewing platform is made from large granite plates **[297]**, into whose surfaces seven more gourds are carved. The design of the gate is derived from the Chinese characters in "Hôkoku" (豊国), the shrine's name **[305]**. The garden was named Shûseki-tei (秀石庭), which is what Mirei Shigemori had proposed. *Shû* (秀) is taken from *Hideyoshi* (秀吉), and *Seki* (石) is from *Ishiyama-dera* (石山寺), the name of the temple that had previously stood on the site.

Interpretation: As he had already done quite often in his career, here Mirei Shigemori got to work on a site that had been a place of worship for many centuries. This meant he needed to understand the previous layers of history, and at the same time could draw inspiration from them. In this case a temple named Ishiyama-dera, literally "Stone Mountain Temple," had existed on this site in ancient times. From this he learned two things. First, there had most likely been a stone mountain or hill here before the first castle was built; and, second, this was usually an indication that there had probably been an *iwakura* here long before that, since, after Buddhism came to Japan, temples were frequently built on what were already ancient religious sites.

As Mirei Shigemori was now faced with the task of designing a garden for a Shinto shrine, he felt it was entirely appropriate to use an *iwakura*-like stone setting to make those old religious roots visible again. Thus his design refers back to the ancient Shinto belief that *kami* come to visit on particular rocks at certain times of the year. But with the Buddhist trinity stone setting, he incorporates a Buddhist layer into his design as well.[6] Because of the site's proximity to the ocean and Osaka's very old harbor, Mirei Shigemori also thought it was appropriate to recall an ocean scene here. He explains: "Since ancient times foreign culture entered Japan through these ports, so the notion of the sea was also important for me."[7] This was the motivation to design the garden in *karesansui* style, creating a landscape of islands set within a huge ocean of sand. By designing the biggest island in the shape of a gourd, he establishes a link to Toyotomi Hideoshi and thus layers what is historically the site's newest aspect into the garden's design. Remaining true to his principles, Mirei Shigemori does this in his own modern way by using concrete and thereby offending all the traditionalists who are convinced that the ancient garden element of the *tsukiyama* can only be made out of soil. The outcome not only reflects the power of Toyotomi Hideyoshi's character, as Mirei Shigemori would like us believe, but also very much the character of the garden's designer.

[305] **The *kanjis* of the temple's name are to be found in the gate's complex design**

Next page:
[306] **Overview of the garden as seen from the viewing platform**

6 The Japanese have the great ability to integrate several religions in their everyday lives (and gardens): they grow up with Shinto rituals, marry in Christian chapels, and get buried by a Buddhist priest.

7 From *Nihon Teienshi Taikei*, vol.30, p. 94.

[306]

1973 Shinto and Buddhism Meet on Mount Kôya: Fukuchi-in

福智院

The summit of Kôya-san is 800 meters above sea level and is pleasantly cool in summer, when most of the low-lying parts of Japan are humid and hot. Any time between April and November is great for a visit, with the cherries blooming two weeks later and fall colors starting two weeks earlier than in Osaka. If you do not mind snow, winter can be very impressive on Kôya-san with everything white and blanketed. High on Mount Kôya, Shinto and Buddhism have long coexisted and influenced each other. The temple garden at Fukuchi-in, which is a Buddhist temple, combines a variety of cultural and religious references in a quite distinctive way. Extensive use of color and form is balanced with vast numbers of clipped azaleas.

In AD 816 Kôbô Daishi returned from studying Buddhism in Tang China and was given a piece of property by the emperor. Its isolated location on top of Mount Kôya seemed the perfect environment for the study and practice of religion. Since it was the emperor, considered the head priest of the nation's Shinto cult, who had bestowed the land, from the outset the emphasis at Mount Kôya was on the coexistence of the two religions. By the 17th century the colony on the mountain had grown to nearly 2,000 small huts. After the Meiji Restoration in 1868 the temples there were reorganized, and Kongôbu-ji emerged as the largest among them. The founding date of Fukuchi-in is unknown, but today it is the second largest temple on Mount Kôya.

Left page:
[307] A beautiful *karikomi* and some maples form the backdrop in Fukuchi-in's North Garden

In 1973 Mirei Shigemori was commissioned by the temple's head priest to draw up a design for the pond garden and the courtyard garden north of the main building. He finished the plan on June 27 and construction began as soon as August 21. By December 3, 1973, the entire back garden was finished. Mirei Shigemori must have pleased his clients very much, because within a few months he was asked to design the front garden as well. On October 1, 1974 the plan was complete, and construction began in mid October. But because of Mirei Shigemori's declining health as well as scheduling problems with other projects, everything was put on hold on November 16 and work on the garden did not resume until September 12, 1975, resulting in a ten-month break during which the garden remained half finished. After Mirei Shigemori's death in March 1975, a team led by his longtime head of construction, Okamoto Yukio, finished the work in accordance with the plans on November 4, 1975.

[308] A spectacular framed view from one of the rooms along the South Garden

Description: The garden at Fukuchi-in consists of three main sections: the front garden to the south of the building **[309]**, a pond, and a courtyard garden in *karesansui* style to the north **[316]**. As you enter the temple's precincts though the main gate, two paths, one straight and the other curved, lead toward the main building. The straight path draws a diagonal line through the garden and is paralleled by an ornamental fence. The curved path takes you around a group of plants up to the main entrance. Not accessible to visitors is the section behind the bamboo fence **[318]**, where a straight gravel path leads right up the middle to the temple's *hôjô*, the strong symmetry of the layout emphasizing the importance of that building. A white-and-red grid pattern covers part of the ground between the path and the main building as well as the area right in front of the *hôjô* **[311]**. The backdrop to this consists of a series of *tsukiyama* covered in clipped azaleas and occupied by several stone settings, all of which stretch along the earthen wall on the

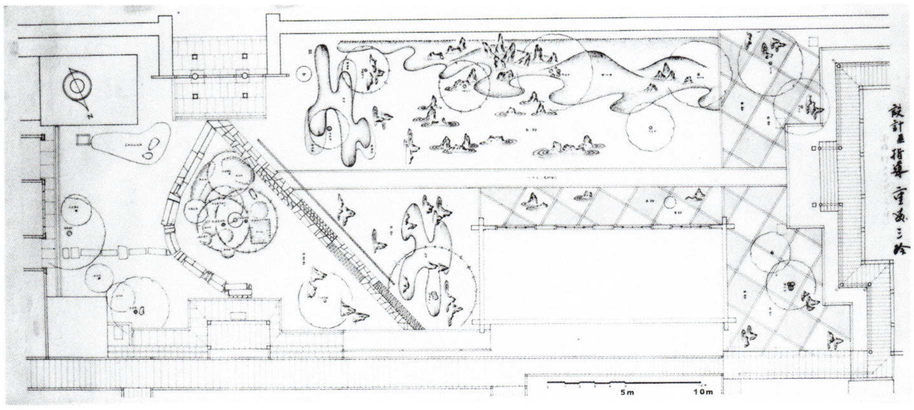

[309] Plan of the Front Garden at Fukuchi-in (south of the building)

[310]

[311]

Left page:
[310] A *karikomi* with extensive stone settings are the main features of the South Garden
[311] A red and white grid pattern mediates between the buildings and the *karikomi*

[312] Stone settings provide accents and viewpoints at various spots in the South Garden

garden's southern border [310]. The stone settings extend into the gravel plane and continue all the way into the grid, thereby connecting the different features of this section of the garden.

The pond at the back is mostly viewed from the main lobby and contains the usual tortoise-and-crane-island grouping that symbolizes longevity and luck [315]. To the rear a gradual slope is planted with a large *karikomi* consisting of two types of azaleas [307]. From the west a river flows via a dramatic waterfall into the pond below. An ornamental water basin makes a quiet accent near the building [313]. Adjacent to the east is the courtyard garden, surrounded on three sides by buildings and separated from the pond garden by a bamboo fence. It features an imaginary *karesansui* landscape in two colors of gravel with longish mounds of moss. The winding lines give a feeling of a river meandering between mountains [314]. In a narrow spot between the buildings Mirei Shigemori created a spectacular scene of rocks and waves [317].

[313] A small *karesansui* garden makes the transition between the pond and the building

Interpretation: An interesting aspect of Japanese temples is that many of the buildings actually started out as residences and were only later converted into temples. Hence temple gardens often had a distinctly residential feel to them, which was further enhanced once guest facilities were added. Fukuchi-in is a good case in point as the line between temple and residential garden is especially blurred here. The front garden presents an interesting juxtaposition of forms and styles, apparently inspired by the history of the place. Mirei Shigemori's son Kanto explains: "The unusual design represents the idea of a mixture of Shinto and Buddhism, as this is what has been practiced on Mount Kôya

[314] An imaginary landscape with a river winding through the space

[315] The pond in the North Garden with the crane island in front

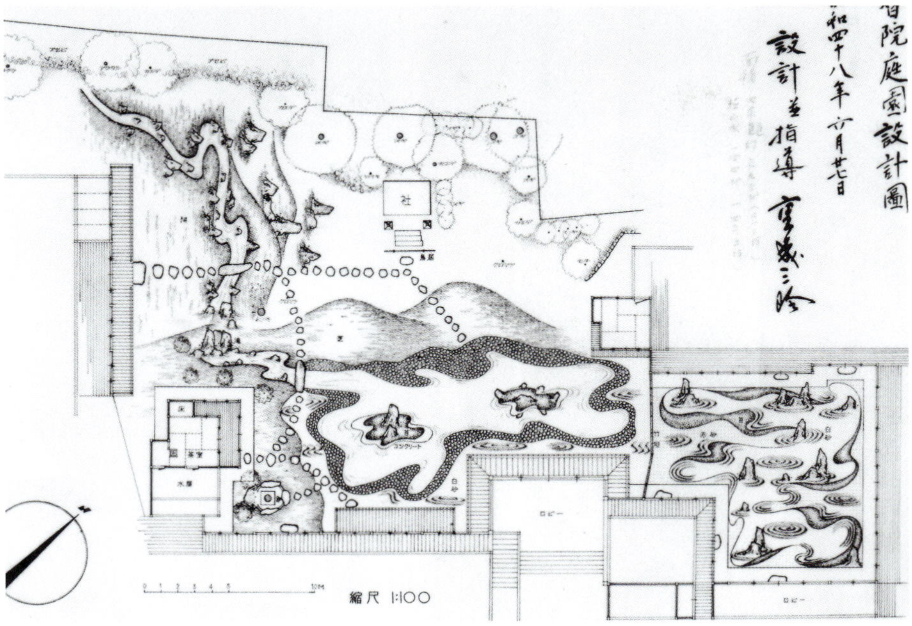

[316] **Plan of the pond and courtyard gardens at Fukuchi-in (north of the building)**

since its establishment. So the garden here represents both the solemnity of Buddhism [in the form of the grid] and the ancient *iwakura* of Shinto."[8] The grid marks the front of the building, thereby highlighting the connection between the two. As the temple of Fukuchi-in is dedicated to a god named Aizen Myôô,[9] Mirei Shigemori named the front garden Aizen-tei (愛染庭), literally "Garden in the Color of Love," which also explains the red sand, inspired by the color associated with this god. Taoism is represented in the garden in the form of a Hôrai style[10] stone setting, a reference to the cult of immortality in ancient Chinese philosophy.

The pond behind the main building is an interesting combination of real water with a *karesansui* theme around it: the paving along the shore implies a beach, which is then followed by actual sand. The *karikomi* at the back complements the scene well and makes for a dramatic mountain and sea composition, a classic motif executed with a contemporary twist. The garden was named Tôsen-tei (登仙庭), meaning "Ascending to Paradise Garden," a reference to the way the *karikomi* mountains are rising toward the distant background, starting from the ocean and the beach near the building. In the back garden, as well as in the front, the mounds of clipped azaleas also fulfill another important role: they serve to balance the visual activity created by the various shapes and colors.

The courtyard garden's river landscape could well be inspired by the famous hills around Yangshou[11] that are so often depicted on Japanese scroll paintings. Mirei Shigemori named this garden Yûsen-tei (遊仙庭), which can be translated as "Paradise Garden." For him this was where the human soul would go to play and seek the truth, which is just what the designer himself did before he could finish this garden.

[317] **This is a tiny extension off the courtyard garden to the north of the main building**

Next page:
[318] **A *karikomi* interspersed with stone settings, a straight path and the two colored grids are the main features of the South Garden**

8 Kanto Shigemori in *Nihon Teienshi Taikei*, vol. 33, p. 52.

9 The god Aizen Myôô is originally from India and was later adopted into esoteric Shingon Buddhism.

10 Mount Hôrai is said to be located in the East China Sea. This legendary sacred island is the home of the immortals and is often depicted in Japanese gardens. In Mirei Shigemori's gardens it is usually depicted by the tallest group of stones.

11 A scenic landscape where the wide Lijiang River meanders between narrow but very tall limestone mountains; located south of Guilin, in China's Guangxi Province.

[318]

TRADITIONAL, BUT NEW

What is traditional and what is new? It is the duality of Mirei Shigemori's work that may prove to be its only constant factor. In the chapter on traditional and new design elements we have seen the range of design elements that his work includes, and many of them can be found throughout the gardens portrayed in this book. It seems that Mirei Shigemori was able, at the same time, to conserve and renew the inheritance of the Japanese garden by reusing many of its typical design elements and translating them into a more contemporary form. Clearly, the two strongest influences on Mirei Shigemori were the big survey and his education as a painter. While both are of similar importance, it was the big survey that taught him the fundamentals about the Japanese garden and its history, and it was his education as a painter that gave him the tools to look at the garden as an art that could be modernized. In addition, the latter also provided him with inspiration as well as specific approaches for the artistic renewal of the garden. So, in a nutshell, the experience of the survey provided for a deep understanding of the garden's tradition, while art school opened his eyes to new influences and artistic trends. This duality can be found in many if not most of his works, and there are some in which an interesting balance of the two aspects is reached. This last group of three gardens consists of works that fit this description better than all the others in the book. The selection includes a temple, a residence and even a museum.

1961 A Garden as a Present: Zuihô-in

瑞峯院

The south garden at Zuihô-in depicts an impressive coastal mountain, with the whole scene extending from the turbulent waters of the ocean to a protected inland bay. The north garden features a hidden Christian cross in the form of a stone setting, an allusion to the suppression of Christianity in medieval Japan. It is a garden that was made as a present.

Zuihô-in is one of 22 subtemples within Kyoto's Daitoku-ji Temple complex and was founded in 1546 by Sôrin Ôtomo,[1] who at the time was a feudal lord in Kyûshû and a devoted follower of the Rinzai school of Zen Buddhism. He later became a fanatic Christian. The current *hôjô* dates back to 1535 and is registered as an important cultural asset. In 1960 the Kyoto Garden Association[2] began raising money from their members for the construction of a garden to commemorate the association's thirtieth anniversary. A committee was established whose purpose was to find a suitable site. The ideal location would be at a well-visited temple, on a site that was neither too big nor too small, and ideally adjacent to a temple dating from the Momoyama period (1568–1600) that was still in good condition. The committee members visited many temples and after a long discussion selected Zuihô-in for the commemorative garden. As Mirei Shigemori was then president of the association, he naturally adopted the project and drew up a design for the garden. Construction started on April 16, 1961 and was finished by May 11, for the temple's 400th anniversary. The stone setting in the south garden was done in only two days, April 16 and 17, and by April 19 most of the south garden was complete. To coincide with the temple's own celebrations, the garden association's present to itself was actually finished a year early. The thirtieth anniversary of the Kyoto Garden Association was thus celebrated the following year in June 1962.

[320] Seen from the side, the stones are leaning toward the viewer

Left page:
[319] The theme of the garden is the Blissful Mountain at the edge of the sea

Description: The south garden is long and narrow and extends along the southern border of the property **[324]**. Inspired by the temple's name, Zuihô (瑞峯), which translates as "Blissful Mountain," the garden's main focal point is a tall stone setting, symbolizing the legendary sacred peak of Mount Hôrai **[319]**. From there a ridge extends down and out into the sea, eventually taking the form of a low stone peninsula. The ocean of sand is always raked rather dramatically **[325]**, creating the appearance of a rough sea at the foot of the mountain. The base around the main stone setting, as well as the garden

1 Sôrin Ôtomo (1530–1589) was a Christian *daimyô* (a feudal lord) and in 1550 became the 21st generation head of the Ôtomo clan in Bungo, now Ôita Prefecture. He was baptized at the age of 48 and named Don Francisco.

2 The *Kyoto Garden Association*, or Kyoto Rinsen Kyôkai, founded by Mirei Shigemori and others in 1932 to study and protect the heritage of the Japanese garden, was initially an interdisciplinary and rather progressive study group with many like-minded people.

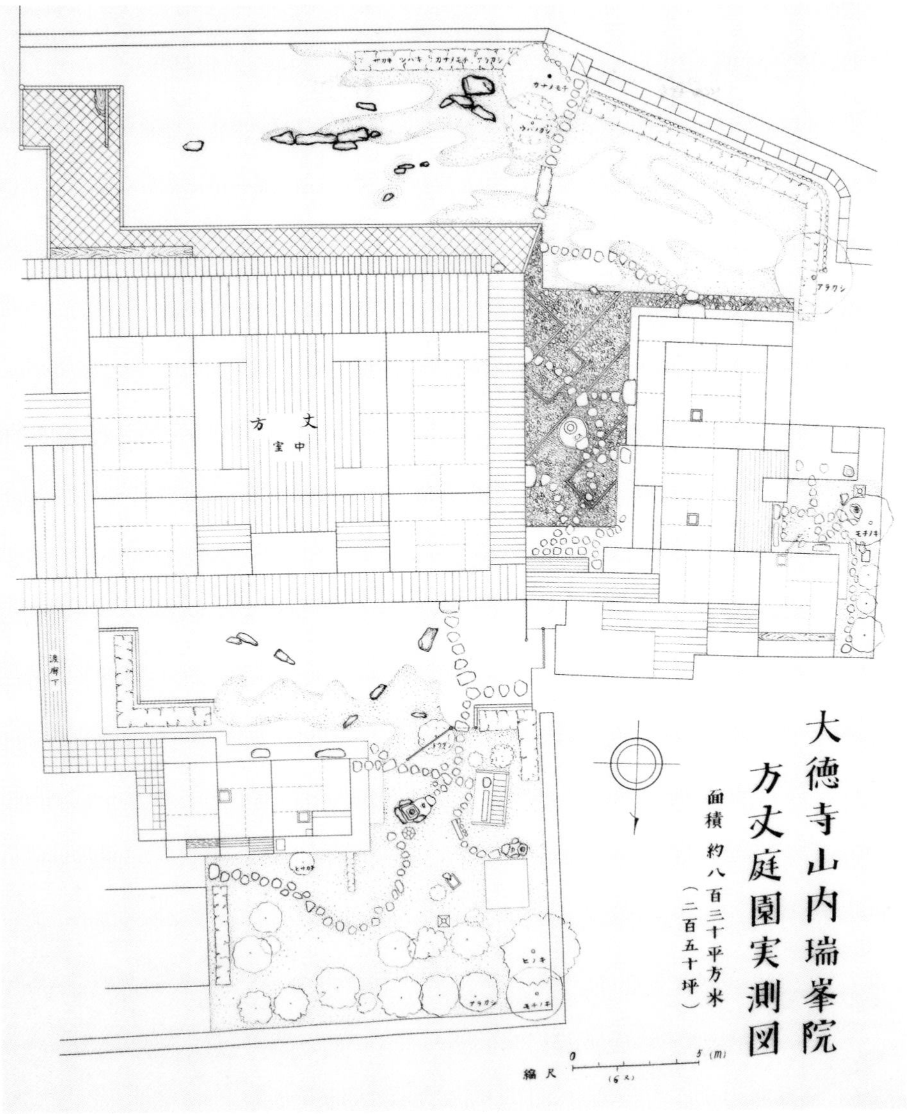

Left page:
[321] A quiet inlet bay with hills covered in moss

[322] Plan of Zuihô-in with the previous version of the tea garden between the buildings

section to the west, is mostly covered with moss. In the western section there are no stone settings, apart from a few stepping-stones, giving the landscape here more the feel of a quiet bay **[321 | 326]**. To screen the entire coastal scene from the neighboring property, a long *karikomi* was planted as a backdrop, part of which takes the form of a double hedge. Further north, squeezed in between the *hôjô* and the tea house, is a rectangular tea garden with a stone basin **[322]**. The initial design by Mirei Shigemori, a very abstract all-stone garden with diagonal geometric lines, must have been too extreme for the temple. Over the course of some renovation work on the building in the early 1970s, it was replaced by a more conventional tea garden with extensive planting. Behind the *hôjô* is the mysterious Kanmin no Niwa (閑眠の庭), known as "Garden of the Cross" **[327]**. Located on the north side of the building, it consists basically of the same elements as its counterpart to the south, but here the stone setting symbolizes a Christian cross in reference to the founder's conversion to that religion. It is set in a sea of gravel and balanced by two different hedges and a low *tsukiyama* covered in moss. A short stepping-stone path leads to another tea garden further north, behind the hedge.

Interpretation: Zuihô-in is the quintessential Zen garden. The south garden is even named Dokuza no Niwa (独坐の庭) **[323]**, or "Garden of Solitary Meditation." The garden's main purpose is thus to offer a place to sit alone in meditation, in front of an impressive landscape. According to Zen, being in solitude in this kind of environment helps a person become conscious of his or her existence in the world.[3] In terms of design, the south garden of Zuihô-in is perhaps the most traditional among the gardens presented in this book. Although much abstracted, the design depicts a seaside landscape in a relatively naturalistic way. A little closer to Mirei Shigemori's later approach to the *karesansui* garden is the north garden at Zuihô-in; here he is actively looking for other themes that can be depicted using the elements of the dry landscape garden. The north garden is

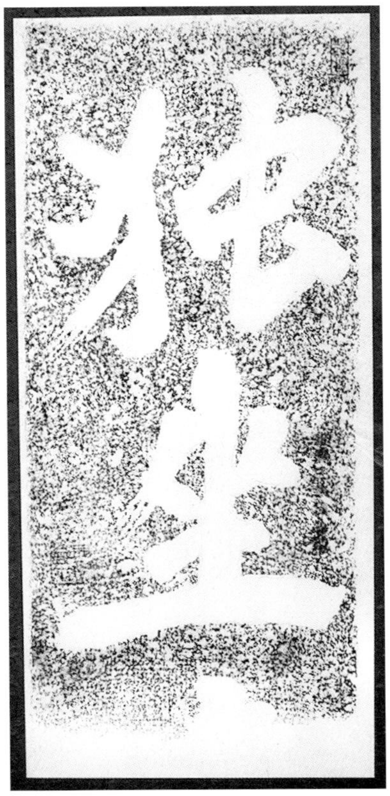

[323] *dokuza*: to sit alone (see page 45)

3 *Dokuza yûhô* is a famous expression in a catechism, meaning to sit alone on a great mountain, realizing your own existence. It says that a Zen Buddhist priest can find the greatness of human existence while sitting alone and meditating.

[324] Overview of the entire South Garden from the adjacent temple building

[325] An island in the dramatically raked, stormy ocean

[326] The quieter inlet in the western part of the garden

[327] **The North Garden, also in *karesansui* style, with a stone setting symbolizing a Christian cross**

named Kanmin no Niwa (閑眠の庭), actually meaning the "Quietly Sleeping Garden," but more often simply referred to as the Garden of the Cross. The name hints at the fact that with regard to Christianity things were only quiet and peaceful on the surface in Japan. The Japanese government in the 17th century banned Christianity and attempted to stamp out all visible signs of its practice. Over the next 250 years, Christianity in Japan flourished undercover and in secret. One could only recognize it if one knew it was there. The same is now true for Mirei Shigemori's stone setting in the form of a cross; you can only see it if you know it is there.

Another interesting point regarding Zuihô-in is that Mirei Shigemori did not hesitate to integrate Buddhist and Christian references into his designs for gardens at the same temple. Similarly, in the garden at Fukuchi-in, described earlier in this book, he incorporates Shinto and Buddhist references into the very same garden space. All this points to a refreshing degree of religious tolerance that is often found in Japanese culture. To build a garden at one of Daitoku-ji's famous old temples, and on top of that as a commemorative work, paid for by the members of the Kyoto Garden Association, placed considerable pressure on Mirei Shigemori to produce an outstanding composition. He notes: "There are many famous and old gardens at Daitoku-ji, so this one couldn't possibly be just an ordinary classic style. If it were, the Garden Association would lose face. I had to build the absolutely best garden I could, even though it was all voluntary work for me and was also on a very tight construction budget. To be able to make a garden at Daitoku-ji was a milestone in my life, so I did my best to leave something interesting behind and put a lot of effort into the job."[4] The result at Zuihô-in speaks for itself. The Mount Hôrai stone setting is certainly among Shigemori's best and most powerful works. The constant stream of visitors to the temple is ample testimony to the garden's reputation.

4 From *Nihon Teienshi Taikei*, vol. 29, p. 97.

1958–1965 **A Shoin and a Tea House for a Garden: Kogawa Residence**

小河松吉氏邸

This is a project of superlatives: it is probably the largest private garden that Mirei Shigemori designed in his career and also the slowest as it took eight and a half years to complete. In addition, it is a total art work as it not only consists of the garden, but also a unique *shoin* and two tea houses. The client, Mr Kogawa, was a true patron, and therefore Mirei Shigemori shaped no other place, apart from his own house in Kyoto, to such an extent. But, for both men, it was by no means an easy process.

Mr Kogawa, president of the Iwami Kôtsû Bus Company, first visited Mirei Shigemori in his hotel in Masuda when the latter was doing restoration work at the two local temple gardens of Ikô-ji and Manpuku-ji. On that occasion, he asked Mirei Shigemori to redesign the garden at his estate. Since Mr Kogawa was a true garden enthusiast, the old garden contained a motley collection of stones, plants and lanterns that had accumulated for over thirty years. But there was nothing that Mirei Shigemori liked and he also doubted that the client would understand his work. So, anticipating that it might be a tough project, he decided to turn the job down. But Mr Kogawa was so insistent that Mirei Shigemori finally gave in and accepted.

The construction of the first round started on October 14, 1958 and the front garden of the *shoin* was finished the same year. Mirei Shigemori was very busy at the time, so he limited the work to this part for the moment. Half a year later, on July 13, 1959, he then started to work on the rest of the garden. The more the construction progressed, the more Mr Kogawa wanted to extend the project. He decided to enlarge the garden and bought additional land, equal to about a third of the existing garden. In the north part he wanted to build a new *shoin* and tea house, which he also asked Mirei Shigemori to design. Eventually everything had to be renovated, all the walls, the gates, the entry path, the paving stones, the front garden and the bamboo fences. This meant that Mirei Shigemori not only had to design the garden but everything else as well. The supervision of the construction for such a big project kept him very busy for a while. But Mr Kogawa apparently was a great client to have and he understood all the plans better than anybody else on the construction site. He had eventually accepted Mirei Shigemori's direction, was studying a lot of books and came with new questions every day. He tried to spend as much time on the construction site as he could. However, this was not an easy project for Mirei Shigemori, also because he was so busy and had to travel all the way from Kyoto, even in winter. On July 23, 1959 about 20 people came and removed the old stones as well as some trees. Then on August 23 the new stones arrived from Awa, a quarry on the island of Shikoku, and were placed. The stone setting was finished within a few days and subsequently the earthwork was done. Next the moss was planted, the stone bridge set in place and the fences erected. At last the white sand was spread out and the whole garden at once looked completely different.

From August 16, 1959 work started on the construction of the *shoin* and tea house and both were completed by February 1960. After that, on February 25 the tea garden was started. Everything on the site was finished by June 14, 1960, and on June 20 the *sekibiraki* or opening ceremony of the tea house was celebrated. Even after all these major improvements, Mr Kogawa kept wanting to change or renovate further parts of his gardens. Between 1961 and 1963 Mirei Shigemori went there several times to consult on garden matters. In November 1963 the tea house behind the main house was also renovated. And once more there was an opening ceremony, this time on December 5, 1963. Finally, in March 1965 Mirei Shigemori went to Masuda one last time to consult on a change to part of a stone setting. The work on all the garden's parts as well as the numerous buildings had taken more than eight years to complete.

Left page:
[328] This garden contains many dramatic stone settings made with *aoishi*

Description: According to Mirei Shigemori this is a *karesansui* garden in stroll style (the latter we know from large pond gardens), with some parts of the garden fashioned as tea gardens.[5] The main garden measures 1645 square meters, which is a very large private plot for Japan. The building itself is in the Japanese-Western style of the early Shôwa period, showing quite a bit of Western influence **[333]**. Also inside there is a mix of

5 From *Nihon Teienshi Taikei*, vol. 29, p. 60.

[329] The access to the main garden is through this gate

[330] Different stepping-stones paths offer to lead the visitor through the garden

[331] Many different views open up along the way

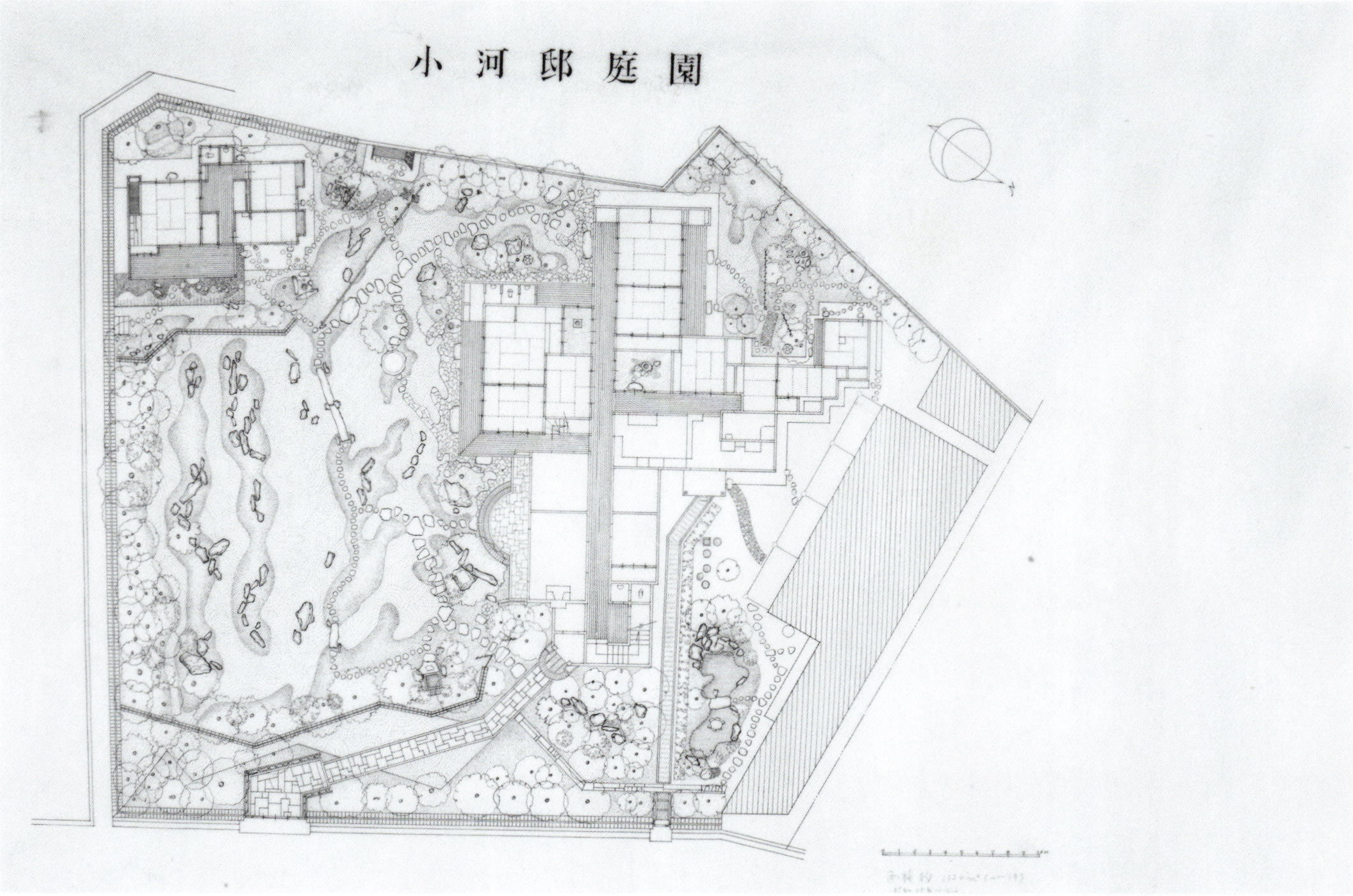

Western and Japanese-style rooms, as can be seen from the plan. With the residence located in the northern half of the property, the main part of the garden is situated to the southeast. The *shoin* with its integrated tea house is located in the southernmost corner of the property, and the tea house later renovated by Mirei Shigemori is adjacent to the main building in the northwest corner of the site.

On entering this garden in the east corner of the property, there is a unique granite path that leads along a mysteriously winding fence towards the main house **[334]**. Shortly before arriving at the residence, a view through a small gate invites the visitor to a stroll in the garden **[329]** . If you accept the invitation and follow the stepping-stones, a breathtaking view opens up: the sea, hills and distant mountains, as if overlooking a grandiose landscape **[330 | 335]**. This is also the view from the rooms on the southeast side of the house. Continuing along the path, choices have to be made at intersections, bridges have to be crossed and many different views appreciated **[331]** . Unexpectedly, a well appears, a *chôzubachi* attracts attention or a special stone needs to be inspected. The richness of the garden is slowly revealed **[328]**. A triad stone setting is a first highlight and marks the gravitational center of the space **[336 | 337]**.

While navigating through the middle of the ocean and island landscape, a small structure becomes visible among a few trees behind an elaborate bamboo fence. To get there one has to cross a long bridge made of two very flat and low-lying stones **[335]**. Then, passing the corner of another beautifully crafted fence, you arrive at the garden's main treasure: the new *shoin* building and the tea house that took six months to build **[337 | 341]**. But looking at the space and its amazing detailing the time it took to complete is no longer a surprise. The *shôji* are decorated with a modern-looking blue-silver grid **[344]**, while some are overlaid with Mirei Shigemori's trademark, the undulating line **[340]**. The doorknobs are designed as *kanji* characters making reference to the owner's name and the theme of the room (moon) **[343 | 344]**. The carpet that stretches out in front of the *shoin* is made from pebbles, with a wave pattern imbedded in it **[342]** . The structure not only serves the family as an elaborate guesthouse, but the northern half is also the setting for tea ceremonies. A small tea garden, complete with *tsukubai* and waiting area, lies directly to the north of the structure **[338]**. In order to get to the tea house later renovated by Mirei Shigemori, you have to follow the stepping-stones northward, slip along the house and turn right. A small tea garden with a *tsukubai* framed by a beautiful pine tree and stone setting surprises the visitor **[339]** . Ms Kogawa still teaches her tea ceremony classes here.

[332] Plan of the Kogawa residence showing the main part of the garden to the southeast
[333] The residence is a Japanese-Western mix of styles
[334] A unique granite path leads along a mysteriously winding fence

[335]

[336]

Left page:
[335] The garden forms a grandiose landscape consisting of the sea, hills and distant mountains
[336] The view from the second floor of the house with the main stone setting in the center

[337] Sketch showing the entire scene with the *shoin* and tea house in the background
[338] The small tea house located on the north side of the *shoin*.

Interpretation: The sheer size of this garden allowed Mirei Shigemori to design a space that you can actually walk through and explore, just like the famous stroll garden at Katsura Rikyû in Kyoto. The major difference being that here, in true *karesansui* style, the water is replaced by sand; moreover, even though this is a large private estate, it is still only a fraction of the size of its famous model. Nonetheless, the reference is a valid one, as I am about to show. So, while the concept of walking around a large pond, enjoying different views as they come up, is certainly not new and neither is the idea of the *karesansui* garden, this combination of the two in a residential garden is. Moreover, the symbolism in this garden is rather interesting. The theme of the stone setting is once more the local landscape, this time the area along the Japan Sea, from Izumo to Iwami.[6] Of course, making reference to a local landscape of special beauty is neither new nor at all unusual in a Japanese garden, but, as so often in Mirei Shigemori's work, it is the way it is done that is so striking. Combining upright and flat-lying stones, in such massive and powerful settings, is simply overwhelming for some Japanese. Others, like the garden maker himself, like their impressiveness and feel that anything else would be just boring. Although we can find similarly strong stone settings throughout history, Mirei Shigemori really celebrated mass and power with his way of arranging stones. So again, much of it is traditional, but his specific techniques (and their results) are at least thought-provoking.

Another detail worth pointing out is the design of the *fusuma*, or sliding doors, in the *shoin*. The design features a prominent, modern-looking grid pattern that may be familiar to some readers from Katsura Rikyû. But just copying would not have been acceptable, so Mirei Shigemori plays with the reference and modifies the appearance. One side is contrasted with a strong diagonal line, giving it a contemporary feel, while the other is overlaid with a rising moon. Behind the *fusuma* is the *mizuya*, literally the water room, which is the space where the utensils for the tea ceremony are prepared. Therefore, on the back of the doors is a dynamic five-color grid pattern with a dramatic wave superimposed. With regard to the use of color, the silver mining in the Iwami area

6 From Nihon Teienshi Taikei, p. 63.

[339] Small garden in front of the second tea house in the western corner of the property

[340] *Fusuma* in the *mizuya* featuring a grid pattern overlaid with waves

[341] The entrance of the *shoin* with a wide wooden deck

[342] Unique paving pattern with elongated pebble stones in front of the *shoin*

[343] **Doorknob made of the second *kanji* of the owner's name, pronounced "gawa" (river)**

might be the reason for the silver color used on the *fusuma*, as the historic original is in blue and white. It is also worth noting that the same moon we saw inside on the *fusuma* also appears on the wall at the end of the platform outside, hinting at the famous moon-viewing platform in the previously mentioned Kyoto garden. So in the end, through these references, the Kogawa garden pays real homage to Katsura Rikyû. Incidentally, although Mirei Shigemori admired it so much for its modernity, the garden of Katsura Rikyû dates from the early 17th century.

To a traditionally minded Japanese (gardener) of the 1950s, Mr Kogawa's garden definitely felt very new. From the paving and fences to the powerful but unconventional stone arrangement, all the way to the modern details of the *shoin*, the tea houses and surrounding tea gardens. Although most of these elements could be found in older gardens as well, there is always a twist or modern touch to them. On the other hand, to a modern-minded Japanese visitor, even today, this garden can still feel quite traditional, especially compared to some of what is currently being built. Therefore, many things in this garden must be traditional, but new.

Next page:
[344] ***Fusuma* in the shoin featuring a grid pattern and the moon**

[344]

1965 The Setonaikai Among Mountains: Kitano Bijutsukan

北野美術館

In the boom years after WWII many modern museums were built in Japan, but when it comes to their surroundings there is often little in the form of a garden that could compete with either the building or the collection. Mirei Shigemori noticed this lack of commitment on behalf of the museum owners, and late in his career he was lucky to find a client who wanted the garden to be of the same quality as the building and the collection. For this reason, the garden at the Kitano Museum had to become a piece of art.

Mr Yoshito Kitano was a successful businessman from Nagano, a town in the mountains to the northwest of Tokyo. For many years he had collected modern Japanese and Western paintings, sculpture, Edo period military clothing, Japanese swords and other handicrafts. Then one day he decided to build a museum for his collection and open it to the public. In reverse of the usual order, the garden was built in 1965 and the building two years later in 1967.

On May 17, 1965 Mr Kitano sent his son Ikuzô to Tokyo, where Mirei Shigemori was working on the garden of the Fukusen-ji Temple, to ask him to design the garden for their new museum. A few days later Mirei Shigemori came to see the site, was pleased with the plans the client had and eventually accepted the commission. He started work on the garden on June 15 and most of the stone settings were already in place by the end of the month. The overall layout was finalized on July 2 and the planting started on July 16. Work on the elaborate stone paving along the edge of the garden continued from July 22 onward. At the same time the crew worked on another part of the garden behind the museum, which unfortunately was later abandoned when the museum was extended. Both parts of the garden were finished by the end of August, only three months after Mirei Shigemori had formally accepted the work. The contractor was Kitano Construction Corp., of which Mr Kitano was the president.

Left page:
[345] High humidity allows the moss to grow between the pebbles

Description: The museum is an L-shaped modern structure **[349 | 351]**, built from reinforced concrete, that faces toward the garden situated to the southeast. The ground floor was slightly elevated as if it were on stilts, and a two-meter wide *engawa* follows the side where the garden meets the museum. This veranda-like space offers the best appreciation of the garden's scenery, a technique already found in many traditional buildings in Japan. In addition, as Japanese buildings often have no gutter, a ditch filled with black pebbles also follows the building and collects the rainwater. The garden itself is approximately 396 square meters in size and nearly rectangular. A white concrete wall delineates the two sides not bordered by the house. However, the pavement follows the house as well as the wall, allowing the visitor to encircle the garden **[348]**. This was an option envisioned and welcomed by the designer, but it is no longer encouraged by the current museum management.

[346] Pockets of stick-shaped pebbles complement the dynamics of the undulating line

Although this place lies in the middle of Japan's most beautiful mountains, Mirei Shigemori decided that for him contrast was the right design strategy here, and once again he chose the sea landscape of the Setonaikai, the Inland Sea, as the theme for a garden. Similar to the Maegaki Residence (see pages 98–105), two moss-covered peninsulas reach into the space of the garden, from the southeast and the northwest, and overlap in the center for part of their length **[347]**. This creates a beautiful sense of depth. Stone settings and pine trees accentuate the important spots on these *tsukiyama* peninsulas. The sand is raked with whirls suggesting a dynamic ocean surface. A very unique detail is the marvelous paving pattern along the two sides facing the museum **[346 | 348]**. This elaborate stonework immediately catches the visitor's attention, as it is perfectly situated to be admired from the *engawa* along the building. In old photographs an orchard behind the garden walls makes for a beautiful transition to the hills in the background. As often in this situation in Japan, the surrounding environment is used as borrowed scenery in the garden. But, unfortunately, this idyllic backdrop has ceased to exist and instead has given way to new houses and power lines, a disappointing visual impact for an otherwise magnificent view **[347]**.

Only three kinds of tall plants were used in this garden: *Pinus thunbergii* (Japanese black pine), *Pinus densiflora* (Japanese red pine) and *Cryptomeria japonica* (Japanese cedar). The ground cover initially planted by Mirei Shigemori was *Buxus microphylla*

[347]

[348]

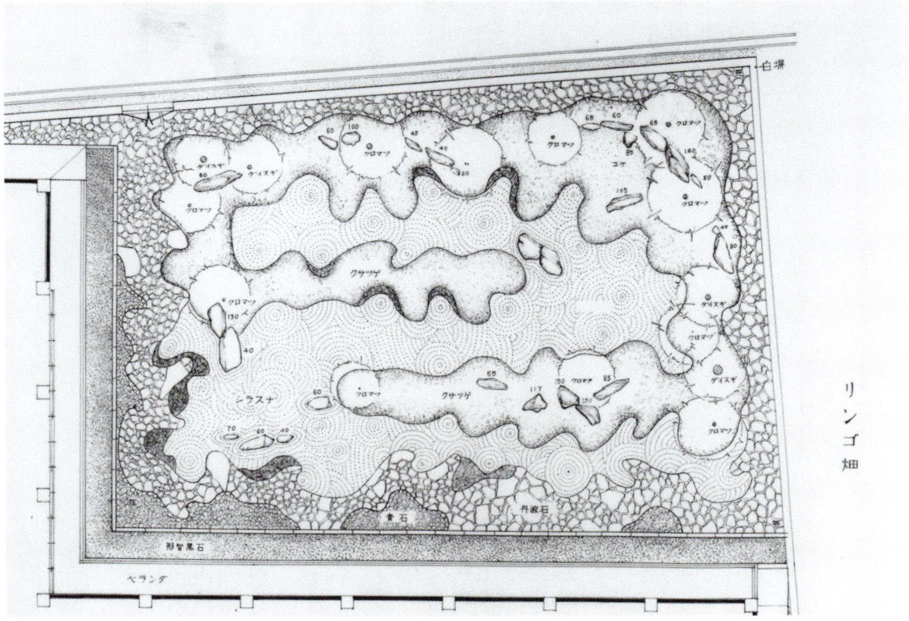

Left page:
[347] Long peninsulas, stone settings and pine trees dominate the center of this garden
[348] A highly elaborate paving pattern traces the edge of the garden

[349] Plan of the Kitano Bijutsukan garden with the museum building at two sides

(littleleaf boxwood), which spread over the ground in a beautiful patchwork of small hand-pruned shrubs. *Ophiopogon japonica Tamaryu* (lilyturf), a low, evergreen, grass-like plant later replaced this, as it is more resilient and therefore does better in the harsh environment of an exposed *karesansui* garden in Nagano prefecture. The stone settings are made of Mirei Shigemori's favorite stone, *aoishi* from the Awa area, the red stones for the paving are *akaishi* from the Tamba area, and the sand is, as always, the famous *Shirakawa suna* from Kyoto.

[350] View across the garden from the museums *engawa*

Interpretation: Ten years after the undulating line first appeared in the garden of the Maegaki Residence, another aspect was added to it. Pockets of stick-shaped pebbles, recalling the moving effect the waves have on a beach, now complement the dynamic of the line. This not only adds a certain visual complexity, but might also indicate a growing awareness of specific natural processes by the designer, a topic usually much neglected in the Japanese garden. This garden, too, is more coherent as a scene. The stone settings, which here come in groups of 2–3–5, are less dominant than in other gardens by Mirei Shigemori. They noticeably subordinate themselves more to the overall landscape. Also, to a greater extent than elsewhere, this *karesansui* garden is a painting in both two and three dimensions. The paving pattern clearly ornaments the plane, where the two peninsulas planted with pine trees immediately recall ink paintings of the famous Amanohashidate (see footnote, page 105). The light gray stone line enhances this by literally framing the image for the viewer. Looking at the overall layout of the site, the importance of the view from the *engawa* and the design elements, such as the *tsukiyama*, make this very much a traditional Japanese garden. But then the ostentatious play of the undulating line opposite the contemporary interpretation of the Setonaikai gives the whole composition an unmistakable air of the wild and new. Hoping to complement the architecture as well as the collection at the museum, Mirei Shigemori here strove for the ultimate contrast between the traditional and the new.

Next page:
[351] The modern building provides an excellent backdrop for this contemporary Japanese garden

[351]

1,900
2,750
1,000
370

GLOSSARY

aoishi (青石): a general term for blue-green colored stones that are usually used in the garden. In most cases they are green schist. Depending on their area of production they are called *Kishû aoishi*, *Awa aoishi*, *Iyo aoishi*, etc. It is a metamorphic rock and naturally occurs in a vein from Tokyo to Wakayama, Shikoku and on to Kyûshu. So, for variety, it can be found in the valleys, as well as near the ocean.

chadô (茶道): the way of tea, the study or doctrine of the tea ceremony as an art.

chôzubachi (手水鉢): a basin designed to hold water for washing one's hands and rinsing the mouth. It is usually made from stone and often used in tea gardens.

engawa (縁側): an elevated veranda space that often surrounds a traditional Japanese house; usually built from wood.

fusuma (襖): a sliding door inside the house, made from paper or cloth, often beautifully painted.

geta (下駄): a pair of wooden clogs, Japanese sandals with two bars on the sole.

gohei (御幣): white zigzag paper streamers, usually hanging from a *shime-nawa* which is tied around trees or rocks, representing the brilliance of the sun and the glare of its light; a talisman against evil, demarking a purified place.

haiku (俳句): a 17-syllable Japanese poem in 5–7–5 form.

hakama (袴): a Japanese skirt for formal wear; traditional attire for men.

hakke (八卦): a tent-like structure made from bamboo and rice straw, used at the Yoshikawa Tôban Matsuri for the reception of the gods.

hatsugama (初釜): the first tea gathering of the new year; a very important event in the calendar for everybody who practices chadô seriously.

himorogi (神籬): a place where the *kami* decend, usually marked by a rice-straw rope and folded paper strips, used in Shinto as a temporary altar for the celebration of a particular deity. When worshippers wished to summon a *kami* to earth they prepared a holy place, called *himorogi*, by setting four posts in the earth to mark the corners of a rectangle. At the center of the space stood a column where the *kami* dwelled, *yorishiro*, and a rope *shime-nawa* was tied around the four posts that enclosed the space.

hiragana (平仮名): an alphabet used in Japanese writing, often in combination with *kanji*. Also if there is no *kanji*, or it is not known, *hiragana* is used instead.

hôjô (方丈): the main hall or building in a temple complex.

iemoto (家元): a hierarchical school system with many patterns that is dominated by a family and its head for many generations and is known for a certain style or way of doing things.

Ikoma ishi (生駒石): a type of granite found on the border of Ôsaka and Nara prefecture. It is similar to the stones found at Tsukuba. It contains some iron and therefore oxidizes naturally over time, but is a popular stone for use in the garden.

iwakura (磐座): a shrine rock and stage for the gods; often used for a prominent natural stone outcrop where a god is thought to descend in primitive beliefs. Used since ancient times as a prayer site, the *iwakura* is thought to contain a *kami* at certain times of the year and is therefore a link to the world of the gods. This is thought to be the origin of stone arranging in Japanese gardens.

iwasaka (磐境): a sacred place with a boundary of rocks, in use similar to the *iwakura*; twin rocks evoke the image of the female sex; one theory sees the *iwakura* as a place to pray to ancestral gods and *iwasaka* for prayers for progeny. Both are spiritual or holy areas where the gods descend.

kameshima (亀島): lit. tortoise island, a representative form of island in pond gardens or dry landscape gardens. Under the influence of the Chinese cult of immortality, it came to be made together with the crane island an augury for long life and happiness, and was frequently built from the Muromachi to the Edo periods. It is composed of a tortoise head stone, foreleg stones, hind leg stones and a tail stone.

kami (神): god(s), of which there are about eight million in the Shinto religion.

kanji (漢字): the Chinese characters that the Japanese adopted in the Heian period and that are still used in the modern logographic writing system.

karesansui (枯山水): a dry landscape (garden), dry garden; a garden style that probably appeared first in the Muromachi period and that is unique to Japan. Using neither ponds nor streams, it makes symbolic representations of natural landscapes using stone arrangements, white sand, moss and pruned trees. The term is mentioned already in the ancient *sakuteiki*, where it indicates a stone arrangement in part of the garden without water.

karikomi: (刈込み): trees and shrubs shaped by trimming; often to be found in dry landscape gardens of the mid-Muromachi period. Sometimes similar to Western topiary, but generally used for more abstract forms.

katakana (片仮名): an alphabet used for writing foreign words. It is the simplest of the Japanese scripts and is easily recognized by its short straight strokes and angular corners.

konnyaku (蒟蒻): a jelly-like food made from the starch of devil's tongue.

Kurama ishi (鞍馬石): a granodiorite from the area around Kurama in Kyoto, characterized by rust-colored bands that look like layers of onion skin. It is appreciated as a garden stone and often used as a shoe-removing stone, an ornamental stone or stepping stone, etc. The same stone is to be found in Tamba and Kôshû, but of lesser quality as it sometimes peels off in thick layers.

maccha (抹茶): a very foamy, green drink made from hot water and the ground leaves of *Camellia sinensis* (formerly also *Thea sinensis*, *Camellia thea*); this evergreen plant is native to China and the Himalayas and grows to a height of about 1m. In Japan it is mainly cultivated in the Uji area south of Kyoto, as well as in the Shizuoka prefecture.

matsuri (祭り): a festival or celebration.

mikoshi (神輿): a portable shrine.

mizuya (水屋): a room in the tea house where the tea utensils are prepared.

mochi (餅): a flat and very chewy rice cake that is often grilled and served in winter.

nihonga (日本画): Japanese-style painting in which only colors based on natural pigments are used, so the aspect of the paintings is very subdued and the color palette somewhat limited.

sakuteiki (作庭記): *The Book of Gardening* is the oldest textbook on the secrets of gardening in Japan. There is no established theory regarding its authorship or time of compilation. It is generally accepted that Tachibana no Toshitsuna (1028–1094), third son of Fujiwara no Yorimichi, compiled it from his rich experience in seeing and hearing many things about Shinden-style gardening from childhood, and from his keen observations of nature.

sensei (先生): a teacher, master or professor.

shime-nawa (七五三縄): lit. the 7–5–3 rope; shime means to occupy or bundle, *nawa* comes from *nau*, which is to twist or bind a rope ; so the word *shime-nawa* stands for a rope made from rice straw that usually signifies the place where a *kami* decends. The numbers 7–5–3 indicate the actual count of rice straw, often hanging from around the middle of the rope in three individual bundles.

shinden (寝殿): the main hall of the residences of the Heian period aristocracy, from which the term *shinden-dukuri* is derived, denoting that style of architecture. In front of the main hall there was usually a garden with a rather large pond, including an island connected to the land by a bridge.

shin-gyô-sô (真行草): formal, semiformal, informal; a ranking system first applied to design styles by the tea masters of the medieval period.

Shirakawa suna (白川砂): lit. white river sand; small pebbles of weathered granite taken from the Kitashirakawa area in Kyoto. It has been used in gardens at least since the early 13th century, and has become an essential element in the *karesansui* style. As the original material is becoming increasingly rare, machine-crushed sand is used instead.

shite (仕手): the main character in a Noh drama.

shoin (書院): lit. the writing room or writing alcove, a ceremonial room for meeting guests; an architectural feature found first in the Zen temples and warrior residences of the Muromachi period; part of an architectural style called *shoin-dukuri* which developed from the *shinden* style.
shôji (障子): a paper sliding door, a *shôji* screen.
suhama (洲浜): denotes a beach consisting of a sand bar jutting out into the sea; in Japanese gardens it indicates a pebbled beach sloping gently into a pond, serving both to protect the shore and enhance the view.
tatami (畳): a mat made from rice straw, used as flooring in traditional Japanese architecture since medieval times; one mat is approximately 1.8 x 0.9m in size.
tokonoma (床の間): an alcove in some rooms of the house where a scroll and an *ikebana* piece are usually on display. The *tokonoma* is a place of honor, so the highest ranking guest always gets to sit closest to it.
tsukiyama (築山): an artificial earthen hill made in the garden, in actual size anything from a one-meter mound to a small hill; created with soil and for larger hills, with rock infill.
tsure (連れ): the second supporting character in a Noh drama.
tsurushima (鶴島): lit. crane island, a representative island style in the Japanese garden, symbolizing a crane. Wing stones are often stood on both sides, or at the center of the island. It has an auspicious meaning, like the tortoise island.
waka (和歌): a 31-syllable Japanese poem in the order 5–7–5–7–7.
waki (脇): the main supporting character in a Noh drama.
yarimizu (遣水): a comparatively narrow and shallow winding stream made in the garden. First used in the *shinden*-style gardens of the Heian period; the technique of using a small natural stream as its model is described in the *sakuteiki* in detail.
zaibatsu (財閥): a giant financial combine or group owned by one family; for example, Mitsui.

TIMELINE OF MIREI SHIGEMORI'S LIFE

The following table summarizes the milestones in Mirei Shigemori's life:

1896 Born in Okayama-ken, Jôbô-gun, Yoshikawa-mura (today Kibi Chûô-chô), Ôaza Yoshikawa, 4983 Banchi. His father was Genjirô Shigemori, and his mother was Tsuruno. He was named Kazuo.

1911 Started taking Fumai style tea and Ikenobô style flower arrangement lessons with Mrs Aizawa who lived in the next village.

1914 Designed his own tearoom called Tenrai-an at his parents' house. It was four and a half tatami in size and also had a garden. This was his first work.

1915 At the age of 19 he designed a *karesansui* garden called Sôran-tei for his friend Iga; the garden featured mounds and a main stone setting. Later he also made a *karesansui* garden called Gyokuraku-tei at his friend Nishitani's house.

1917 Moved to Tokyo and entered Tokyo Fine Arts School to study *nihonga*. At the same time he continued to study ikebana and also started to get interested in philosophy.

1919 Graduated from the undergraduate program of Tokyo Fine Arts School and continued into the graduate program.

1920 At Tôyô University he also took classes in Indian philosophy; graduated from the Research Department of Tokyo Fine Arts School.

1922 Made great efforts to establish the University of Japanese Culture (Bunka Daigakuin), aiming to synthesize culture.

1923 Married Matsue Ochi; their first son Kanto was born on May 19. (Kanto eventually followed in his father's footsteps and became a garden maker while publishing several books on his own.) The massive Kantô earthquake interrupted his plans for the University of Japanese Culture and he moved back to his hometown.

1925 Changed his name from Kazuo to Mirei on May 6; finished the garden at his house in honor of Dr Sekino's visit. Yoshikawa Hachimangû was registered as an "Important Cultural Property" on April 24. Dr Tamura introduced Mirei Shigemori's work in the June issue of the magazine *Teien* with an article titled "Karesansui and Mister Shigemori's first work."

1926 His second son Kôen was born on July 27. (He went on to become professor of photography at Tokyo College of Photography and followed his father as an ikebana artist and critic; he also wrote poetry.)

1929 Mirei Shigemori moved with his family to Kyoto and rented a house at 45 Shimoôji-chô, Sakyô-ku. He intended to create a new style ikebana and to develop his criticism.

1930 The New Ikebana Association was founded. He also wrote a book on the history of flower arrangement and published the *Complete Works of Japanese Flower Arrangement Art* (9 vols) by himself. His only daughter Yûgo was born on April 15. (Yûgo eventually became an *iemoto* in the field of Japanese dance.)

1932 Kyoto Rinsen Kyôkai founded together with Mr Nakano, Dr Amanuma, Mr Kanshûji and Prof. Sekiguchi

1933 Made a strong case for the artistic character of ikebana by outlining a new formative way of flower arrangement when he published the *New Ikebana Declaration* together with Sôfû Teshigahara and Bunpo Nakayama.

1934 The Muroto typhoon devastated many gardens in and around Kyoto on September 21. Mirei Shigemori asked the government to survey the gardens in order to have records at hand in case of future disasters.

1935 His third son Geite was born on December 19. (He would eventually publish the only large format retrospective in book form that is available on his father's work.)

1936 As the government showed no intention of agreeing to his request, Mirei Shigemori decided to start the first survey of all the gardens in Japan on his own, supported by a small group of friends and helpers.

1938 Finished publishing the results of his historical survey of approximately 250 gardens all over Japan in the 26-volume *Illustrated Book on the History of the Japanese Garden*.

1939 Built the garden at Tôfuku-ji's Hôjô and seven more gardens in the Kinki area within the next two years. His fourth son Bairon was born on February 6. (He was later educated as a filmmaker and ultimately had his own business in Tokyo called Iwanami Audio-Visual Media Inc.)

1942 Decided to buy the former house of the well-known Suzuka family in Kyoto-shi Sakyô-ku, Yoshida, Kamiôji-chô. The house, which was almost two hundred years old, was originally part of the Yoshida Shrine and was the place where he lived for the rest of his life.

1946 Published *Japanese Garden Art* on August 15 only one year after the war; continued to write many books in the following years.

1948 First winner of the Kyoto Bunka-in prize (from the Kyoto Cultural Society).

1949 Established an ikebana study group called Byakutôsha, bringing in Nakagawa Yukio and other ikebana artists.

1950 Started publishing the *Ikebana Geijutsu* magazine. Played the role of opinion leader in avant-garde ikebana together with Teshigahara Sôfû, Nakayama Bunpo and Ohara Hôun.

1951 Resumed full-scale garden-making; moved energetically around the Kinki area.

1952 The first Byakutôsha Exhibition was held.

1953 Built the garden at Kishiwada castle and for the Muji-an tearoom at his residence. The second Byakutôsha exhibition was held.

1956 The gardener Yukio Okamoto joined the construction team; together they built more than 130 projects over the next 19 years. Mr Okamoto eventually became Mirei Shigemori's right hand, taking over much of the on-site responsibility for building the gardens.

1957 Met Isamu Noguchi for the first time on April 18 and helped him to find suitable stones for the UNESCO garden in Paris.

1958 Started collaboration with the photographer Haruzô Ôhashi and resumed his publishing efforts after an eight-year break by writing the book *Gardens* together with his son Kanto. His wife opened a shop named "Mitsumori" selling tea utensils in Osaka.

1964 Published his only book that focuses entirely on his own work: *Shigemori Mirei's Collected Works (Gardens)*.

1969 The Kôkoku-an Shoin was built at his house in Kyoto; he donated Tenrai-an, the first tea house he built with his father, to his hometown Yoshikawa.

1971 Started the second survey of all the gardens in Japan and published the results in the 35-volume *Japanese Garden History Survey*.

1975 Died in Kyoto University Hospital at the age of 79 on March 12.

CATALOGUE OF WORKS

Gardens Designed by Mirei Shigemori

This chronological list contains 239 gardens all designed or altered by Mirei Shigemori. It was initially based on the list that Tadakazu Saito and Geite Shigemori published in their book (*Mirei Shigemori's Collection of Works*) in 1976. Many gardens were added through new evidence I found among his original design drawings and in his diary.

Each entry uses the following scheme: owner or garden name, name in *kanji* characters, location, year. Where no location is given, it is unknown.

Mr Shigemori, Shôrai-en, 重森邸松籟園庭園, Kayô-chô, Okayama Prefecture, 1915/1924
Mr Iga, 伊賀氏邸庭園, Kayô-chô, Okayama Prefecture, ~1925
Mr Nishitani, 西谷氏邸庭園, Kayô-chô, Okayama Prefecture, ~1925
Mr Andô, 安藤氏邸庭園, Ôsaka, 1933
Mr Yomo Usaburô's Second House, 四方氏海印山荘, Nagaokakyô, Kyoto Prefecture, 1934
Mr Horino, 堀野氏邸庭園, Sakyô-ku, Kyoto, 1934
Mr Yamauchi, 山内氏邸庭園, Ukyô-ku, Kyoto, 1934
Mr Sakano, 坂野氏邸庭園, Sakyô-ku, Kyoto, 1934
Mr Kajino, 梶野氏邸庭園, Kôbe, Hyôgo Prefecture, 1934
Oiso Jinja, 老蘇神社, Fushimi-ku, Kyoto, 1934
Kasuga Taisha, Shamusho Garden, 春日大社社務所庭園
Shôden-ji, 正伝寺, Kita-ku, Kyoto, 1935
Mr Itô Kisaburô, 伊藤喜三郎氏邸庭園, Kameoka, Kyoto Prefecture, 1935
Mr Kôbe Masao, 神戸正雄氏邸庭園, Kyoto, 1935
Mr Suzuki Keitarô, 鈴木慶太郎氏邸庭園,1936
Tôfuku-ji Temple Grounds, 東福寺境内整理計画図, Higashiyama-ku, Kyoto, 1939
Tôfuku-ji Hôjô, 'Hassô no Niwa', 東福寺方丈, Higashiyama-ku, Kyoto, 1939
Funda-in, Tôfuku-ji, 芬陀院庭園, Higashiyama-ku, Kyoto, 1939
Mr Kitagawa, 北川氏邸庭園, Nishinomiya, Hyôgo Prefecture, 1939
Kômyô-in, 光明院（雲嶺庭・波心庭・蘿月庵露地), Higashiyama-ku, Kyoto, 1939/1963
Mr Saibara, 祭原氏邸庭園, 1939
Mr Nishiyama Ushinosuke, 西山丑之助氏邸庭園（青竜庭), Toyonaka, Ôsaka Prefecture, 1940
Mr Onohara Toshio, 斧原敏夫氏邸庭園（曲水庭), Nishinomiya, Hyôgo Prefecture, 1940/1958
Mr Nakada (formerly), 旧中田氏邸庭園, Nishinomiya, Hyôgo Prefecture, 1940
Mr Inoue Seiichi, 井上成一邸庭園（巨石壷庭), Ôsaka, 1940
Mr Nishida, 西田氏邸庭園, 1940
Mr Nakata, 中田氏邸苦楽園庭園, 1940
Mr Koga, 古賀氏邸庭園, 1940
Mr Inui Kôyô-sansô, 乾氏甲陽山荘庭園, Nishinomiya, Hyôgo Prefecture, 1940
Mr Nagasaki, 長崎氏邸庭園, 1940
Mr Yoshida Kaichi, 吉田嘉一氏邸庭園, 1940
Kennin-ji Hôjô, Sand Pattern Design, 建仁寺方丈庭園砂紋, Higashiyama-ku, Kyoto, 1940
Memorial Stone in Sakamoto village, 坂本村忠魂碑, Sakamoto, Shiga Prefecture, 1940
Kisshôin Tenmangû, ruin restoration, 吉祥院天満宮菅公硯ノ井遺跡復元図, 1940
Tominaka Clinic, 富中医院庭園, 1940
Sakurai Girls Highschool, 桜井女子高等学校庭園, Sakurai, Nara Prefecture, 1941
Mr Akira Saichirô, 明楽佐一郎氏邸庭園（又楽庭), Wakayama, Wakayama Prefecture, 1941
Mr Miyaji, 宮地氏邸庭園, Kôbe, Hyôgo Prefecture, 1943
Mr Minami, 南氏雲雀別墅庭園, 1941
Mr Kumagai Kôyô-sansô, 熊谷氏甲陽山荘庭園, Nishinomiya, Hyôgo Prefecture, 1941
Mr Shinza, 新佐氏邸庭園, 1942
Nishimura Tarôemon Memorial Garden, 西村太郎右衛門供養塔庭園, Ômihachiman, Shiga Prefecture, 1942
Mr Ôta, 太田氏露地庭園, 1942
Mr Nomura, 野村氏邸家庭園, 1946
Mr Murakami Masatsune, 村上允常氏庭園（曲泉山荘), Nishiwaki, Hyôgo Prefecture, 1949
Mr Ikegaki Iwatarô, 池垣岩太郎氏邸庭園, Nakagyô-ku, Kyoto, 1950
Mr Yamamoto, 山本氏邸庭園, 1950
Mr Ogura Yutaka, 小倉豊氏邸庭園, Kayô-chô, Okayama Prefecture, 1951
Mr Uchida Ichirô, 内田一郎氏邸庭園, Nishinari-ku, Ôsaka, 1951
Edokko Ryokan, 江戸ッ子旅館庭園, Kita-ku, Ôsaka, 1951
Mr Kaji Orinosuke, 鍛冶織之助氏邸庭園, Sennan, Ôsaka Prefecture, 1951
Mr Nakamura, 中村邸御船入屋敷庭園, Okayama, 1951
Shôchi-in, 正智院庭園, Kôya-san, Wakayama Prefecture, 1952
Sainan-in, 西南院, Kôya-san, Wakayama Prefecture, 1952
Ôuchi-in, 櫻池院, Kôya-san, Wakayama Prefecture, 1952
Mr Akira Saichirô, 明楽佐一郎氏邸庭園（有楽庭), Wakayama, Wakayama Prefecture, 1952
Mr Ysuda Shintarô, 安田信太郎氏邸庭, Nara, 1952
Mr Kanbayashi Hisao, 上林久雄氏邸庭園, Sennan, Ôsaka Prefecture, 1952
Iwashimizu Hachimangû Teien, 石清水八幡宮庭園（鳥居の庭), Yawata, Kyoto Prefecture, 1952/1966
Matsuo Clinic, 松尾医院, 1953

Tsukushi-ya, つくし家庭園, 1953
Jôchi University, 上智大学図書館, Tokyo, 1953
Shiratori Shrine, 白鳥神社, 1953
Mr Shimizu, 清水氏邸庭園, 1953
Mr Ôsawa, 大澤氏邸庭園, 1953
Kishiwada Castle, Hachijin no Niwa, 岸和田城（八陣の庭）, Kishiwada, Ôsaka Prefecture, 1953
Honkaku-in, 本覚院庭園, Kôya-san, Wakayama Prefecture, 1953
Saizen-in, 西禅院庭園, Kôya-san, Wakayama Prefecture, 1953
Ryûsen-in, 竜泉院, Kôya-san, Wakayama Prefecture, 1953
Kôdai-in, 光台院新書院庭園, Kôya-san, Wakayama Prefecture, 1953
Mr Nakamura Ken, 中村健氏邸庭園, Okayama, 1953
Ryokan Uehara, 上原旅館庭園, Minami-ku, Ôsaka, 1953
Muji-an Teien, Kôkoku-an Teien (Mirei Shigemori's Home), 無字庵庭園、好刻庵庭園, Sakyô-ku, Kyoto, 1953/1969/1970
Shôrin-ji, 少林寺庭園, Minami-ku, Ôsaka, 1954
Sakyô Ward Fire Department, 左京区消防署庭園, Sakyô-ku, Kyoto, 1954
Mr Kinoto Hideyoshi, 木野戸秀吉氏邸庭園, Takamatsu, Kagawa Prefecture, 1954
Mrs Sasai Kimiyo, 笹井君代氏邸庭園, Matsumoto, Nagano Prefecture, 1954
Ryokan Goshûkaku, 五洲閣（旅館）庭園, Higashi-Ôsaka, Ôsaka Prefecture, 1954
Mr Handa, 半田氏邸庭園,1954
Mr Kawaguchi, 河口氏邸庭園, Higashiyama-ku, Kyoto, 1955
Fudô-in, 不動院庭園, Kôya-san, Wakayama Prefecture, 1955
Mr Maegaki Hisao, 前垣壽男氏邸庭園, Higashi-Hiroshima, Hiroshima Prefecture, 1955
Mr Kawata Genshichi, 河田源七氏邸庭園, Amino-chô, Kyoto Prefecture, 1955
Mrs Higashi Tamiko, 東民子氏邸庭園（鱸庵）, Takahashi, Okayama Prefecture, 1955
Ryokan Eirakuan, 永楽庵（旅館）庭園（三楽庭）, Misasa Onsen, Tottori Prefecture, 1955/1966
Mr Iwasawa Tetsuya, 岩澤徹誠氏邸庭園, Ukyô-ku, Kyoto, 1955/1966
Zuinô-in, 瑞応院庭園（楽紫の庭・如々庭）, Sakamoto, Ôtsu-City, Shiga Prefecture, 1956
Mr Fujii Takuzô, 藤井琢三氏邸庭園, Hyôgo Prefecture, 1956
Mr Tomita Takumi, 富田精氏邸庭園, Kita-ku, Kyoto, 1956
Ryokan Nohara, 野原旅館庭園, Yamaguchi, Yamaguchi Prefecture, 1956
Mr Miyashina Kyûsaburô, 宮階久三郎氏邸庭園, Kamigyô-ku, Kyoto, 1956
Ryûzô-ji, 竜蔵寺庭園, Yamaguchi, Yamaguchi Prefecture, 1956
Mr Nagaogi Yoshimitsu, 長萩吉光氏邸庭園, Tokushima, 1956
Mr Masui Tsutomu, 増井励氏邸庭園（雲門庵）, Takamatsu, Kagawa Prefecture, 1956
Mr Usuki Sakae, 臼杵栄氏邸庭園（露結庵）, Takamatsu, Kagawa Prefecture, 1956/1960
Kômyôzen-ji, 光明禅寺庭園, Dazaifu, Fukuoka Prefecture, 1957
Bodai-ji, 菩提寺庭園, Tennoji-ku, Ôsaka, 1957
Mr Tomiya, 富屋氏邸庭園, Ôsaka, 1957
Shôgo-in Goten-sô, 聖護院御殿荘, Sakyô-ku, 1957
Mr Okamoto Hajime, 岡本一氏邸庭園（仙海庭）, Saijô, Ehime Prefecture, 1957
Mr Ochi Yôta (Kyokusui-tei), 越智庸太氏邸庭園（旭水庭）, Saijô, Ehime Prefecture, 1957
Mr Ochi Eiichi, 越智栄一氏邸庭園（牡丹庵）, Saijô, Ehime Prefecture, 1957
Mr Orita Akitarô (Tôsen-tei), 織田秋太郎氏邸庭園（島仙庭）, Mibugawa-chô, Ehime Prefecture, 1957
Hotel Takarasô, ホテル宝荘庭園, Matsuyama, Ehime Prefecture, 1957
Mr Katayama Kaoru, 片山薫氏邸庭園, Kishiwada, Ôsaka Prefecture, 1957
Mr Shimazu, 島津氏邸庭園, Kyoto, 1958
Mr Wakasa Hisakichi (formerly), 旧若狭久吉氏邸庭園, Amino-chô, Kyoto Prefecture, 1958
Suntory Tamagawa Kôjô, サントリー多摩川工場, Kawasaki, 1958
Ikô-ji, 医光寺庭園, Masuda, Shimane Prefecture, 1958
Manpuku-ji, 万福寺庭園, Masuda, Shimane Prefecture, 1958
Mr Ebi Kurio, 衣斐栗雄氏邸庭園, Nishinomiya, Hyôgo Prefecture, 1958/1963
Mr Kogawa Matsukichi, 小河松吉氏邸庭園, Masuda, Shimane Prefecture, 1958-1965
Mr Murakami Sadatsugu, 村上定次氏邸庭園（青山庭）, Muikaichi, Shimane Prefecture, 1959
Mr Kuroda Yasaburô, 黒田弥三郎氏邸庭園, Kamigyô-ku, Kyoto, 1959
Mr Kurisu Shigeru, 栗須殖氏邸庭園, Tennôji-ku, Ôsaka, 1959
Mr Kuwata Masami, 桑田真三氏邸庭園（宗玄庵）, Fukuyama, Hiroshima Prefecture, 1959
Mr Matsumoto Saburô, 松本三郎氏邸庭園, Okayama, 1959
Mr Tanaka Sensaku, 田中専策氏邸庭園, Kita-ku, Kyoto, 1959
Mr Matsumoto Tadahira, 松本忠平氏邸庭園, Sennan, Ôsaka Prefecture, 1959
Mr Tamoi Yûji, 田茂井勇治氏邸庭園, Amino-chô, Kyôto Prefecture, 1959/1970
Eikô-ji, 栄光寺庭園, Utsumi-chô, Kagawa Prefecture, 1960
Yonehara Shôten, 米原商店庭園, Shimogyô-ku, Kyoto, 1960
Mr Fukuda Tomokazu, 福田智一氏邸庭園（鴨月庭）, Sakyô-ku, Kyoto, 1960
Mrs Miyatake Fusa, 都竹ふさ氏邸庭園, Ikuno-ku, Ôsaka, 1960
Mr Kiraoko Sansô, 北岡山荘庭園, 1960
Mr Amino, 網野氏邸庭園, 1960

Daimaru Second Houses, 大丸別荘, 1960
Zuihô-in, 瑞峯院庭園（独座庭・閑眠庭）, Kita-ku Kyoto, 1961
Shinnyo-in, 真如院, Shimogyô-ku, Kyoto, 1961
Mr Matsubayashi Toyohiko, 松林豊彦氏邸庭園, Uji, Kyoto Prefecture, 1961
Kôri-danchi, 香里団地庭園（以楽苑）, Hirakata, Ôsaka, 1961
Rinshô-ji, 林昌寺庭園, Sennan, Ôsaka Prefecture, 1961
Mr Yamaguchi Iwao, 山口巖氏邸庭園, Nishiwaki, Hyôgo Prefecture, 1961
Mr Hosoda Shigeru, 細田繁氏邸庭園, Abeno-ku, Ôsaka, 1961
Mr Tateoka Kôichi's second house, 立岡孝一氏別邸庭園, 1961
Shido-ji, 志度寺（曲水庭・無染庭）, Shido-chô, Kagawa Prefecture, 1962
Mr Mitani Shinzô, 三谷進三氏邸庭園, Kanazawa, Ishikawa Prefecture, 1962
Mr Kuwamura Toshirô, 桑村敏郎氏邸庭園, Naka-chô, Hyôgo Prefecture, 1962
Mr Matsushita Kônosuke, 松下幸之助氏邸庭園, Nishinomiya, Hyôgo Prefecture, 1962
Shitennô-ji Gakuen, 四天王寺学園, Tennôji-ku, Ôsaka, 1963
Kôzen-ji, 興禅寺庭園（看雲庭）, Kisofukushima-chô, Nagano Prefecture, 1963
Hotel Shôwa-en, ホテル昭和園 庭園, Beppu, Ôita Prefecture, 1963
Kyôhô-in, 教法院庭園, Kamigyô-ku, Kyoto, 1963
Mr Iwamoto Tosio, 岩本年生氏邸庭園, Fukuyama, Hiroshima Prefecture, 1963
Mr Hirai Yasuo, 平井康雄氏邸庭園, HigashiÔsaka, Ôsaka Prefecture, 1963
Mr Ozawa, 小澤氏邸庭園, 1963
Niihama Cultural Center Courtyard, 新居浜文化センター中庭, 1963
Ryôgin-an, 龍吟庵, Higashiyama-ku, Kyoto, 1964
Mr Ariyoshi Yoshikazu, 有吉義一氏邸庭園（有心庭・吉泉庭）, Abeno-ku, Ôsaka, 1964
Mr Aono Kazuyuki, 青野一幸氏邸庭園, Kashiwara, Ôsaka Prefecture, 1964
Mr Iwasawa Shigeo, 岩沢重夫氏邸庭園, Kita-ku, Kyoto, 1964
Mrs Kobayashi Hideko, 小林秀子氏邸庭園, Okayama, 1964
Mr Yamada Teruo, 山田輝郎氏邸庭園, Ashiya, Hyôgo Prefecture, 1964
Mrs Tokuya Kiyo, 徳矢きよ氏邸庭園, Ashiya, Hyôgo Prefecture, 1964
Mr Hiratsuka, 平塚氏邸家庭園, 1964
Kongôbu-ji Lotus pond, 金剛峰寺蓮池, Kôya-san, Wakayama Prefecture, 1964
Ôtori Taisha Teien, 大鳥大社庭園, 1964
Kibune Jinja, 貴船神社, Kita-ku, Kyoto, 1965
Fukusen-ji, 福泉寺（四十八願の庭）, Minato-ku, Tokyo, 1965
Kitano Bijutsukan and Mr Kitano Yoshito Residence, 北野美術館庭園/北野吉登氏邸庭園, Nagano, 1965/1971
Mr Mori Kôtarô (formerly), 旧森康太郎氏邸庭園, Shimogyô-ku, Kyoto, 1965
Mr Narita Noboru, 成田昇氏邸庭園（望州楼）, Handa, Aichi Prefecture, 1965
Mr Kiyohara Seinosuke, 清原清之助氏邸庭園, Ashiya, Hyôgo Prefecture, 1965
Ankoku-ji, 安国寺庭園, Fukuyama, Hiroshima Prefecture, 1965
Mr Iwata Yukio, 岩田幸雄氏邸庭園, Hiroshima, 1965
Mr Nishikawa, 西川氏邸庭園, Yao, Ôsaka Prefecture, 1965
Mr Koromogawa Yasunobu, 衣川安信氏邸庭園, Kaiduka, Ôsaka Prefecture, 1965
Mr Hirano Norihito, 平野徳人氏邸庭園, Sennan, Ôsaka Prefecture, 1965
Mitaki-dera, 三瀧寺, 1965
Mr Takizawa, 滝澤氏邸庭園, 1965
Mr Kaneshige, 金重氏邸庭園, 1965
Sumiyoshi Jinja, 住吉神社（住之江の庭）, Sasayama-chô, Hyôgo Prefecture, 1966
Mr Okamoto Rui, 岡本類氏邸庭園, Fukuyama, Hiroshima Prefecture, 1966
Mr Nishikawa Sotoyoshi, 西川外吉氏邸庭園, Kanazawa, Ishikawa Prefecture, 1966
Kôso no Ie, 酵素の家, Kamigyô-ku, Kyoto, 1966
Takagamine Sansô, 鷹ヶ峰山荘庭園, Sakyô-ku, Kyoto, 1966
Kôsei-ji, 光清寺（心字庭）, Kamigyô-ku, Kyoto, 1967
Mr Asano Yoshikazu, 浅野義一氏邸庭園, Kita-ku, Kyoto, 1967
Mr Katsukawa, 勝川氏邸庭園, Suita, Ôsaka Prefecture, 1967
Mr Ishii Umekazu, 石井梅一氏邸庭園, Nara, 1967
Mr Matsumura Jirô, 松村次郎氏邸庭園, Suita, Ôsaka Prefecture, 1967
Mr Asano, 浅野氏邸庭園, 1967
Tôkô-an, 東行庵前池庭, 1967
Mr Akitani Iori, 秋谷伊織氏邸庭園, Takaraduka, Hyôgo Prefecture, 1967
Ôishi Jinja Teien, 大石神社庭園, Akô, Hyôgo Prefecture, 1967
Jôei-ji, 常栄寺庭園（南溟庭）, Yamaguchi, Yamaguchi Prefecture, 1968
Shôgen-ji, 正眼寺, Minôkamo, Gifu Prefecture, 1968
Mr Yokoyama Hideyoshi, 横山秀吉氏邸庭園, Komono-chô, Mie Prefecture, 1968
Mr Shimada Hisashi, 島田久氏邸庭園, Sennan, Ôsaka Prefecture, 1968
Sôrin-ji, 宗隣寺庭園, Ube, Yamaguchi Prefecture, 1968
Yûrin Kaikan (rebuilt in 2002), 友琳会館, Ukyô-ku, Kyoto, 1969
Mr Izuhara Yôzô, 出原陽三氏邸庭園, Shinichi-chô, Hiroshima Prefecture, 1969

Mr Sasai Genei, 笹井源衛氏邸庭園, Matsumoto, Nagano Prefecture, 1969
Mr Nakata Mitsuo, 中田三雄氏邸庭園, Matsumoto, Nagano Prefecture, 1969
Mr Hatake Sôshi, 畑宗志氏邸庭園 (逢春庭), Sasayama-chô, Hyôgo Prefecture, 1969
Mr Akagi Norihei, 赤木憲平氏邸庭園, Okayama, 1969
Mr Hanafusa Masao (Shirasagi-an Senraku-tei), 英政夫氏邸庭園 (白鷺庵仙楽庭), Himeji, Hyôgo Prefecture, 1969
Tenrai-an, 天籟庵露地, Kayô-chô, Okayama Prefecture, 1969
Kanyô-ji, 漢陽寺庭園 (曲水庭・蓬莱庭・九山八海庭・地蔵遊戯庭・門前庭・蕭湘八景庭), Kano-chô, Yamaguchi Prefecture, 1969/1973
Mr Imanishi, 今西氏邸庭園, 1969
Shôkaku-ji, 正覚寺, Tamba-Sasayama , Hyôgo Prefecture, 1970
Yashima-ji, 屋島寺庭園 (座忘庭), Takamatsu, Kagawa Prefecture, 1970
Mr Kubo Takehisa, 久保武久氏邸庭園, Itami, Hyôgo Prefecture, 1970
Mr Yamamoto Kiichirô (Taisan-tei, Seiran-tei), 山本紀市郎氏邸庭園 (泰山庭・晴嵐庭), Imabari, Ehime Prefecture, 1970
Mr Fukamori Toshio, 深森俊夫氏邸庭園, Toyonaka, Ôsaka Prefecture, 1970
Mr Takenaka Masao, 竹中正夫氏邸庭園, Kita-ku, Kyoto, 1970
Reiun-in, Tôfuku-ji, 霊雲院 (九山八海の庭・臥雲の), Higashiyama-ku, Kyoto, 1970/1971
Ôita Junkyô Kôen, 大分殉教公園, Ôita Prefecture, 1970
Mr Uchigaki Yasuhiro, 内垣健祐氏邸庭園, 1970
Mr Ashida Suejirô, 芦田末次郎氏邸庭園, Amagasaki, Hyôgo Prefecture, 1971
Mr Kobayashi Hyakutarô, 小林百太郎氏, Sakai, Ôsaka Prefecture, 1971
Hiroshima Yûenchi (Juka-en), 広島遊園地 (聚花園), Hiroshima, 1971
Mr Shinoda Tôji, 信田藤治氏邸庭園, Sakai, Ôsaka Prefecture, 1971
Hôkoku Jinja Shûsekitei Teien, 豊国神社秀石庭庭園, Ôsaka Castle, 1972
Sekizô-ji, 石像寺 (四神相応の庭・句碑の庭), Tanba, Hyôgo Prefecture, 1972
Zennô-ji, 善能寺 (遊仙苑), Higashiyama-ku, Kyoto, 1972
Seiraku-ji, 清楽寺庭園 (没滋味の庭・帆風の庭・青竜の庭・三楽室露地・七賢の庭), Fukuoka, 1972
Mrs Ishibashi Satoko, 石橋里子氏邸庭園, Hamada, Shimane Prefecture, 1972
Taishô-ji, 大正寺, Kitakyûshû, Fukuoka Prefecture, 1972
Mr Shikata Yonekichi, 志方米吉氏邸庭園, Kôbe, Hyôgo Prefecture, 1972
Mr Kishimoto Shigeo, 岸本繁雄邸庭園, 1972
Sennyû-ji, 泉涌寺, Higashiyama-ku, Kyoto, 1973
Shizuoka Royal Hotel Rooftop Garden, 静岡ロイヤルホテル屋上庭園, Shizuoka Prefecture, 1973
Fukuchi-in, 福智院庭園 (愛染庭), Kôya-san, Wakayama Prefecture, 1973–1975
Mr Konishi, 小西氏邸庭園, 1973
Mr Sato Nobuhiro, 佐藤慶寛氏邸庭園, Tokuyama, Yamaguchi Prefecture, 1973/ 1975
Mr Nakanishi, 中西氏邸庭園, 1973
Honkyû-ji, 本休寺庭園, Sasayama-chô, Hyôgo Prefecture, 1974
Mr Yagi Gentarô, 八木源太郎氏, Higashiyama-ku, Kyoto, 1974
Mr Higashiguchi Tsuruji, 東口鶴次氏, Sakai, Ôsaka Prefecture, 1974
Mr Matsuyama Sôzu, 松山宗都氏 (山月庭露地), Kôriyama, Fukushima Prefecture, 1974
Mr Chiba Keiichi, 千葉慶一氏 (千波庭), Mizusawa, Iwate Prefecture, 1974
Mr Ishii, 石井氏邸家庭園, 1974
Matsuo Taisha Shrine, 松尾大社 (松風園), Ukyô-ku, Kyoto, 1975

Projects Without Year Information:
Mr Tani Shiro, 谷四郎氏邸庭園
Inari Jinja, 稲荷神社
Mr Ôwatari, 大渡氏本邸庭園
Mr Yoshimoto, 吉本氏邸庭園

Books Published by Mirei Shigemori

This chronological list contains 81 published books all written by Mirei Shigemori. It is largely based on a list Mirei Shigemori provided in the very last book of his *Japanese Garden History Survey* in 1975, which was finished after his death by his son Kanto. Several books were added though as I found missing works, partially with the help of Mitsuaki Shigemori.

Each entry uses the following scheme: book title translated into English, original title in *kanji*, location, publisher, year.

Lecture on the Trend of Thought on Art, 美術思潮講座, Tokyo, Bunka Daigakuin, 1922
Lecture on the Trend of Thought on Philosophy, 哲学思潮講座, Tokyo, Bunka Daigakuin, 1922
Outline of the Aesthetics of Flower Arrangement, 美学大系 '花道美学', Kyoto, Kokufusha, 1927
Japanese History of the Unification of Opposites, 日本母陰史, Kyoto, Tôshinkaku Shobô, 1930
Complete Works of Japanese Flower Arrangement Art (in 9 Vol.), 日本花道美術全集、(全9巻), Kyoto, Kadô Bijutsu Kenseikai, 1930–1932
Lectures on Modern Decorative Flower Arrangement, 近代花弁装飾講座, 1932
Art in Kyoto (Garden Version), 京都美術大観 (庭園編), Tokyo, Tohô Shoin, 1933
The Art Flower Arrangement in Japan, The Art Flower Arrangement in Japan, Kyoto, Nigyokudô, 1933
A Short History on Japanese Gardens, 寺院の庭園 (日本宗教講座), Tokyo, Tohô Shoin, 1933
Selected Arrangements of Moribana and Heikwa (Vol. II), 盛花瓶華図集, New York, Yamanaka & Co., 1933
The Magnificence of Temples and placing Flowers before the Memorial Tablet (Lecture on Japanese Religions), 寺院の荘厳と供華 (日本宗教講座), Tokyo, Tohô Shoin, 1934
Tea Ceremony Rooms and their Gardens, 茶室　茶庭, Kyoto, Kawahara Shoten, 1934
History of Japanese Tea Ceremony, 日本茶道史, Kyoto, Kawahara Shoten, 1934
The Appreciation of Japanese Gardens, 日本庭園の観賞, Kyoto, Suzukake Shuppan Sha, 1935
Tea Ceremony by Rikyû (Complete Works of the Tea Ceremony), 利休の茶会　他数編 (茶道全集), Ôsaka, Sôgensha, 1935
The Appreciation of Ikebana, 挿花の観賞, Kyoto, Daiichi Geibun Sha, 1936
Illustrated Book on the History of the Japanese Garden (26 Vol.), 日本庭園史図鑑 (全26), Tokyo, Yûkôsha, 1936–1939
The Garden of Jikô-in, 慈光院庭園, Nara, Jikô-in, 1936
Drawings of Hedges (5 Vol.), 垣根之図 (全5冊), Kyoto, Kyoto Rinsen Kyôkai, 1938
Tea Gardens (Tea Ceremony Edition), 茶庭 (茶道文庫), Kyoto, Kawahara Shoten, 1939
A Short History on Japanese Gardens, 日本庭園小史, Kyoto, Kawahara Shoten, 1939
The Aesthetics of Ikebana, いけばな美学, Tôkyo, Dai Nihon Kadôkai, 1940
The Study of Ikebana, 挿花の研究, Kyoto, Daiichi Geibunsha, 1940
Gardens of Temples, 社寺の庭園, Kyoto, Kawahara Shoten, 1940
The Beauty of the Garden, 庭の美, Kyoto, Daiichi Geibunsha, 1942
100 Gardens in the Old Capital (=Kyôto), 古都百庭, Ôsaka, Keihan Denki, 1942
The Development of Japanese Gardens, 日本庭園の発達, Kyoto, Kôbunsha, 1942
The Gardens of the Imperial Palace in Kyoto, 京都皇居の御庭園, Kyoto, Kôbunsha, 1942
Thoughts on the Tea Ceremony Rooms and their Gardens, 茶席茶庭考, Kyoto, Kôbunsha, 1943
Japanese Gardens, 日本庭園, Kyoto, Ichijô Shobô, 1943
The History of Japanese Gardens, 日本庭園歴, Kyoto, Kôbunsha, 1943
Gardens in the Yamato Area, 大和の庭園, Tenri, Tenri Jihôsha, 1943
A Reader for Flower Arrangement, いけばな読本, Tokyo, Dainihon Kadôkai, 1944
On the Appreciation of the Gardens in the Kinki Area, 近畿名園の鑑賞, Kyoto, Kyoto Inshokan, 1946
An Introduction to Tea Gardens, 茶庭入門, Kyoto, Kyoto Inshokan, 1946
The Architecture of Tea Ceremony Buildings in Japan, 日本の茶席建築, Kyoto, Tomi Shoten, 1946
Gardens in Kyoto, 京の庭, Kyoto, Takagiri Shoin, 1946
Japanese Garden Art, 日本の庭園芸術, Kyoto, Tomi Shoten, 1946
Karesansui (Old Cultural Collection Publication), 枯山水 (古文化叢刊), Kyoto, Ôyasu Shuppan, 1946
A Study on the Gardens in Kyoto, 京都庭園の研究, Kyoto, Kawahara Shoten, 1947
Famous Gardens of Kyoto, 古都の名園, Tokyo, Takara Shobô, 1947
Flowers in the Tea Ceremony Room, 茶室花, Kyoto, Kôbunsha, 1947
The Lifes of Tea Ceremony Masters, 茶人伝, Kyoto, Kawahara Shoten, 1947
Japanese Gardens, 日本の庭園, Kyoto, Tomi Shoten, 1948
Tales of Gardens, 庭園の話, Tokyo, Hôbunkan, 1948
New Tendencies in Flower Arrangements (7 Vol.), 新しい投入と盛花 (7巻), Kyoto, Kôbunsha, 1948
Introduction to Creative Flower Arrangement, 創作投入盛花入門, Kyoto, Kôbunsha, 1949
Kobori Enshû, 小堀遠州, Kyoto, Kawahara Shoten, 1949
A Study on Flower Arrangement (A complete work on Flower Arrangement), 立花の研究 (花道全集), Kyoto, Kawahara Shoten, 1949
Japanese Tea Garden Art, 日本の茶庭芸術, Kyoto, Usui Shobô, 1949
How to Arrange and Appreciate Flowers, 花の生方と見方, Kyoto, Kôbunsha, 1949
New Flower Arrangement, 新しい生け花, Tokyo, Isobe Shoten, 1949
On the Skill and the Appreciation of Flower Arrangement, 挿花の技法と鑑賞, Kyoto, Kôbunsha, 1949
Gardens of Japan, Kyoto, Nihon Shashin Insatsu, 1949
A Selection of the Best Modern Flower Arrangement, 現代挿花名作集, Kyoto, Tôkasha, 1950
Ikebana Bunko (5 Vol.), いけばな文庫 (5集), Kyoto, Ikebana Geijutsu Henshûbu, 1953
Japanese Gardens, 日本の庭園, Tokyo, Kadokawa Shoten, 1956
Gardens (written by Mirei and Kanto Shigemori), 庭 (重森完途共著), Tokyo, David's Company, 1958
Tea Garden and Tea Ceremony Today (A Compendium of the Tea Ceremony), 茶庭　今日の茶の湯、他 (茶の湯全書), Tokyo, Shufunotomosha, 1959

Tea Ceremony Rooms and their gardens (Education Series), 茶室と庭（教養文庫）, Tokyo, Shakai Shisôsha, 1962
Mirei Shigemori's Collected Works (Gardens), 重森三玲庭園作品集（庭）, Tokyo, Heibonsha, 1964
Karesansui, 枯山水, Kyoto, Kawahara Shoten, 1965
Tea Ceremony Rooms and their Gardens—How to Create and Appreciate them, 茶室と茶庭一見方　作り方一, Tokyo, Seibundô Shinkôsha, 1966
An Illustrated Book on Flower Arrangement (by Mirei Shigemori and Yamane Yûzô), 立華図鑑（山根有三、重森三玲共著）, Tokyo, Bishutsu Shuppansha, 1966
Guidebook for Gardens in Japan, 全国庭園ガイドブック, Tokyo, Seibundô Shinkôsha, 1966
On the Beauty and Appreciation of Gardens, 庭園の美と鑑賞法, Tokyo, Hôbunkan, 1967
Gardens—Spirit and Form, 庭一こころとかたち一, Tokyo, Shakai Shisôsha, 1968
Contemporary Japanese Style Gardens—Living in the Garden, 現代和風庭園　庭に生きる, Tokyo, Seibundou Shinkôsha, 1969
Famous Japanese Gardens (Deluxe Edition), 豪華本日本の名園, Tokyo, Seibundô Shinkôsha, 1969
Famous Japanese Gardens, 日本の名園, Tokyo, Seibundô Shinkôsha, 1969
Survey Plans of Famous Japanese Gardens, 実測図日本の名園, Tokyo, Seibundô Shinkôsha, 1971
A Recommendation of famous Japanese Gardens (Kyoto and Chûgoku Area), 推賞日本の名園（京都、中国編）, Tokyo, Seibundô Shinkôsha, 1971
Japanese Garden History Survey (30+5 Vol.), 日本庭園史大系（全35巻）, Tokyo, Shakai Shisôsha, 1971–1976
A Recommendation of famous Japanese Gardens (Shiga, Nara and Rest Japan), 推賞日本の名園（滋賀、奈良、全国編, Tokyo, Seibundô Shinkôsha, 1971
Tea Room and Tea Garden Dictionary, 茶室茶庭事, Tokyo, Seibundô Shinkôsha, 1973
Gardens (by Mirei and Kanto Shigemori), 庭（重森完途共著）, Tokyo, Seibidô Shuppan, 1973
Japanese Garden History Dictionary, 日本庭園歴覧辞典, Tokyo, Tôkyodo Shuppan, 1974
Every Moment is Special', 刻々是好刻, Niigata, Hokuetsu Shuppan, 1974
Visiting Kyoto's Gardens, 京の庭を巡る, Kyoto, Shirakawa Shoten, 1975
The Japanese Garden, 日本の庭（２）, Tokyo, Mainichi Shinbun, 1975
Mirei Shigemori's Collection of Works, Gardens—Approach to Gods, 重森三玲作品集　庭　神々へのアプローチ, Tokyo, Seibundô Shinkôsha, 1976

BIBLIOGRAPHY

Note: The works by Mirei Shigemori are not listed again as they already appear in the catalogue of his works.

Asano, K.; Takakuwa, G; Dickinson, F. R. and Matsuyama, N., *Invitation to Japanese Gardens.* Tokyo: Tuttle, 1970.

Bary, Wm. Theodore de. *Sources of Japanese Tradition*. New York: Columbia University Press, 1958.

Berthier, Francois. *Reading Zen in the Rocks: The Japanese Dry Landscape Garden.* Chicago, London: The University of Chicago Press, 2000.

Blaser, Werner. *Structure and form in Japan.* New York: Wittenborn, 1964.

Blaser, Werner. *The Temple and the Teahouse in Japan.* Basel, Boston, Berlin: Birkhäuser, 1988.

Bring, Mitchell and Wayembergh, Josse. *Japanese Gardens: Design and Meaning.* New York: McGraw-Hill, 1981.

Cave, Philip. *Creating Japanese Gardens.* Rutland, Tokyo: Charles E. Tuttle Co., 1993.

Chamberlain, Basil Hall. *The Kojiki: Records of Ancient Matters.* Rutland, Tokyo: Charles E. Tuttle Co., 1981.

Condor, Josiah. *Landscape Gardening in Japan.* Tokyo, New York, London: Kodansha International 2002.

Davidson, A. Keir. *Zen Gardening.* London: Rider, 1982.

Davidson, A. Keir. *The Art of Zen Gardens.* Los Angeles: J. P. Tarcher, 1983.

Eliade, Mircea. *The Sacred and the Profane.* San Diego, New York, London: Harcourt, Inc., 1987.

Engel, David H. *Japanese Gardens for Today.* Rutland, Vermont: Charles E. Tuttle, 1959.

Fujioka, Michio and Tsunenari, Kazunori. *Japanese Residences and Gardens: A Tradition of Integration.* New York: Kodansha International, 1982.

Fujishima, Gaijiro. *Katsura Rikyû: Katsura Detached Palace.* Kyoto: Suiko Shoin, 1950.

Greenbie, Barrie B. *Space and Spirit in Modern Japan.* New Haven, London: Yale University Press, 1988.

Gropius, Walter; Ishimoto, Yasuhiro and Tange, Kenzo. *Katsura—Tradition and Creation in Japanese Architecture.* Tokyo, New Haven: Yale Press, 1960.

Hale, Gill. *The Feng Shui Garden.* Singapore: Asiapac Books Pte. Ltd., 1998.

Harada, Jiro. *Japanese Gardens.* London: The Studio Limited, 1956.

Haug, Christoph. *Vom Klassischen Trockenlandschaftsgarten und der Suche nach Modernen Gartenkunstwerken.* Nürtingen: thesis, 2006.

Hayakawa, Masao. *The Garden Art of Japan.* New York, Tokyo: Weatherhill/Heibonsha, 1973.

Hearn, Lafcadio. *In a Japanese Garden—Glimpses of Unfamiliar Japan.* Rutland, Tokyo: Charles E. Tuttle, 1993.

Holborn, Mark. *The Ocean in the Sand: Japan, from Landscape to Garden.* New York: Random House, 1978.

Horiguchi, Sutemi; Harada, Jiro and Sato, Tatsuzo. *The Katsura Imperial Villa.* Tokyo: Mainichi Press, 1952.

Ishikawa, Tadashi. *Imperial Villas of Kyôto: Katsura and Shugaku-in.* Tokyo: Kodansha, 1970.

Itoh, Teiji. *Japanese Garden: An Approach to Nature.* New Haven: Yale University Press, 1972.

Itoh, Teiji. *Space and Illusion in the Japanese Garden.* New York, Tokyo: Weatherhill/Tankosha, 1973.

Itoh, Teiji. *Imperial Gardens of Japan.* Second edition. New York, Tokyo: Weatherhill/Tankosha, 1978.

Itoh, Teiji; Arai, Masao and Ogawa, Taisuke. Katsura: *A Quintessential Representative of the Sukiya Style of Architecture.* Tokyo: Shinkenchiku-Sha, 1983.

Itoh, Teiji. *The Gardens of Japan.* Tokyo, New York, London: Kodansha International Ltd., 1984.

Jakob, Michael. *Mirei Shigemori and the Reinvention of the Japanese Garden.* Verbania: Tarara Edizioni, 2012.

Johnson, Norris Brock. Tenryu-ji: *Life and Spirit of a Kyoto Garden.* Berkeley: Stone Bridge Press, 2012.

Katsuhiko, Mizuno. *Masterpieces of Japanese Garden Art.* Kyoto: Kyoto Shoin Co., 1992.

Kandinsky, Wassily. *Point and Line to Plane*, New York: Dover Publications, 1979.

Keane, Marc P. *Japanese Garden Design.* Rutland, Tokyo: Charles E. Tuttle, 1996.

Keane, Marc P. *The Art of Setting Stones.* Berkeley: Stone Bridge Press, 2002.

Kuck, Loraine. *The Art of the Japanese Garden.* New York: The Japan Society, 1941.

Kuck, Loraine. *The World of the Japanese Garden.* New York, Tokyo: Walker/Weatherhill, 1968.

Kuitert, Wybe. *Themes, Scenes, and Taste in the History of Japanese Garden Art.* Amsterdam: J.C. Gieben, 1988.

Kuitert, Wybe. *Themes in the History of Japanese Garden Art.* Honolulu: University of Hawai'i, 2002.

Hayakawa, Masao. *The Garden Art of Japan.* New York: Weatherhill/Heibonsha, 1973.

Main, Alison. *The Lure of the Japanese Garden.* Kent Town: Wakefield Press, 2002.

Mason, Penelope. *History of Japanese Art.* New York: Harry N. Abrams, Inc., 1993.

Mizuno, Katsuhiro. *Shigemori Mirei's Artistic Garden Design.* Kyoto: Mitsumura Suiko Shoin, 2015.

Mori, Osamu. *Photo Collection: Katsura Imperial Villa.* Tokyo: Mainichi, 1970.

Morse, Edward S. *Japanese Homes and Their Surroundings.* New York: Dover, 1961.

Naito, Akira. *Katsura: A Princely Retreat.* Tokyo, New York, San Francisco: Kodansha International Ltd., 1977.

Newsom, Samuel. *A Thousand Years of Japanese Gardens.* Tokyo: Tokyo News Service, 1953.

Newsom, Samuel. *Japanese Garden Construction.* Tokyo: Domoto, Kumagawa and Perkins, 1939.

Newsom, Samuel. *A Japanese Garden Manual for Westerners: Basic Design and Construction.* Tokyo: Tokyo News Service, 1965.

Nitschke, Günter. *The Architecture of the Japanese Garden: Right Angle and Natural Form.* Cologne: Benedikt Taschen, 1991.

Nomura, Kanji. Kobori Enshu: *A Tea Master's Harmonic Brilliance.* Kyoto: Kyoto Tsushinsha Press, 2008.

Nosé, Michiko Rico. *The Modern Japanese Garden.* London: Octopus Publishing Group, 2002.

Ohashi, Haruzo. *The Japanese Garden: Islands of Serenity.* Tokyo: Graphic-sha, 1997.

Okada, Norihisa. *Nihon no Niwa Kotohajime.* Tokyo: Toto Shuppan, 2008.

Okakura, Kakuzo. *The Book of Tea.* Tokyo: Charles E. Tuttle Co., 1956.

Ono, Kenkichi and Edwards, Walter. *Dictionary of Japanese Garden Terms*, Kansai Process, Nara, 2001.

Ono, Masao. *Katsura Rikyû.* Tokyo: Mainichi Shinbunsha, 1982.

Ono, Sokyo. *Shinto: The Kami Way.* Rutland, Tokyo: Charles E. Tuttle Co., 1993.

Ota, Hirotaro. *Traditional Japanese Architecture and Gardens.* Tokyo: Kokusai Bunka Shinkokai, 1972.

Picken, Stuart. *Shinto: Japan's Spiritual Roots.* Tokyo, New York, San Francisco: Kodansha Kodansha International, 1980.

Picken, Stuart. *Buddhism: Japan's Cultural Identity.* Tokyo, New York, San Francisco: Kodansha International, 1982.

Picken, Stuart. *Shinto Meditations for Revering the Earth.* Berkeley: Stone Bridge Press, 2002.

Platzek, Carola. *Teachings of the Garden,* Wien: Schlebrügge.editor, 2019.

Rambach, Pierre and Rambach, Susanne. *Gardens of Longevity in China and Japan.* New York: Skira and Rizzoli, 1987.

Richards, Betty W. and Kaneko, Anne. *Japanese Plants.* Tokyo: Shufunotomo Co. Ltd., 1991.
Richie, Donald and Georges, Alexandre. *The Temples of Kyôto.* Rutland, Vermont: Charles E. Tuttle Co., 1995.
Sadler, A. L. Cha-No-Yu: *The Japanese Tea Ceremony.* Rutland, Tokyo: Charles E. Tuttle Co., 1994.
Saito, Katsuo and Wada, Sadaji. *Trees and Stones: Secrets of Japanese Gardening.* New York, San Francisco, Tokyo: Japan Publications Trading Company, 1964.
Saito, Tadakazu and Shigemori, Geite. *Mirei Shigemori's Collection of Works, Gardens—Approach to Gods*, Seibundou Shinkou Sha, Tokyo, 1976.
Schaarschmidt-Richter, Irmtraud. *Japanese Gardens.* New York: William Morrow, 1979.
Sen, Soshitsu. *Chado—The Japanese Way of Tea*. New York, Tokyo, Kyoto: Weatherhill/Tankosha, 1979.
Shigemori, Geite. *Shigemori Mirei—Modern Karesansui*, Tokyo: Shogakkan, 2007.
Shigemori, Kanto. *The Japanese Courtyard Garden*, New York: Weatherhill, 1981.
Shimoyama, Shigemaru. *Sakutei-ki.* Tokyo: Town & City Planners, 1976.
Shirahata, Yozaburo. *Ueji, The Genius of Water and Stone.* Kyoto: Kyoto Tsushinsha Press, 2008
Soshitsu Sen XV. Chanoyu: *The Urasenke Tradition of Tea.* New York, Tokyo: Weatherhill, 1988.
Slawson, David A. *Secret Teachings in the Art of Japanese Gardens.* Tokyo, New York: Kodansha International Ltd., 1987.
Takakuwa, Gisei and Okamoto, Toyo. *Katsura Rikyû: Detached Palace.* Kyoto: Suiko Shoin, 1950.
Takei, Jiro and Keane, Marc Peter. *Sakuteiki: Visions of the Japanese Garden.* Rutland, Tokyo: Charles E. Tuttle Co., 2001.
Tamura, Tsuyoshi. *Art of the Landscape Garden in Japan.* Tokyo: Kokusai Bunka Shinkokai, 1935.
Tange, Kenzo. *Ise: Prototype of Japanese Architecture.* Cambridge: MIT Press, 1962.
Taniguchi, Yoshiro; Harada, Jiro and Sato, Tatsuzo. *The Shugakuin Imperial Villa.* Tokyo: Mainichi, 1956.
Taut, Bruno. *Fundamentals of Japanese Architecture.* Tokyo: Bunka Shinkokai, 1936.
Taut, Bruno. *Houses and People of Japan.* Tokyo: Sanseido Co. Ltd., 1936.
Tashibana-no, Toshitsuna. *Sakuteiki: The Book of Garden*, Tokyo: Town and City Planners Inc., 1976.
Treib, Marc and Herman, Ron. *A Guide to the Japanese Gardens of Kyôto.* Tokyo: Shufunotomo Co. Ltd., 1980.
Usui, Shiro. *A Pilgrim's Guide to Forty-Six Temples.* New York, Tokyo: Weatherhill, 1990.
Watanabe, Yasutada. *Shinto Art: Ise and Izumo Shrines.* New York: Weatherhill, 1974.
Wright, Tom. *Zen Gardens: Kyôto's Nature Enclosed.* Kyoto: Mitsumura Suiko Shoin, 1990.
Yamamoto, K.; Wright, T.; Asano, Y. and Takagi, M. *Invitation to Kyôto Garden.* Kyoto: Mitsumura Suiko Shoin, 1989.
Yoshida, Tetsuro. *The Japanese House and Garden.* New York: Frederick A. Praeger, 1955.
Yoshida, Tetsuro. *Gardens of Japan.* New York: Frederick A. Praeger, 1957.
Young, David and Michiko. *The Art of the Japanese Garden.* North Clarendon: Tuttle Publishing, 2005.

ILLUSTRATION CREDITS

Editor, author and publisher thank the following photographers, architects and organizations for their kind permission to reproduce the photographs in this book.

Sutemi Horiguchi	**103**
Sumiyoshi Jinja	**224, 225**
Kyoto Rinsen Kyôkai	**076–078**
Christian Lichtenberg	**001 (Cover), all three images on page 8 and 9, 003, 020–025, 032–035, 043, 047, 048, 062, 080, 083, 095, 097, 148, 162, 164–167, 172, 174, 175, 177–179, 181–189, 193–196, 199, 200, 204–216, 218, 219, 221, 222, 226–231, 235, 236, 238–255, 258–268, 270, 272–276, 278–280, 282–285, 287–298, 300–303, 305–308, 310–315, 317–321, 324–331, 333–336, 339–348, 350, 351**
Haruzo Ôhashi	**002**
Pierre Rambach	**026, 040–042, 044–046**
Chisao Shigemori	**038, 039**
Shigemori family	**006–008, 010–015, 017, 018, 027, 036, 037, 050–056, 075, 084, 092–094, 100, 104–109, 112, 113, 116, 117, 120–125, 128, 132–141, 144–147, 150, 152–154, 156, 158, 160, 163, 168–171, 173, 176, 180, 190–192, 197, 198, 201–203, 217, 220, 232, 237, 256, 257, 269, 271, 277, 281, 286, 299, 304, 309, 316, 322, 323, 332, 337, 338, 349**
Mr Suzue	**089, 090**
Christian Tschumi	**004, 005, 009, 016, 019, 028–031, 049, 057–061, 063–074, 079, 081, 082, 085–088, 096, 098, 099, 101, 102, 110, 111, 114, 115, 118, 119, 126, 127, 129–131, 142, 143, 149, 151, 155, 157, 159, 161, 223, 233, 234**
unknown	**091**

Every effort has been made to trace the copyright holders and we apologize in advance for any unintentional omission and would be pleased to insert the appropriate acknowledgement in any subsequent edition.